"As licensed mental health therapists and parents, we've seen firsthand how essential it is to engage our children in honest and hopeful conversations about bodies, desires, and identity—conversations many of us would rather avoid due to our own unresolved stories and the complex cultural narratives we navigate. *Raising Wise Kids in a Sexually Broken World* offers a lifeline for those of us seeking thoughtful ways to begin. With practical tools and gospel-centered insight, Laurie and Matt Krieg show how to transform moments of uncertainty into sacred opportunities for growth—both for parents and children. Their wise guidance equips you with the language you need to approach these conversations with clarity, courage, and grace."

Jay Stringer, licensed mental health therapist and author of *Unwanted* and *Desire,* and **Heather Stringer,** licensed mental health therapist and author of *Life in Ritual*

"Laurie and Matt Krieg offer a rich, biblical framework for parents navigating the complicated terrain of talking about sexuality with children. The Kriegs provide a breadth of wisdom from their own parenting journey and incorporate key insights from psychology, all the while helping parents feel more effective and less alone. There is no shortage of parenting books available today, but *Raising Wise Kids in a Sexually Broken World* is one that sifts through the noise and offers concrete, practical guidance and modeling of critical conversations around human sexuality."

Julia Sadusky, licensed clinical psychologist and author of *Start Talking to Your Kids about Sex: A Practical Guide for Catholics*

"This book is a gift to all parents trying to navigate the complexity of raising children in today's world. In *Raising Wise Kids in a Sexually Broken World,* Laurie and Matt Krieg have shared invaluable wisdom, insight, and understanding that is crucial in these times. I wish I could make this book required reading for every parent."

Christine Caine, founder of A21 and Propel Women

"I'd love for every Christian parent to read this book. It covers not only what to say but also how to understand and communicate the important whys of God's plan for sexuality. This is a rich read, providing a powerful combination of personal experience, theological depth, and practical application."

Juli Slattery, president and cofounder of Authentic Intimacy and author of *Rethinking Sexuality*

"With wisdom, humility, gentleness, and the proper confidence of those who know their subject and the fraught landscape it can sometimes bring, Laurie and Matt Krieg have, with *Raising Wise Kids in a Sexually Broken World*, offered their readers a book that we ought not simply read. Rather, we would do well to meditate upon it, carefully and with the same humility with which it has been penned. For all of us who long for our offspring to joyfully follow Jesus, this is a book that is no mere manual about children and sexuality; it is an invitation to partnering with God as he forms them into the image of the King."

Curt Thompson, psychiatrist and author of *The Soul of Desire* and *The Deepest Place*

"In a shaky world, Laurie and Matt Krieg offer parents an unshakable foundation. In *Raising Wise Kids in a Sexually Broken World*, the gospel is not just mentioned, it is unveiled as our real and practical hope. Like Jesus taught in Matthew 7, the Kriegs remind us that storms will come to every house, yet when we are grounded in God's truth, we remain unshaken. They lay a solid foundation and then walk us through how to live on it, equipping us to be parents who are full of faith, antifragile, firm in truth, and free from fear. We do not have to be intimidated or stressed about the future for our children. Grounded in God's truth, we stand unshaken and can raise kids who do the same."

Megan Fate Marshman, author of *Relaxed* and teaching pastor at Willow Creek Community Church

Foreword by DAN ALLENDER

RAISING WISE KIDS
—IN A—
SEXUALLY BROKEN WORLD

A Gospel-Centered Approach

LAURIE KRIEG with MATT KRIEG

ĩvp

An imprint of InterVarsity Press
Downers Grove, Illinois

InterVarsity Press
P.O. Box 1400 | Downers Grove, IL 60515-1426
ivpress.com | email@ivpress.com

InterVarsity Press® is the publishing division of InterVarsity Christian Fellowship/USA®. For more information, visit intervarsity.org.

Unless otherwise indicated, all Scripture quotations are taken from the Holy Bible, New Living Translation, copyright ©1996, 2004, 2007, 2013. Used by permission of Tyndale House Publishers, Inc., Carol Stream, Illinois 60188. All rights reserved.

While any stories in this book are true, some names and identifying information may have been changed to protect the privacy of individuals.

Published in association with the literary agency of Wolgemuth & Wilson.

The publisher cannot verify the accuracy or functionality of website URLs used in this book beyond the date of publication.

Cover design: Faceout Studio, Tim Green
Interior design: Jeanna Wiggins
Cover images: © ivetavaicule / DigitalVision Vectors via Getty Images

ISBN 978-1-5140-1214-7 (print) | ISBN 978-1-5140-1215-4 (digital)

Printed in the United States of America ∞

Library of Congress Cataloging-in-Publication Data
Names: Krieg, Laurie, 1986- author | Krieg, Matt, 1985- author
Title: Raising wise kids in a sexually broken world : a gospel-centered
   approach / Laurie Krieg with Matt Krieg.
Description: Downers Grove, IL : IVP, [2026] | Includes bibliographical
   references.
Identifiers: LCCN 2025028078 (print) | LCCN 2025028079 (ebook) | ISBN
   9781514012147 paperback | ISBN 9781514012154 ebook
Subjects: LCSH: Child rearing–Religious aspects–Christianity |
   Parenting–Religious aspects–Christianity | Sexual
   orientation–Religious aspects–Christianity
Classification: LCC BV4529 .K75 2026 (print) | LCC BV4529 (ebook) | DDC
   248.8/45–dc23/eng/20250827
LC record available at https://lccn.loc.gov/2025028078
LC ebook record available at https://lccn.loc.gov/2025028079

31   30   29   28   27   26 | 13   12   11   10   9   8   7   6   5   4   3   2

THIS BOOK IS DEDICATED TO all of the moms, dads, grandparents, caregivers, and children's pastors who are looking around at this wild world wondering,

"How do we equip the next generation with a gospel vision for sexuality?"

May the Holy Spirit work through these pages to empower you to do exactly that.

CONTENTS

FOREWORD

Dan Allender

MY WIFE, BECKY, AND I built one home together. We had heard it was an endeavor that often divided couples even to the point of divorce. We walked into the endeavor with some degree of wisdom but utterly unaware of what it would cost. If you have built a home or hired someone to do upgrades or repairs, you have heard the axiom: "Double the cost, double the time." The cost may not be as severe as the axiom, but knowing that even the most experienced and honest builder can't predict the exact outcome is essential.

In our case, we had not only an experienced and honest builder but one who was wise, talking to us often about the process, challenges, risks, and decision points that required our active involvement rather than making those decisions on his own. It took him more time and labor, and it would have been vastly more straightforward to execute our initial plans according to his desire.

I felt the same respect and appreciation while reading this holy, brilliant, and wise book. Laurie is a brilliant architect, builder, and reader of the human heart. She knows her craft. What she is building is infinitely more important than a house—she is inviting you to the holy enterprise of helping your children make sense of their bodies, desires, struggles, and sexuality in a Christian world that too often commands purity, ignores the inner war of desire, and hopes for the best.

That is similar to telling a child, "Here is the blueprint—let me know when you finish the house to my specifications." Telling a child to be faithful and do what is right when the world constantly alters the plan and offers visions of better design is at least foolish if not passive and even cowardly.

But other than building a few bookshelves, I have no clue how to build a whole home. I need help in one of the most crucial building projects I will ever endeavor to form—the building of a holy, sensuous, God-honoring, playful sexuality that enters the reality of both brokenness and beauty. What I do for myself will lead to what I offer for my children.

Laurie understands that the good fruit we desire to give to our children must grow from the soil of our healing and redemption. Where there is ignorance or, worse, fear and shame, we cannot offer the goodness in word and deed that will help our children and grandchildren come to themselves and negotiate a world that seldom offers the glory and honor God has written into our bodies.

We need holy freedom, and we need keen wisdom. This glorious book offers both. Laurie tackles every hurdle that needs to be engaged to help you as a parent talk with your children about where babies come from; address issues of sexual orientation, gender dysphoria, and transgenderism; and navigate sexual abuse and sleepovers. Every knob, handle, light switch, and tile choice gets engaged to help you make good decisions.

She humbly offers a glimpse into the process she and Matt have created to give you a picture of what and how you might want to build. You may not agree with every choice, but the depth and breadth of her biblical foundation are substantial enough to help you shape your language and discern the next step when the moment's challenges feel overwhelming.

Are you saving money for your children's education? Do you regularly insist they brush their teeth and clean up their rooms? Do you parent to help your children know and desire God? If so, you need to step into some of the hardest and holiest discussions earlier and more profoundly than you likely received from your parents. It will lead to your children's provision and build glory for yourself and your whole family.

INTRODUCTION

ONE OF THE BEST PARTS of parenting is watching our kids grow: that first look into their open eyes, that first smile, that first word, the first bike ride, that first word read, that first day of school.

One of the hardest parts of parenting is there is no 24/7 human parenting coach to help us as our kids grow. That does not keep us from trying to find one. Those middle-of-the-night feedings when we don't know if our baby is still hungry, has to burp, or just needs to go to sleep? We desperately text friends who may be awake or ask the internet to help us. Those moments where we don't know if a fever is "just a fever" or something more serious that requires a visit to urgent care? We reach out to any nurses or doctors we may know while typing symptoms into Dr. Google (who always tells us those symptoms require emergency care and probably an amputation or two). Those years we are discerning what God might have for our kids' education? We solicit a jury of our peers, pray, and research online.

Then we face questions about sex, gender, and sexuality. We ask our friends their opinions, and we can be surprised at what they say. Sometimes they believe something contrary to our views. Or they live it out differently. Or they were actually going to come to us with the same question! In desperation, we start to go to ask the internet but quickly see that the onslaught of opinions and statistics is overwhelming and unhelpful to our real lives right now.

So we close the laptop and leave our conversations with friends, but we realize we are still parents. We are responsible for raising our kids in this wild world with wisdom.

And it is wild.

Currently, 28 percent of Generation Z identify as LGBTQ, compared with 10 percent of all adults.[1] At least one study found that 87 percent of Christian singles on religious dating sites believe it is okay to have sex outside of marriage,[2] while Christians who do not regularly watch pornography are in the minority (54 percent sometimes watch it and 49 percent are "comfortable with how much they watch").[3] One in five teenagers see pornography by the time they are ten years old, and roughly three out of four see it by the time they are seventeen.[4] There has also been a 2,400 percent increase in referrals for children wanting to gender-transition between 2010 and 2019 in the UK (75 percent of whom are natal girls),[5] while one in four women and one in ten men experience unwanted sexual touch by the time they are eighteen.[6]

When we hear these statistics, questions pour out of our brains like:

- "How do I talk to my kids about God's design for marriage and singleness?"
- "What do I say when my kid asks about the rainbow flags at the library?"
- "How do I talk with my five-year-old about her aunt who now identifies as her uncle?"
- "When are we supposed to talk to our kids about sex—and how?"
- "How do I keep my children's bodies safe?"
- "How can I talk about the evils of pornography without scarring my children?"

We desperately look around for our personal parenting coach who can tell us what to say, but the coach never shows up. So our brains go straight to trauma responses. Some of us choose to fight. You see us show ourselves in rants on social media. Some of us choose flight. You can pick us out by how many jokes we make to avoid teaching our kids. Others of us fawn. We desperately try to people-please our way into peace with everyone in this conversation. And still others of us freeze. Picking up this very book was an absolute act of faith.

But then we take our fear to our kids and try to figure out how to bubble wrap them or fight the enemy of the day for them. Or we simply curl up in a fetal position while scrolling Instagram until the anxiety lessens.

Later, after our kids are in bed and the phone is tucked away, the tears start to fall. We come face-to-face with our helplessness and find ourselves begging Jesus to come back and make it all better.

Me too.

But he hasn't come back yet. So what are we supposed to do?

This is why we wrote this book: to help parents discover and implement gospel wisdom in one of the most controversial spaces of our age.

I have professionally been in this conversation for ten years, and our oldest child is ten years old. Every person I have interviewed for our podcast, every book I have read, and every coaching conversation I have taken part in I have filtered through my mom lens to see how I can teach our own kids bite-sized biblical truth. Not only have I engaged these conversations in ministry, but my own story includes ongoing same-sex attractions and surrender of those attractions to Jesus. My husband, Matt, who offers his wisdom in this book as well, is a licensed mental health therapist who specializes in marriage, sex, and sexuality. He has his own story of pornography addiction and freedom from it. Further, when we went through marriage struggles, it was the theology of marriage that saved our marriage. (You can read more of our story in *An Impossible Marriage: What Our Mixed-Orientation Marriage Has Taught Us About Love and the Gospel.*[7])

Matt and I perhaps have had more opportunities than most Christian parents to think about these topics, to talk with experts, and to practice what we learn in real time in our home. Do you know what we have discovered?

The gospel is the secret.

I'm not saying that because "the gospel" is some sort of code word to get us into Christian spaces. I truly believe it. Every time I start to think about teaching my kids about God's design for marriage and sex or scramble for what to say when their male friend suddenly identifies as their female friend—and I feel my prefrontal cortex begin to shut down with anxiety—I remember the gospel. I remember how God created the world, and it excites me. I remember how God knows about the brokenness in this world, and it calms me. I remember how Jesus rescued and is rescuing the world, and it empowers me to teach my kids with peaceful courage.

It gives me confidence to teach because that's how God taught us. The Bible does not begin with, "In the beginning sin distorted everything, so avoid sin." It begins with, "In the beginning God created the heavens and the earth, and it was good." God created the world good! He created gender, marriage, sex, and bodies good, and then sin distorted them. Breathe in his goodness. His beauty. And then respond in peaceful confidence when sin seeks to invade his beauty.

This beautiful, peaceful, gospel-saturated theology of "yes" is the anchoring lens with which I want my kids to view this broken world. An anchoring bias is a cognitive pattern in which the first piece of information we encounter on a topic is the one we compare every subsequent idea to when that topic comes up again.[8] No matter what we hear afterward, it is extremely hard to shake that initial concept. What is the first anchoring piece I want my kids to hear about gender, marriage, sex, and sexuality? Is it the darkness? The evil? The fearful things that keep me up at night? Or is it the gorgeousness of God's design and the knowledge that his will, plan, and sovereignty over the entire world—including over our sexuality—will not be thwarted?

Yes, that one. I'll take that last one.

It's interesting to me that when we focus on this theology of "yes," it shapes our kids' brains and personalities for the better. In Jonathan Haidt's work on how to help kids thrive without debilitating anxiety, he talks about curbing "defend mode" in them. Defend mode is where kids grow up with a default to be suspicious of new things, always look for threats, and approach life defensively. This leads to anxiety, and long term it can inhibit learning and growth. "Discover mode," on the other hand, is where kids' default is to view the world with open eyes, look for new opportunities, and become eager for new experiences. These kids tend to be happier and more sociable, and such a viewpoint fosters learning and growth.[9]

How do we cultivate "discover mode" in our kids? How do we help them approach the world not fearfully but walk into it confidently—even in the world's most controversial spaces? I'll offer two ideas on which this book is written. First, kids need good soil. They need an anchoring gospel foundation that focuses on God's beauty. We parents lay this foundation with the power of the Holy Spirit. Half of this book is going to be focused on laying that foundation in us as parents first so that when we parent our kids on topics related to marriage and sexuality, we are truly parenting, not parroting.

Second, as parents we need to know how to walk those foundations with our kids—that's the other half of the book. Our kids need bite-sized, age-appropriate introductions to the brokenness in our world. They need wind to make their roots strong. To highlight this necessity, Haidt cites a 1980s experiment where scientists sought to create a closed artificial ecosystem. They gave it the ideal amount of air, water, and soil nutrients. This shrink-wrapped system failed for many reasons, but one of the most significant was that trees need wind to grow.[10] Without wind, trees' roots do not become strong enough, and the trees fall over from their own weight.

Trees are "antifragile." And they are not the only antifragile things in the world. Our immune systems are antifragile, needing germs around them to grow stronger. So are our muscular systems. And so are our kids. "Children are intrinsically antifragile," Haidt says, "which is why overprotected children are more likely to become adolescents who are stuck in defend mode. In defend mode, they're likely to learn less, have fewer close friends, be more anxious, and experience more pain from ordinary conversations and conflicts."[11]

Kids need to bump into the world in age-appropriate ways in order to thrive. They cannot be bubble-wrapped. They also should not be tossed to the world to be taught by its ideals. They should be planted in gospel soil and offered enough wind to strengthen their roots. I cannot even begin to count how many hyper-sheltered-kids-turned-adults are in my husband Matt's mental health office because of a sexual addiction. The research says that when kids are not taught about sex, they turn to pornography—30 percent say they learned "a lot" to "everything they know" about sex from it.[12] That is truly disturbing when we also know that anywhere from one in three to nine in ten pornography videos depict violence, and watching such violent content can lead to real-life violent actions in a person.[13]

The good news is kids want to talk and learn, and when they do, it is beneficial. In just one secular study, researchers found that when teens talked with their parents about pornography, almost three in four (71 percent) said the conversation "made [them] feel like there are helpful resources other than pornography to explore [their] sexuality."[14] Yes. There are helpful resources. We parents, through the power of the gospel, are that helpful resource.

That is the trajectory of this book: We are going to lay the foundation and then walk the foundation. To get more specific, the book is split up into six gospel foundations: the gospel, marriage and singleness, sex, gender, honoring God with our bodies (body safety), and honoring God with our minds (porn prevention). Each foundation is split into two chapters—what I call "Lay the Foundation" and "Walk the Foundation." The "Lay the Foundation" chapters teach us as parents the beautiful gospel concepts God lays out for us in the Bible, and the "Walk the Foundation" chapters teach us how to practically teach it to our kids, not just so they avoid sin and harm, but so they live confidently and peacefully out of God's gospel design for their bodies.

Each "Lay the Foundation" chapter begins with specific questions parents are asking in these spaces. Each "Walk the Foundation" chapter begins with a key teaching for parents to implement with their kids. When I get specific about how to implement, feel free to adopt my ideas completely, adjust them, or use the foundational wisdom and find a completely different way to use the gospel teaching. We will not be offended. The important thing is that our kids are being tenderly taught with God's wisdom.

Let's define what I mean when I say "kids." This book is focused on helping Christian parents of kids aged twelve and under who hold to a historically biblical view of human sexuality. Why are we cutting it off at twelve? There are several great books out there that help parents talk about these topics with their teenagers, but they understandably tend to be written in reaction to culture as opposed to proactively laying foundations. As a mom of young kids and a leader in this space, I have often wondered, "Is there anything we can teach before they are thirteen that will help us have those conversation more easily?" I believe there is. Therefore, this book.

Saying that, having conversations about topics related to gender identity, marriage, and sexuality with adults is not easy.

Explaining them to little kids is even more challenging. We have tried our best to take these complex, nuanced topics and explain them in a robust but simple way so parents not only understand them themselves but can teach them. If a reader wants to learn more or dive more deeply into each topic so they can walk with their kids through more specific questions, we have Next Step Resources listed at the end of this book. We have also included discussion questions at the end of each chapter for reflection alone, with our spouses, or with a small group of friends.

Additionally, because at times this book describes our own parenting decisions as we've tried to walk wisely in a sexually broken world, I want to say we have received permission from our kids for every story we share.

Well, here we are: I haven't found a 24/7 human parenting coach for us, but I hope we can be fellow parents in the trenches walking through this book together.

And, truly, we do have a parenting coach. His name is the Holy Spirit, and he is our counselor, friend, and advocate. He is not only with us every minute of every day, but he goes before us and behind us, and he is within us. He cares more about these conversations than we do. He loves our kids more than we do.

And even when we are anxious, he is never biting his nails.

The goal of this book is to equip our kids so that no matter how they experience sexual brokenness within them and around them, they have the tools they need to walk in the way of Jesus no matter what.

It starts with us as parents learning it first.

By the power of the Holy Spirit, we will teach it to our kids in incremental ways.

Lay the foundation. Walk it.

Ready to dive in?

I am.

1. THE GOSPEL

Lay the Foundation

> "How do I teach my kids about Jesus? I'm so overwhelmed. And how does telling my kids about the gospel relate to sexuality and gender? I'm sure I've heard a sermon about all of this at some point, but I'm just me. I don't know how to teach this."

SAY WE WERE TO SIT DOWN together with a cup of coffee and I asked, "What is your greatest hope for your kids?" What might you say? I'd wager most parents would say something along the lines of, "I want my kids to know and love Jesus for all of their days." Or if they're feeling extra spiritual, "I want them to glorify God and enjoy him forever." I would agree.

Now, what if the apostle John rolled up with his own espresso? I'm thinking he would nod with us, talking about his spiritual children. "I could have no greater joy than to hear that my children are following the truth" (3 Jn 4). If we kept the conversation going (John can stay—I mean, he brought his own espresso), I wonder if we would start talking about less on-the-nose spiritual hopes for our kids like, "I hope they get good jobs. If God calls them to marriage, I hope they marry someone amazing. I hope they have sweet friends and that they have a joyful, long life."

When would our coffee chat turn fearful? As parents, we are hyper-aware that we have no guarantees our kids will do any of these things. As we look at each other over our coffee, smiling anxiously now, we might start subtracting years in our heads. "What is eighteen minus how old they are?" Our eyes widen, and we realize we have only so many years to help them know all they need to know to navigate this wild world with wisdom. If we're close friends, we might start praying fervently together. More likely, we pack up our cups and go home to sit in a corner terrified or quickly try to teach our kids some sort of lesson to make ourselves feel better.

Does that sound about right?

Recently, U.S. Surgeon General Vivek Murthy issued an advisory about the mental health and well-being of parents. His warning cites research stating that 48 percent of parents find daily life completely overwhelming compared with 26 percent of other adults, and 33 percent of parents report high levels of stress in the past month compared with 20 percent of other adults.[1] That feels kind of affirming to hear, doesn't it? The reasons given for our anxiety include financial strain (amen), economic instability (yep), time demands (we're spending 40 percent more time with our children than we did in 1985, yet we're also working more), our children's health (in the United States, one in five children have a special healthcare need), their safety (shudder), parental isolation and loneliness (up to 77 percent of parents experience loneliness compared with 55 percent of nonparents), technology issues (don't even get us started on screen time fights), and cultural pressures and fears about our children's future (we *know*).[2]

Dr. Murthy adds commentary to these statistics, saying, "As technological and economic forces have reshaped the world at a dizzying pace, it has . . . become harder for parents to prepare children for a future that is difficult to understand or predict." Thank you, Mr. Kindhearted Surgeon General. We should have invited you to coffee. "Parents across all backgrounds want to provide their kids with a foundation for happiness and success. Yet too many fear they won't be able to provide what's necessary or their kids won't be able to access what they need in order to lead a fulfilling life."[3] In other words, we want to give our kids every possible advantage in life, but we are freaking out because we can't.

Cool, we might be thinking. But what can we do about it? We hear these statistics and Dr. Murthy's affirmations, but then our kids wake up, or they get home from school, or they turn off whatever screen we let them watch, and we are neck-deep back in the crazy. We cannot read these things and conclude, "Great! I think I'll pass."

This is the job. We cannot outsource it. We cannot walk away and, of course, we don't want to. But is there a way to make it better? A way that doesn't just make us feel better about managing the chaos of parenting but helps with the original conversation we were having about our hopes and goals for our kids? Yes. And the gospel is the key.

Let's Go Back to the Coffee Question

If we roll back the tape on this chapter, back before the apostle John joined our coffee chat and I answered the question about my greatest hopes for my kids, I would probably answer, yes, "I want my kids to know and love Jesus all of their days." But when I start looking at that countdown clock of eighteen years old and think about the insanity of sending these little treasures into the wild world at that point, I find another goal surfacing: I want my kids to be wise. I want them to know God's wisdom so that no matter how they experience the effects of this sexually broken world within or around them, they have the tools they need to walk in the way of Jesus no matter what.

Why am I saying this? Because as much as we dislike it for them, our kids will encounter evil. Suffering. Brokenness. Sexual sin. Temptation. No matter how protective we are, we cannot protect our kids from their own flesh. "For I was born a sinner—yes, from the moment my mother conceived me" (Ps 51:5). We cannot keep them safe from relational, physical, or even sexual suffering. I hate this for us. And before anyone pipes in with, "God can transform suffering into good!" (a true statement, but unhelpful in this moment), I want to affirm that our desire for a suffering-free life for our kids is good. That's God's desire, too. He did not want evil when he created the world. There will be no more "death or sorrow or crying or pain" in the end (Rev 21:4). Our protective hearts resemble the heart of the Father for us. And yet . . . there is evil. Neither we nor our kids can avoid it. So we need wisdom.

What Is Wisdom?

For most of my life I thought wisdom was Jesus smarts. Not IQ smarts but, "I know how to answer WWJD—what would Jesus do—all the time! And then I do it!" The funny thing is, it almost is that. Theologian Daniel Ebert says biblical wisdom "invites people to a way of life that is in harmony with both the created order and God's redemptive work."[4] In other words, God has a path of flourishing in this world, and following the way of Jesus is going to lead to a flourishing life. Douglas Moo adds that wisdom "refers to practical knowledge, the ability to understand reality from God's perspective and to act on that understanding."[5] Wisdom is walking in the way of Jesus. His path is not a tightrope, but it's also not a free-range chicken field. How do we know when we are running off God's path and into barbed wire? We know where not to walk toward by reading his Word. "Your word is a lamp to guide my feet and a light for my path" (Ps 119:105). God put his law into the Bible not because he loves to be a cop but because he wants us to flourish. Following in the wisdom of God is how we flourish.

Let's put this in the context of the gospel. It is important that we have the basic gospel narrative in our heads because it will be the main foundation for this book. It is the basis for why my husband and I hold to a traditional view of marriage, why we believe our sexed bodies determine whether we are male or female in God's eyes, why we don't look at pornography, why we want to keep kids' bodies safe—all of it.

Specifically, there are two major gospel themes we will focus on as we talk about sexuality: God wants to be one with us, and God has a job for us. When I think about raising my kids in the wisdom of God in a sexually broken world, I think of these two gospel themes constantly. I never want to say to my kids, "This is the rule—because I said so"; I want to have the gospel behind everything I say, and these two themes are especially helpful as we talk about marriage, sexuality, sex, gender, body safety, and porn prevention.

With that in mind, let's dive into the gospel.

What Is the Gospel?

The gospel is the story of King Jesus. It is the good news of what God has done through Christ to ensure our salvation and redeem the world unto King Jesus. The story of the Bible takes place in four acts. Act one: In the beginning there was union between God and his creation. Act two: The fall introduced a major fissure to that union called sin. Act three: Jesus made a path for union again when he came to earth. Act four: There will be eternal union between God and his bride, the church, when Jesus returns.

Let's dive deeper into each part of the gospel and how it applies to teaching our kids about sexuality.

Act one—creation: Unity through difference. In the beginning, out of great love for the Father, Son, and Holy Spirit,

God—three-in-one—created the world (Gen 1–2). Right away we see unity through difference, the triune God creating the world as one. This theme continues in his creating night and day—different but unified. Land and sea—different but unified. Male and female—different but unified.

Later in Scripture we directly hear God's longing heart for unity through difference when Jesus (the fullness of God in human form) prays for it in John 17:20-23:

> I am praying not only for these disciples but also for all who will ever believe in me through their message. I pray that they will all be one, just as you and I are one—as you are in me, Father, and I am in you. And may they be in us so that the world will believe you sent me.
>
> I have given them the glory you gave me, so they may be one as we are one. I am in them and you are in me. May they experience such perfect unity that the world will know that you sent me and that you love them as much as you love me.

When we are unified with God, each other, and the world in and through our differences, "the world will believe you sent me." Unity is so core to the heart of God and wired into our flourishing that it preaches "God loves you!" to all who see it.

This unity-through-difference theme is woven throughout the Bible in the form of a big metaphor of marriage. The Bible begins with a marriage between two different beings coming together (man and woman) and ends with a marriage between God and his creation (Rev 19:6-10).

The holistic biblical marriage theme that can be seen from Genesis to Revelation, especially throughout Hosea, Jeremiah, Isaiah, Ezekiel, and Song of Solomon and in the words of Jesus. Pastor and author Tim Keller says of this holistic Bible marriage theme, "If a book begins with something and ends with the same thing, the author is telling you, 'That's what the book is all about.'

The Bible is saying to you, in a marriage between a husband and a wife, you have a clue to the meaning of the universe and of history."[6] Theologian and author Christopher West adds, "Here is the whole Bible in five words: God wants to marry us."[7]

In the newly created world, Adam and Eve were perfectly jiving with each other and God, and they were given jobs to do: "Be fruitful and increase in number; fill the earth and subdue it. Rule . . . " (Gen 1:28 NIV). They were given jobs before the fall, which means work is a good part of our eternal role in the world. Their jobs were to serve as kings, priests, and prophets. Another way to say this is that they (and therefore all of humanity after them) were to be "vice-regents." Besides sounding like a bad guy in Star Wars, a vice-regent is a person who acts in place of a ruler, governor, or sovereign. As image bearers of God, humans govern on his behalf, acting in alignment with God's path of flourishing and toward his mission for the world.

What is God's mission for the church? That in perfectly loving relationship to God and each other we rule as he would rule until everyone everywhere is living in joyful submission to King Jesus for God's glory and our good. In the Great Commission found in Matthew 28:18-20, Jesus does not eliminate this original task for humanity; he reinforces and expands on it: "I have been given all authority in heaven and on earth. Therefore, go and make disciples of all the nations, baptizing them in the name of the Father and the Son and the Holy Spirit. Teach these new disciples to obey all the commands I have given you." Jesus wants the whole world to know and love and be joyfully submitted to him. That was his design from the beginning, and that is still his design. This is for God's glory and our good.

Although we cannot tangibly see this kingdom of God before Jesus returns (Luke 17:20-21), we can see the fruit of it when justice wins, when peace reigns, when there is union between parents and kids and between husbands and wives, and when churches shine light in the darkness. This is known as the shalom of God on earth as it is in heaven, or "the way things ought to be."[8] One day God will be king of his kingdom in the city of God—a real place. Heaven and earth will be unified, and we, the church, will be one with God (Rev 21:10-11). God wanted Adam and Eve and therefore all humanity after them to work together, empowered by the Spirit, to advance God's kingdom until everyone everywhere is living in joyful submission to King Jesus.

This work, this advancing the rule and reign of King Jesus business, is how we can walk in the way of wisdom to the glory of God. To follow in God's path of flourishing—including in our God-given tasks—is to walk in wisdom. The author of Proverbs repeatedly says something along the lines of, "The fear of the Lord is the foundation of wisdom" (Prov 1:7, 9:10, 15:33), and that's not code for "Be scared straight into doing good stuff." It means if we begin with proper awe and respect for God, we will want to follow God's path of flourishing (wisdom). This is similar to how we might feel about standing at the edge of the Grand Canyon. Walking next to it with awe-filled fear leads to wanting to follow the rules (i.e., we won't foolishly close our eyes and start running wherever we want). Foolishness is going wherever we think is best based on our own insight. Wisdom is following in alignment with how we were created based on God's path of flourishing. Part of walking in God's path of flourishing is to fulfill our eternal tasks to further God's kingdom over all the earth.

Act two—the fall: Disunity. Continuing the gospel narrative, it's time to sadly bump into the fall. Instead of working in perfect union with God and others to advance God's kingdom, Adam and Eve stared at what they were told not to have: "The Lord God placed the man in the Garden of Eden to tend and watch over it. But the Lord God warned him, 'You may freely eat the fruit of every tree in the garden—except the tree of the knowledge of good and evil. If you eat its fruit, you are sure to die'" (Gen 2:15-17).

But they do it, as we see in Genesis 3:1: "The serpent was the shrewdest of all the wild animals the LORD God had made. One day he asked the woman, 'Did God really say you must not eat the fruit from any of the trees in the garden?'" (Note: God didn't say that. He said not to eat from the tree of the knowledge of good and evil. Satan is sneaky, using half-truths to trick us.) Adam and Eve fall for it, and instead of taking their role as vice-regents seriously and bringing God's rule and reign to the serpent, they try to take God's place. Theologian Scot McKnight says, "Instead of mediating God to the serpent, instead of taking our assignment of ruling God's good garden on God's behalf, Adam and Eve tried to elevate themselves to God's role. The issue is not just that we were sinners; we were usurpers in the garden."[9] Adam and Eve do not live into their calling, and everything gets cursed: work, relationships, childbearing, and the entire world (Gen 3:14-19).

But the fundamental human assignment does not change. The creation mandate to be fruitful, multiply, subdue, and rule transfers through covenants from Adam to Noah to Abraham to Israel. God gives Moses, the leader of the Israelites, the task of leading the rescue of God's now-enslaved people. He gives the Torah to Israel and helps them find the Promised Land. "But it's all the same task: in the heart of Exodus we find this assignment all over again: to be kings and priests—as a people," McKnight says.[10] Israel fails to rule and subdue as kings and priests, and so a literal king, Saul, takes up the mantle but fails. King David, his successor, does okay, but the subsequent kings lead mostly dismally.

Act three—redemption: Jesus makes a path for unity. Finally, God sends Jesus. He is the true Israelite, the rightful priest and king, and the only perfect image bearer of God. The task that began with Adam is fulfilled in the new Adam, Jesus. He lives, dies on the cross, and rises again, taking the evil of the world on himself always and forever. Through Christ we now have a path of redemption and a pathway to eternal unity with God. Believing on the Lord Jesus Christ (our salvation moment) is a part of this gospel whole: The story of King Jesus.

Jesus is king now, and his kingdom on earth has begun but not yet fully come. We live in the already-but-not-yet time. God did not leave us alone, however. He gave us the Holy Spirit and commissioned his people, the church, to show the world a glimpse of what eternity will be like when we live as brothers and sisters forever with Jesus as our king.

Act four—restoration: We will be unified. There is a real-life future restoration coming for us. One day the city of God will be on earth, where there will be a marriage between God and his people, the church. All evil will be gone. Justice will prevail. And there will be no more sorrow, mourning, tears, or relational pain. "Look, God's home is now among his people! He will live with them, and they will be his people. God himself will be with them. He will wipe every tear from their eyes, and there will be no more death or sorrow or crying or pain. All these things are gone forever" (Rev 21:3-4). This is not theory. This is not merely a story. This is a future fact. *The* story.

A Cross-Shaped Pause

Before moving on to how the gospel informs how we speak about sexuality, I want to pause and look us parents in the eye to talk about how the gospel informs real life, imperfect, exhausting, 24/7 parenting. We need this if we are going to learn more together.

One night I got sick of cycling through my daily failures and began to implement a practice that curbs my perfectionism and toxic shame like nothing else: I picture hiding behind the cross. As condemnation, sin, and mistakes start to pile up in my mind, I picture them like arrows coming toward me. Instead of pummeling me, I hide behind Jesus on the cross. He dies for them. He takes the punishment. His blood covers everything.

All I have to do is receive the gift of that grace.

It feels oddly uncomfortable, but also like what I've needed my whole life. There is nothing so gloriously uncomfortable as being loved and given grace when we don't deserve it.

So now, each night instead of meditating on my failures, I give each arrow to Jesus. Practically this means I confess sin, but I don't wallow in shame. I receive the uncomfortable-wonderful gift of grace.

We can receive this gift, parents. Right now. As we are learning, as we are teaching, and as we stumble-parent in one of the most challenging parenting spaces of our age.

Let's receive it. Let's give it to our kids. Let's teach them to share it with the world.

Two Foundations

This book speaks in the language of foundations and wisdom, and Matthew 7 brings both together. After giving his most famous teaching, the Sermon on the Mount, which describes how disciples of God should live, Jesus concludes with four warnings about applying the sermon. The final warning describes foundations:

> Anyone who listens to my teaching and follows it is wise, like a person who builds a house on solid rock. Though the rain comes in torrents and the floodwaters rise and the winds beat against that house, it won't collapse because it is built on bedrock. But anyone who hears my teaching and doesn't obey it is foolish, like a person who builds a house on sand. When the rains and floods come and the winds beat against that house, it will collapse with a mighty crash. (Mt 7:24-27)

What do we notice in this passage? What immediately stands out to me is that "the rain comes in torrents and floodwaters beat against" both houses. There is no escaping the suffering storms. The wind our kids will experience is to be expected. The question is not whether we can avoid the world's evil but whether we can help them build a foundation of wisdom—a foundation of walking in the way of Jesus—so that when they endure the world's evil, they "won't collapse because [they] are built on bedrock."

We are going to try, aren't we? But this is a no-guarantee system I am offering here. I can make zero promises to myself that my kids will follow Jesus in areas of marriage and sexuality, and I am the one writing this book! I can make zero promises that our kids will do like we hoped over coffee together and "know and love Jesus all of their days." But we can pour foundations of wisdom underneath their feet. We can pray our heads off. And at the end of the day, we can hide behind the cross. Because it truly is enough for all of us.

➤ QUESTIONS TO CONSIDER

1. How would you answer the question, What is your greatest hope for your kids? What is your greatest fear?

2. Which gospel theme stood out to you more today: God wants to be one with us or God has a job for us?

3. How might knowing the gospel change how you think about talking with your kids about marriage, sexuality, sex, and so on?

4. What fears do you need to bring to God today? What lies do you need to let him take onto himself on the cross? With what truth can you replace those fears and lies?

2. THE GOSPEL

Walk the Foundation

> **Key teaching:** "Our purpose is to push back the darkness and usher in the light."

EXPLORING ALL OF THE WAYS we can teach the gospel to our kids could fill the rest of the book and probably ten more. Instead of reading ten books, let's focus on the two main gospel themes and how they can be applied to current and future conversations with our kids about marriage, sex, and sexuality. The two themes are: God wants to be one with us, and God has a job for us.

God Wants to Be One with Us

Parents are the first picture of God for their children. No pressure. If out of God's great love he created male and female, then as his image bearers, we bear his image to the world around us—including to our children. As their mom and dad, we are to reflect to them how God loves them as the best Mom and Dad. I often say to my kids, "I love you so much, but in my best moments of my best days, I am the smallest reflection of how much God loves you."

I am glad I say this because, good grief, I fail to represent God many times a day. And they tell me so—energetically. Recently I was driving the kids to school, and I felt convicted about how I'd herded them into the car. I had yelled, been frustrated, and snapped at them. The Holy Spirit prompted me to apologize when we stopped at the traffic light where we usually pray for their school days.

"I am so sorry, guys," I said to the trio seated behind me. I couldn't pray without apologizing first. "I was wrong to yell at you. Will you forgive me?" There was quiet.

"Yeah . . ." they said after a time.

"That was not like God in how I yelled at you. He is kind and patient, and I was not."

From the back, Juliette huffed, "Yeah, you sure are not at all like God."

I chuckled, remembering all the other times I had received a "you're-not-God" reminder from my kids, and also smiling because I was grateful. I want them to know the difference between God and me, and to be able to name it.

Parents do not just teach their kids how God loves them; they show them what it means to be human and how to relate to other humans. God wants us to love each other the way he loves us. "I pray that they will all be one, just as you and I are one—as you are in me, Father, and I am in you" (Jn 17:21). When I look at my kids and think God wants us to be as close as Jesus is to the Father, I feel both excited and like it is impossible. How can I be that close to them? But we need that closeness of heart to earn the relational equity to talk about the most intimate parts of their lives and bodies.

Do I have to earn relational equity? As their parent, I could dictate the truth from on high. But is that the way of Jesus? Did he drop-kick the Bible to us from heaven or did he come down low and experience life with us? These days, the Holy Spirit still journeys closely with us (he is *in* us!), empathizing, helping, convicting, and disciplining us in love. This is how we want to parent.

Heart-close. Earning relational equity through being with them. That way, when we talk about challenging things, it's not like I'm yelling it from afar. We are in the same room, doing life together, and this is simply the next topic of conversation.

How can we do that? How can we show our kids God's desire to be one with them, as well as his desire for union among people, through our pursuit of our children's hearts?

Family Dinners and Devotions

Many of us have heard that it is good to have dinner with our kids regularly and it is beneficial to take them to church. The research shows that eating together three or four times per week lowers rates of obesity, eating disorders, substance abuse, and depression, and it is linked to higher self-esteem and academic performance.[1] One 2020 study found that those who attend church have a 26 percent lower risk of all-cause mortality and are less depressed, suicidal, and anxious than those who do not attend religious services.[2] It seems that eating together and finding a church that preaches and lives the gospel can offer positive outcomes for us and our kids. Why is that? I think it's because we are made for perfect, heavenly union with God and each other, and Christ-glorifying family dinners and a Christ-honoring church give us glimpses of our eternal reality: We will feast with God and each other, worshiping God forever. In their best moments, family dinner and the regular gathering of saints show us exactly that.

In addition to family dinner, we can glimpse our eternal future through family devotions. There we can directly teach the gospel and Jesus' desire to be one with us through resources like *The Jesus Storybook Bible*, which talks about the "never stopping, never giving up, unbreaking, always and forever love" of God. Our very togetherness, our "let's do this together" mentality, models God's desire to be one with us. Here we are, a family, seeking God together as one.

Ellis, our five-year-old, was born with a heart for this sort of union. All he wants is to just be together. "Can you sit with me?" he has asked since he had words. We joke he was born an old man, content to just sit peacefully. If he asked to start smoking a pipe, I might just allow it. (I kid!) When I do finally slow down my too-busy self to sit with him, he often says, "I wish Dad was here, and the girls, and Bingo." He can't forget our hundred-pound Saint Bernard-poodle.

"Me too, buddy," I say. "It's the best when we are all together." His together-loving heart reflects God's together-loving heart.

Ideally, we do devotions together every morning. I recognize this is not realistic for many families—even ours. The goal is not to check devotions off the list; the goal is to be unified as a family in a posture of worship to God to show our kids a glimmer of how God wants to be one with us for his glory and our good.

When we do devotions, they happen more like four times per week for about five to ten minutes. Either during breakfast or after, we get in some sort of circle, and Matt or I ask, "Who wants to read the Bible? Who wants to read the devotional? Who wants to lead prayer?"

The girls are the only strong readers at this point, so they rotate the reading jobs. Ellis, Matt, or I tend to be the prayer leaders. When our kids were very young (ages zero to four), Matt and I did all the reading and invited the kids to respond after we read from a short children's devotional or short section from the Bible. "What did you hear in what we read?" we asked. We tried not to judge the answers even if they were very simple responses like, "Noah. Animals."

"Yeah! Noah built an ark and had animals in it," we encouraged. "Why did God do that?" We waited, listened, and added some guiding insight. Now the girls (ages five to ten) read and are learning to lead the questions.

Parents who did not go to Bible school like Matt and I did don't need to worry. There are some great children's devotionals out there that can help contextualize the stories into the greater story (see Next Step Resources at the end of this book).

As the older kids push into ages eight to twelve, we not only have them lead the devotional time but also ask, "How does that change the way you live today?" After everyone answers (including the parents), we pray together. We ask, "What do you want prayer for and what are you thankful for today?" Each family member responds with a "prayer for and thankful for," and we take all requests seriously. "Yes, we will pray for your cut on your hand. Yes, let's ask God for help with Spanish today. Yes, God cares about your broken scooter." We want our kids to know they can bring all their requests to God. If he wants to be one with us, that means he is in the midst of scooter breakdowns and cut hands. Kids need to know this. I need to know this.

An Identity Rooted in God's Love

Some of the best parenting moments happen in the middle of real life. I'm pretty sure God knows this, so that's why he said, "Commit yourselves wholeheartedly to these words of mine. Tie them to your hands and wear them on your forehead as reminders. Teach them to your children. Talk about them when you are at home and when you are on the road, when you are going to bed and when you are getting up" (Deut 11:18-19). God knows that parenting has intentional "Let's learn a lesson" times, but most of them happen "on the road, while going to bed, and getting up."

So how do we teach our kids that God loves people and wants to be one with them in our real, always-moving lives? To be honest, it starts with our own prayer life. I am by nature a do-er for God instead of a be-er with God, so most mornings, I sit down, grab my $1.99 spiral-bound notebook, and pray, "God, help me to know the love of God, work from the love of God, repent from the love of God, and live from the love of God." Preaching God's love and desire to be one with my kids starts with my meditating on that love first. Then I pray for my family to know his love too. "Help them to know how deeply loved they are," I write underneath each name in the notebook. As I pray this, I remember my favorite verses from Ephesians 3:14-19:

> When I think of all this, I fall to my knees and pray to the Father, the Creator of everything in heaven and on earth. I pray that from his glorious, unlimited resources he will empower you with inner strength through his Spirit. Then Christ will make his home in your hearts as you trust in him. Your roots will grow down into God's love and keep you strong. And may you have the power to understand, as all God's people should, how wide, how long, how high, and how deep his love is. May you experience the love of Christ, though it is too great to understand fully. Then you will be made complete with all the fullness of life and power that comes from God.

The love of God completes us (v. 19). The love of God empowers us (vv. 16, 19). The love of God makes us strong (vv. 17, 19). The love of God roots us in our identity as beloved image bearers of God (v. 17). I desperately want Matt, our kids, and myself to be rooted in this completing, empowering, strengthening, identity-forming love of God. This will be the engine to empower all of us to choose the way of Jesus no matter how we experience the effects of the fall within us or around us.

But "sinking our roots into God's love" is not our default. Shame is. Hiding. Grabbing the fig leaves and running from God. To counteract this default, we pray and speak love over our kids, over and over and over.

"Mom, I am the worst girl!" cried Juliette, six years old at the time, hiding behind her pillow.

"No," I said gently but firmly. "That is not who you truly are. You are created in God's image, and you are loved by Jesus." She had done something wrong, and instead of believing she was still loved in spite of it, she was believing the shame-lie that *who she is* is wrong because of what she did.

These shame spirals can be identity-forming opportunities. Matt and I try to speak eternal truth over our kids—an identity they will carry with them into eternity: "You are beloved. You are chosen. You are beautiful." Not, "You're a bad girl." That's a temporal truth, not an eternal one.

But Juliette wasn't having it. "No!" She told me exactly what she'd done wrong. "See? I am bad!"

Do *we* tell her she's bad because of what she's done? No. But culture does. The enemy of her soul does. So Matt and I focus on telling our kids their eternal identity repeatedly. True, we are "born into sin" and made alive only in Christ (Ps 51:5; Eph 2:1-5). But articulating that to tiny kids who are already in a shame tornado is tough. Instead of *focusing* on their depravity, we focus on Jesus and what he did for them. As our kids get older (nine to twelve), we talk more about depravity, because they can understand even more deeply what Jesus did for them in light of the sin contrast. But in the younger years, we want to establish that their identity is neither achieved nor shaken. It's given.

"I am the worst kid!" Juliette continues.

I almost laugh because I can practically see the cross over her, covering up her self-hateful lies. "That is not who you are! You can't add to your identity or take it away. Your value comes from God making you in his image, and from what Jesus did for you on the cross. You don't have to hide. You can say sorry and God forgives you! When God looks at you, he sees the righteousness of Jesus. So it doesn't matter what you say, dear heart. You are loved. You can't change your value one bit."

She's quiet. Being loved apart from what we do is disarming. God's undeserved love melts hearts. This is probably why we sing about grace being so amazing. I rub her arm. "Buddy, you are going to get a discipline for what you did, but please know that I love you no matter what. God does, too. Nothing can change that."

She snuggles into her comforters and quietly says, "I love you too, Mom."

God Has a Job for Us

We've talked about God's unifying love. Now let's talk about the mission of God. God's mission for people is for us to partner with the Holy Spirit to invite the world to live in joyful submission to King Jesus to the glory of God and to the good of his people.

Our kids get to be a part of that beautiful mission. How in the world do we explain it to them in kid-speak?

"Push back the darkness and usher in the light." Let's go to the kitchen. It's morning. I'm bustling around, getting kids ready for school, Matt is half out the door for work, the oldest and youngest kids are in various states of school readiness, and my second-born, Juliette, is munching slowly on "breakfast." Technically, she's eating breakfast cereal, but it's actually just squares of cinnamon and sugar in a bowl—minus the nutrition of milk. Because who wants to eat cereal the way the good Lord intended? Not my kids.

As I'm rushing about, praying the alleged vitamins promised on the cereal box actually make it into my seven-year-old's bloodstream, Juliette moans, "Mommmm? Why do I have to go to school?"

I have a decision to make in this moment. I can rely on Christian cultural stereotypes and tired mom brain and spit out, "You have to go because you need to become a marketable spouse and move out someday . . . because mommy tired . . . " But while a marriage-oriented life might be the mission of Hallmark movies, it's not the mission of God.

I could say something like, "You have to go to school so you can get a good job and become a valuable contributor to society." This is actually somewhat closer to focusing on the mission of

God. As N. T. Wright says, "To say, 'Jesus died for your sins' ought to lead at once to 'so you can freely pick up your role as a truly human being and discover your particular vocation within God's purposes for his world.'"[3] Humans are made for good work—but toward what end?

With the mission-of-God gospel framework in mind, here is how I responded to my second-born: "Juliette, God has given you and me the same job: to push back the darkness and usher in the light." She looks at me sideways between mouthfuls.

"You know how I told you that God made the world good? It was full of light and was perfect." She nods, likely remembering some of our morning devotional conversations. "But then Adam and Eve ate the fruit, and sin—darkness—entered the world."

She shakes her head, jaw tight. "I wish I was born first," she spits.

"Why?" I ask.

"Because I would take Satan by the throat and say, 'NO!'" (I love this kid. We need like fifty thousand more versions of her.)

"You should have been born first," I sigh. "But sin entered the world, and now there is darkness and evil. My job and your job is to partner with other people who know and love Jesus and push back the darkness and usher in the light of Jesus." She nods again. "God has given you a specific way he wants you to push back the darkness and bring in the light."

I can tell I am starting to lose her focus. "How?" she asks. Bless. She's still listening.

"I don't know yet. You have specific gifts he has given you that we are learning about together. We are going to keep knocking on doors, trying to see what you are good at, what you like, and what God might need you to do in the world." I can tell I have about thirty more seconds before she is lost to a sugar coma. "So you have to go to school because you're getting trained for this good work God has for you."

She shrugs. "Okay."

Bless the Lord, oh my soul, she heard me. "We are called to push back the darkness and usher in the light" is the phrase we use in our house from when they are four years old until they are twelve. When they are in the four to seven range, we stick with the "light and dark" language, helping them see we are in this big mission together. I want them to feel like they belong and are a part of something big with their mom and dad and Jesus.

As they get older (seven to ten), we repeat the big gospel picture, but we start using less "dark and light" language and more "kingdom of God" language: "Pushing back the darkness and ushering in the light is called 'advancing the kingdom of God.' We do that together. I wonder what specific job God has for you?" We ask God about our kids' kingdom role with them, and we pray it over them on our own. Every day I pray, "God, help them to know how loved they are by you and to know their kingdom place in this world." I am not saying this to shine up my parenting résumé but to emphasize that helping our kids know they are part of the mission of God must be a primary parenting focus.

Why? And how does this apply to the sexuality conversation? If I had a dollar for every story I've heard about people who were told, explicitly or implicitly, that their top goal in life was to find a Christian (opposite-sex) spouse, I would be rich. If after many years of searching they do not find "their person," they often go through long seasons of self-doubt or even self-hatred because they feel they have failed God's goal for their lives. If they are same-sex attracted, after years of trying to like the opposite sex, some simply change their trajectory from finding an opposite-sex spouse to finding a same-sex partner. Their journey did not begin with a wholehearted pursuit of a same-sex spouse. It began with prioritizing a human spouse over God.

No other gods. The pursuit of marriage as the ultimate goal is one of the most common forms of idolatry, or putting someone or something before God. Just because it is common does not mean it is godly. We need to repent of our laser focus on marriage more than on the marriage between Christ and the church.

If we want our kids to thrive no matter how they experience their versions of broken sexuality—and *all* of us experience broken sexuality—we must begin by helping them see they are a part of the greatest love story—one that takes them into the mission of God. Our children's journeys with Jesus may lead to a lucrative job, but a gospel mindset will have them see that work as a loving mission field, not as their life. Their pushing-back-the-darkness paths may lead to marriage to someone of the opposite sex or a calling to vibrant singleness, but they will see it as a gift from God and a missional metaphor of God's desire to marry us. Marriage and a good vocation are not our chief aim. God is.

▨➤ QUESTIONS TO CONSIDER

1. Do you do intentional family prayer or Bible time with your kids? What does it look like? How might you want it to look?

2. What are practical ways you could teach your kids the love of God for them?

3. What are practical ways you could teach the mission of God to your kids?

4. How can you help your kids know their identity comes from who God is, not what they do?

3. MARRIAGE AND SINGLENESS

Lay the Foundation

> "My kids see many marital options on TV, at school, and even in our extended family. How do I talk about God's design for marriage to my kids? And singleness? I'm supposed to talk about that too?"

CLEANING A BATHROOM does not seem like the ideal time or place to have a theological conversation about same-sex marriage, but that's parenting, isn't it? Gwyn, my oldest, was three years old at the time and happily "helping me." (By "helping," I mean she was looking at an I Spy book while I attacked the layers of grime that could not be avoided any longer.) Her little sister, one-year-old Juliette, was confined to the bouncy seat downstairs. As I reached for the scrub brush to clean the toilet bowl, Gwyn looked up from her book and asked, "Can girls get married?"

I stopped scrubbing, swallowed, and looked at her. Her blond curls tilted with her head as she looked at me with trusting eyes. *Umm . . . I* thought to myself. *Is this the age we start talking about same-sex marriage?* I'd figured on several more years until I had to talk about this with my kids. And yet here I was, in the middle of scrubbing the bathroom, ready to dive into the theological deep end with my three-year-old.

But wait, what if she didn't mean to ask about same-sex marriage? "Do you mean, can girls get married to boys?"

She shook her head. "No. Can two girls marry each other?"

My heart started racing. *Do I dodge the question until she's older? If I don't respond, will it damage her somehow? If I do, will that make it worse? And how do I even say it in a way she would understand at age three?* I started praying, and my brain quickly landed on what Matt and I were learning in real time within our own marriage: the positive vision. The metaphor of marriage. I decided to go for it.

The Metaphor of Marriage

We will come back to finish the story of how I responded to Gwyn, but let's pause and unpack what I'm talking about related to marriage. What is the positive vision for it? In the last chapters, we said one way we could summarize the Bible is "God wants to marry us." We can see this in the four-act gospel narrative: There was union between God and his creation in the beginning, the fall introduced a major fissure to that union, Jesus made a path for union again when he came to earth, and there will be eternal union between God and his bride, the church, when Jesus returns. The Bible begins and ends with marriage, and so Keller's quote bears repeating: "If a book begins with something and ends with the same thing, the author is telling you, 'That's what the book is all about.' The Bible is saying to you, in a marriage between a husband and a wife, you have a clue to the meaning of the universe and of history."[1]

I had no idea about any of that when our marriage was falling apart right before the time of this bathroom scene with Gwyn. I had been to umpteen weddings by that point in my life—siblings, cousins, friends. My eyes glazed over when pastors started quoting Ephesians 5:31-32: "As the Scriptures say, 'A man leaves his father and mother and is joined to his wife, and the two are united into one.' This is a great mystery, but it is an illustration of the way Christ and the church are one." In my head I thought, *Yeah, blah blah blah, marriage has something to do with Jesus loving us, but it's more about the bride and groom.* After all, the focus of much of my life had been on praying for and finding Mr. Right, so it made sense that that was where my mind focused when listening to sermons about the metaphor of marriage.

After graduating from college, I exchanged finding Mr. Right to longing for Mrs. Right. I had dated Matt after secretly dating a woman in college, but as much as I liked him and felt my heart drawn toward him, when we started talking about marriage, I sensed God saying, "No." It was a good thing, too. After I broke up with Matt, every minute of every day I thought a woman was what I needed. Had Matt and I married then, I'm not sure it would have lasted. When we broke up, my attractions toward women waged war with my theological beliefs about marriage, and it led to a major depressive spiral.

This is when I met Carolyn, a mentor-therapist who helped me understand the richness of God's love. God's love rooted me like nothing else, and empowered (still empowers) me daily to die to self—not just to same-sex desires but to all my other sin issues, as I am not just a one-note sinner. As I joyfully planned out my single future after journeying with Carolyn, I sensed God's hand on my shoulder saying, "I have someone for you." God knows the best mode for us to be in to advance his mission to redeem the world unto King Jesus. Married and single are simply two different ways we can fulfill this mission. Through a bananas series of events, God brought Matt back into my life, and we were soon married, as detailed in our book *An Impossible Marriage.*[2]

Seven years after saying "I do," however, a childhood memory of sexual assault resurfaced. Our kids were growing into the age I was when something happened to me, and I found myself involuntarily shutting down. Such experiences are not uncommon for parents or caregivers who have experienced childhood sexual abuse.[3] Although Matt was not the one who hurt me, the stranger who did was a man, so every time I was near male Matt—even in nonsexual friendship—his presence made me recoil into triggered suffering. Those feelings magnetized to the attractions I was surrendering to Jesus and produced an earthquake of indecision in my life. *Why am I in this marriage? What's the point of doing this hard thing called marriage to a man if my default attractions are toward women?* The attractions reemerged with a vengeance and promised an easy "happily ever after" escape from the growing battle within me.

As the war raged, I found myself wondering along with the apostle Paul, "Oh, what a miserable person I am! Who will free me from this life that is dominated by sin and death?" (Rom 7:24). I did not know if or how God would hear me, but he did. "Thank God! The answer is in Jesus Christ our Lord," Paul answers in the next verse. I discovered the truth of that statement during this second round of intense wrestling with my sexuality. When I had journeyed with my therapist, Carolyn, right after graduating from college, the theme God drew out from the gospel was his deep, unwavering love for me. Seven years later, the primary gospel theme God utilized to save our marriage was the theology of marriage. Yeah. The "boring" part of weddings. To be fair, God also used therapy and amazing friends with whom we were very real to come alongside us, but theology was the engine to even talk with those friends, and it got me in the car to fight for my marriage in therapy.

Then I read Francis and Lisa Chan's *You and Me Forever: Marriage in Light of Eternity.* That book is basically the gospel with some marriage stuff in between, and it was exactly what I needed. I began to understand the gospel vision within the metanarrative of the Bible, and that's what helped me even care about learning communication strategies and the like. The Chans explain the vision of God's desire to be one with us in Ephesians 5:31-32: "As the Scriptures say, 'A man leaves his father and mother and is joined to his wife, and the two are united into one.' This is a great mystery, but it is an illustration of the way Christ and the church are one." Instead of focusing on the husband and wife as the pinnacle of marriage, the Chans put the focus back on the marriage between Christ and the church.

A lightbulb turned on in my head. Wait. Wait a minute. What is the "great mystery"? That men and women fall in love? Yes, some people do see falling in love as a big mystery, and they make jokes about it in wedding reception speeches. But that's not the mystery to which Paul is referring. The "great mystery" is the fact that God wants to and will be one with us in an eternal marriage. We will be unified, complete, and whole forever one day with Jesus as King in a real kingdom within the real city of God (Rev 19–21). For the first time, the reality that God, the Creator of the heavens and the earth, wants to be one with made-from-dust us sank into my soul. I was stunned that God, who is "far above any ruler or authority or power or leader or anything else—not only in this world but also in the world to come," and "who lives in eternity," longs for union with humanity, for whom "the wind blows, and we are gone—as though we had never been here" (Eph 1:21, Is 57:15, Ps 103:16). We are so different from God. And yet he wants to and will be one with us.

I suddenly saw marriage between two opposite-sex people in a one-flesh covenant union for life neither as a cosmic joke nor a cosmic punishment. I understood that even my effort to seek one millimeter of oneness with Matt showed our kids, our neighbors, and strangers in the grocery store a small glimmer of the lengths

Jesus went to in order to be one with us. He died for us. He went to hell and back for us. If God has called us to marriage, then when we love and seek union with our spouses, we get the privilege of preaching the gospel through our marriages. Author Christopher West writes about this reality:

> Here, in Ephesians 5, we learn that the purpose of the sexual difference and the call to union is not only to reproduce the human species, although that's an essential part of it. It's not only for the sake of human companionship, although that, too, is an essential part of it. The ultimate purpose of the sexual difference and the call to union is to signify the difference and call to union of the Creator and the creature, of Christ and his Church. God is infinitely other, infinitely different from his creation. And yet this infinitely different Creator does not hold himself aloof. God wants to be one with his creation. God wants to unite with his creation. God wants to marry his creation. This is what the mystery of Jesus Christ—the mystery of God taking on flesh—is all about: the marriage of Creator and creature; the marriage of divinity and humanity.[4]

People often joke about marriage being the "ol' ball and chain" and roll their eyes about how "men have one thing on their mind" and "women are so controlling," and they laugh about how "God tricks you into marriage by making you want sex" (and marriage makes it Christian-legal)—and I get it. But we need to be careful with our humor and with perhaps our over-emphasis on the frustrating, sanctifying work of marriage. We need to talk about the beauty of it. In creation,

> God created human beings in his own image.
>> In the image of God he created them;
>> male and female he created them. (Gen 1:27)

We are made in the image of God. We call this *imago Dei*. It is an interesting concept if we consider how and where ancient Near East kings put images of themselves. They crafted statues—images—and put them in temples so that people throughout the world would see them as "gods." Our God did not place a statue of himself in the Garden of Eden. He created live-action, image-bearing people. About this, theologian N. T. Wright says:

> Genesis is the creation of a heaven plus earth reality. In the ancient world, a heaven plus earth reality is a temple. Many Old Testament scholars have said that Genesis 1 is describing creation of a temple. And guess what? It has an image in it so that you know who the God is and so that the influence of the God can be felt throughout the world.[5]

God made us to represent him throughout the world. One way we do this as married people is through how we relate to our spouses. Our pursuit of oneness with our different-from-us spouses shows the world a tiny glimpse of God's desire for union with us and desire to produce fruit through us even though he is infinitely different from us. Sin added layers of challenge to this relational barrier crossing, but Jesus went to hell and back to cross the chasm and make a way for union with us. That's a vision I can get behind. That fuels me to work on being one with this different-from-me guy.

But, some may wonder, don't you think two women in a monogamous marriage are different enough to show the world a picture of God's love for the world? To answer this question, we can look deeper into Scripture and to general revelation.

To start with Scripture, Matthew 19 is where I always begin. Here, the Pharisees want to trap Jesus by asking about marriage: "Should a man be allowed to divorce his wife for just any reason?" (Mt 19:3). Jesus responds with what can seem like a too-long answer. Instead of just answering the question, he goes back to the beginning of the Bible and gives us the archetype for marriage.

> "Haven't you read the Scriptures?" Jesus replied. "They record that from the beginning 'God made them male and female.'" And he said, "'This explains why a man leaves his father and mother and is joined to his wife, and the two are united into one.' Since they are no longer two but one, let no one split apart what God has joined together." (Mt 19:4-6)

When Jesus quotes Genesis 2:24, "The two are united into one," that's Bible-speak for "and then they got married." He's essentially saying, "This is what marriage is about: Union. Two different things coming together." But what kind of "different things"? Two women who love each other? How about two men? To find out which two, we look at what else Jesus said: "God created them male and female." Here Jesus is quoting Genesis 1:27 and telling us *the* definition of marriage. "The two" is not two people who love each other; it is male and female. Marriage is the one-flesh covenant union of two sexually different people (male and female) for life.

If we look to general revelation for our arguments, we can ask: What can only one man and one woman produce? Children. Kids are the literal fruit of marriage. If marriage is a picture of God's desire to be one with humanity and produce fruit through them, men and women's ability to produce the fruit of kids reflects God's fruit-producing love and is part of the fulfillment of the creation mandate "to be fruitful, multiply fill the earth and subdue it. Rule . . ." (Gen 1:28 NIV). Yes, sex is meant to be fun, unifying, and covenant-renewing, but ideally it is also meant to produce children.

The reality is that this is not always possible. Infertility is a grief many men and women share. But the fact that they grieve does not negate God's heart to produce the literal fruit of children through marriage; it emphasizes it. A couple's longing for children is a reflection of God's longing. Additionally, parents who choose to foster and adopt show the world a picture of God adopting us into his family. It is an important, beautiful picture of God's love, but it is another picture of God's love for the humanity—not a replacement for how God designed kids to be created. Additionally, God designed kids with a mom and dad in mind not because he is a homophobic jerk, but because he wants the whole world to know and be one with him! When we love our spouses and produce the fruit of kids, we show the world how God wants to be one with us and produce the fruit of disciples through us. Male-female marriage can and ideally should display this vision.

Lest we lose sight of the greater mission of God and start seeing human marriage again as ultimate, let's remember the two parts of the gospel we focused on in chapters one and two: God wants to be one with us, and God has a job for us. Marriage shows the world a picture of God's desire to be one with us, and marriage is the way we lean into our vocational purpose to push back the darkness and usher in the light. However, even though marriage is a beautiful picture of God's love for the world and is a sweet way we can lean into God's purpose for humanity, it is not the only way we can flourish.

The Metaphor of Singleness

Singleness is the other way Christians can show the world a picture of God's desire to be one with humanity, and it is an equally valuable way Christians can advance the kingdom of God. Had I not experienced attractions to the same sex, I am not sure I would have even considered this reality. I was certain I would marry a man someday until the same sex attractions came on strong in college, and then I wanted to marry a woman. Marriage was the focus of my life. But God needed to be the focus. I needed to ask him, "What is the mode you want me in to join your mission for the world?" The apostle Paul knew to ask this question:

I wish everyone were single, just as I am. Yet each person has a special gift from God, of one kind or another. . . . I want you to do whatever will help you serve the Lord best, with as few distractions as possible. . . . The person who marries his fiancée does well, and the person who doesn't marry does even better. (1 Cor 7:7, 35, 38)

Paul says here that singleness is even better than marriage to advance God's kingdom, and in our roughest marriage seasons, we couples may think he's right. My single friends, in their best single seasons, are certain he's right. But it's not what we parents tend to want for our kids, and we need to consider that it might be our kids' path. If the purpose of our lives is not to get married, make Christian babies, tithe, and die but instead to advance God's kingdom for God's glory and our good, we have to remember marriage and singleness are equally valuable ways to do that.

Do we offer both marriage and singleness as equally valuable options for our kids? Or do we talk in "When you get married" language? We don't know if our children are called to marriage, so why do we talk about it in such absolutes? It would be wiser to say, "*If* God calls you to marriage" instead of "*when.*" In our house, we speak so often about God's calling to "push back the darkness and usher in the light" and "God might want you to do this married or single" that our kids have come close to stressing out about it.

"I just don't know if God has called me to marriage or singleness yet, Mom," our five-year-old son said recently. "I just don't know."

My eyes went wide, and I leaned in to comfort his anxiety, saying, "Well, we have a long time to figure it out. God knows. You don't have to worry."

It is wise to talk about the options for marriage and singleness as valuable ways to live into God's mission to restore and redeem the world unto King Jesus. But it's possible to overdo it—and Matt and I are discovering this balance.

Let's go back to how singleness is a gospel picture. Dani Treweek, author of *The Meaning of Singleness*, says, "We are going to be our most perfectly human selves in the next age— perfectly known and knowing perfectly, perfectly loved and loving perfectly—and we are going to do that as men and women with bodies but who are not married to each other and who are not having sex with each other. That actually says that we don't need to be married and sexually active in our lives here and now in this creation in order to be fully human."[6] In eternity there will be no marriage except the marriage between Christ and the church (Mt 22:30). In the new heaven and the new earth, we will be embodied, single, in perfect union with each other, and married to Jesus (Rev 19:6-9).

Singleness also uniquely shows the world the value of the church—the family of God—in the reality that celibate single people may not have biological children, but they do make disciples. As theologian Stanley Hauerwas says:

> One of the few clear differences between Christianity and Judaism is the former's entertainment of the idea of singleness as the paradigm way of life for its followers. . . . Singleness was legitimate, not because sex was thought to be a particularly questionable activity, but because the mission of the church was such that "between the times" the church required those who were capable of complete service to the Kingdom. . . . And we must remember that the "sacrifice" made by the single is not that of "giving up sex," but the much more significant sacrifice of giving up heirs. There can be no more radical act than this, as it is the clearest institutional expression that one's future is not guaranteed by the family, but by the church.[7]

Additionally, Paul says there is something about singleness that allows for a more undivided devotion to the Lord. Single people can have more time to pursue union with Christ in their lives, and they can have more flexibility in how God calls them to advance his kingdom. Some of my single friends model this reality for me in astounding ways; their intimacy with God is palpable. Many of my single friends have beautiful, God-honoring, church-as-sibling relationships that show me a picture of how we will all be in heaven. Several of them are leaning into advancing God's kingdom in astoundingly selfless ways through regular missions, mentoring, and offering their home as a haven to others.

We need to treasure both the vocation of marriage and the vocation of singleness. We need to offer singleness as an equally good option for our kids as they live into the mission of God. This is not only biblical and beautiful, but it also sets our kids up to handle potential attractions toward the same sex. Instead of spending an average of three years in hiding,[8] what if they simply saw their attractions as another version of sexual brokenness, shrugged, and said, "Well, that's not God's picture of love for his church, so I am not called to act on those attractions and find a same-gendered spouse. That's okay. Maybe God will draw me to love someone of the opposite sex and show the world a picture of the gospel through marriage. Or maybe he will call me to singleness, and I will have amazing friends and love God and show the world a picture of the gospel through singleness. Either way, my life is not over, nor will it be lonely. My adventure with Jesus and his church is just beginning."

So, What Did I Say to Gwyn?

Let's finish the story with Gwyn in the bathroom, shall we? What can we say to our kids if they ask about same-sex marriage? Here is an idea: "Yes, honey, two women can technically marry each other in this country, but it is not marriage in God's eyes." Before

I share how I taught her what marriage is, let's break down each part of that answer.

"Yes, honey, two women can technically marry each other in this country," I began. Why do I recommend responding in the affirmative if our kids ask a question like this? First of all, because it's true. I want our kids to know that their parents will share what is true in bite-sized, age-appropriate ways. When two women or two men go to the courthouse and get married, it is legally called "marriage" in the United States, even if it is not biblical marriage. We could say, "The world calls it 'marriage,' but we call it a civil union because it is not marriage in God's eyes." Some parents may choose to do that because it seems more biblical or true. I do not choose to go that route because it does not seem as missional. It could be hard for my kids to share the gospel with someone if the conversation gets caught in semantics, but God can use anyone and anything to advance his kingdom.

A second reason I recommend honestly saying "yes" when our kids ask if same-sex marriage is possible is I want them to know they can bring their tough questions to us. Author and therapist Jay Stringer offers, "Your kids are only going to ask you and come to you about things about which they think you are going to be helpful. If they pick up implicitly that you are nervous about the topic or scared or intimidated, they are more than likely not going to bring you topics with which they think you are uncomfortable."[9] When our kids have questions, we are ChatGPT. We are their anchoring bias. We are their number one top resource for questions about marriage, sexuality, and sex now and in the future. We help them recognize us as this resource when we respond in gracious, age-appropriate truth.

But it's not enough to speak the truth; we need to do it in love. We need to speak with a tone of peaceful gospel confidence that says to our kids, "We are trustworthy. We are not afraid of your questions. You do not need to caretake me in this moment. I am trusting in God who cares for us both." I highlight this for two reasons: If we are afraid, angry, or panicked, our kids are likely going to be afraid, angry, and panicked. Their brains are wired with mirror neurons to copy and be regulated by our emotions.[10] If we are peaceful and confident, God has created their minds to pick up on our confidence and feel at rest.

Another reason we answer questions like these with a peaceful, gospel-confident tone is because our kids may notice our insecurity and try to step in to emotionally regulate us. Ask any therapist if having our kids caretake us as parents is a good thing, and they will shake their heads in sorrow. "Parentification" of kids can lead to anxiety, depression, future boundary issues, and a tendency toward risky behaviors.[11] God never intended for our kids to be our emotional caretakers. We are the parent. They are the kids. If we don't know how to model peace in a tricky moment, instead of panicking, we need to give the Holy Spirit our anxiety and say, "That's a great question, honey. I don't know the answer to that now, but I will find the answer and get back to you." Then, we do it.

Before moving on to how we can cast the beautiful vision for marriage to our kids, one more note on tone: Sometimes when I am doing ministry work, I hear people get riled up about others who do not follow God's design for marriage. They shake their fists, they shout, they scoff about the "LGBTQ agenda." I hear them. I have sympathy. But I often want to ask what is underneath their anger. Anger is often a masking emotion for fear or sadness.[12] When we talk with our kids about God's design for marriage, I would encourage accessing that deeper grief instead of expressing rage or fear. That way our kids do not feel like we are out of control and they have to caretake us.

I call this grief over sin "holy grief." I see it modeled beautifully in Jesus when he is grieving over Jerusalem's murder of his prophets. "O Jerusalem, Jerusalem, the city that kills the prophets and stones God's messengers! How often I have wanted to gather your children together as a hen protects her chicks beneath her wings, but you wouldn't let me" (Mt 23:37). Jesus is embodying peaceful, grieving, gospel confidence. I recommend that be the tone with which we talk with our kids about sexual sin.

I did not end the conversation with Gwyn by telling her, "Yes, two women can technically marry each other in this country." After acknowledging the truth of the world, I needed to cast a vision for God's beautiful design with the theme of "different" in mind. So I added, "But it is not marriage in God's eyes. God wants marriage to be between two people whose bodies are different: a mommy and a daddy. When these different people love each other, they show us a picture of how God loves us."

She stopped, her head tilting to the side again, processing I-have-no-idea-how-much of what I just said. "Okay," she said, and skipped off to find her sister.

It's normal for our kids not to comprehend God's entire design for marriage and sexuality and the bigger picture they represent in one conversation like this. As an adult I needed like twenty teachings on this; our kids will need probably fifty or more bite-sized, age-appropriate, gospel-positive conversations like these.

After talking with Gwyn, I let my head fall back against the shower glass and grabbed my knees in a little hug. *Oof. We did it. Thank you, God.* As she and all my kids grow older, I want them to understand more of this "different" piece that is required in marriage—that is, how kids display the multiplicative, procreative heart of God. I also want them to understand why God's "covenant" in marriage is such a big deal. In the chapters on sex we will explore more of both of those realities and how to share them with our kids, but this was enough for today.

QUESTIONS TO CONSIDER

1. What do you think about the metaphor of marriage being a picture of God's love for the church? How does knowing that change the way you look at marriage or live your marriage?

2. What do you think about the metaphor of singleness being a picture of eternity? How does knowing that change the way you look at singleness or live your singleness?

3. What do you think about saying to your kids, "If God calls you to marriage . . . " instead of "When you get married . . . "?

4. How have you responded to your kids if they've asked about same-sex marriage? Is there anything you might change in your response after reading this chapter?

4. MARRIAGE AND SINGLENESS

Walk the Foundation

> **Key teaching:** *"Marriage is between one man and one woman, so when moms and dads love each other, they show you a picture of how much God loves you."*

"**MOM, WHAT DOES THAT RAINBOW FLAG MEAN?**"

"Dad, where do babies come from?"

"Mom, why were there dinosaurs on the earth but now there aren't?"

It is the reality of parenting that our kids will ask us the most intense questions at the most inopportune times. We're late for school and our kids ask how a man and a woman can have a baby if they aren't married. We're a few minutes from church and our kids notice the rainbow flag on the church next door and want to be educated. We're exhausted after a long day, and they suddenly want to know the entire history of the brontosaurus.

Although my paleontology expertise begins and ends with the sentence above, I can dive into helping our kids wisely walk the foundation of God's design for marriage and singleness.

Work on Our Calling of Marriage or Singleness

One of the best arguments for God's design for marriage and singleness is to live it well. When we married people do the hard work required to love our spouses, valuing them in the way God values us, we show our kids a picture of God's love for them, and we model how to advance the kingdom of God as married people who are a part of the kingdom-advancing work of the church. When single parents do the beautiful, hard, intimate work of pursuing Jesus daily and fostering God-honoring brotherly and sisterly relationships with fellow believers, they not only tell their kids that Jesus is the best spouse ever, they show their kids the viability of advancing God's kingdom as single people who are a part of the kingdom-advancing work of the church.

This hit me when Gwyn, our oldest, was about four years old. Matt and I were starting to climb out of our marriage tumult, and we were causally hugging each other and laughing in front of our kids. Gwyn sighed as she saw us obviously loving each other. "I can't wait to get married someday," she said. "I want to marry someone just like Dad."

I smiled, looking over at Matt. "If God calls you to marriage, Gwyn, you should marry someone just like Dad. He is the best." And I meant it. Then I added, "You know, when Daddy and I love each other, it shows you a picture of how much God loves you."

She smiled. When we say things like that now, our kids can roll their eyes, finishing the line for us: "We know, we know! It shows us a picture of how much God loves us!" I smile sassily, however, happy to annoy our kids with the deeper meaning of marriage. They cannot hear about how much God loves them too frequently.

This likely goes without saying, but this exhortation has no age limit. Whether our kids are five months or fifty-five years old, the best testimony of God's love for the world is for us to be the healthiest people we can in our marriage and singleness.

Find People Who Can Model Gospel-Focused Singleness and Marriage

We cannot fulfill our kids' entire discipleship curriculum. We aren't supposed to. Jesus says, "I pray that [the church] will all be one, just as you and I are one—as you are in me, Father, and I am in you. And may they be in us so that the world will believe you sent me" (Jn 17:21). God does not want just nuclear families to be unified; God wants all people in the church to be so unified and on mission that the world hungers for him.

This means we exhausted parents get to lean on the church to disciple our kids and to see examples of healthy marriage and singleness. This can happen through things like intergenerational mentorship, small groups, church programs, and godparenting. The neat thing is that it is not just wise or biblical for our kids to have other trusted adults teaching them gospel truth; research supports it.

Several years ago, Kara Powell and the team at Fuller Youth Institute noted the alarming statistic that over half of teenagers do not maintain their faith after leaving home.[1] For six years they researched to find the "silver bullet" for helping teenagers transition from home to adult life with resilient, "sticky faith."[2] Although they did not discover such a bullet, they did find four things to be very helpful: parents teaching and living a life-giving spirituality, teenagers learning the whole gospel and how it applies to all areas of life, teenagers having space to wrestle with and doubt their faith, and five adults loving and genuinely caring about each teenager.[3] That last one, intergenerational mentorship from five adults, was the most influential factor in developing sticky faith. "By far, the number-one way that churches made the teens in our survey feel welcomed and valued was when adults in the congregation showed interest in them," Powell says. Specifically, "two variables stood out as significantly related to sticky faith over time: feeling sought out by adults and feeling like those adults 'helped me to realistically apply my faith to my daily life.'"[4]

To parents who are juggling putting dinner on the table, getting to work, keeping the house clean, and helping kids do homework, sports, music lessons, and ten thousand other things, the idea of developing safe adult-to-child relationships for our kids can sound overwhelming at best and impossible at worst. Here is where I suggest we begin: looking more closely at those already in our kids' lives, such as aunts, uncles, godparents, trusted babysitters, and leaders of our kids' church activities. We do not necessarily need to set up weekly coffee conversations for our kids when they are eight years old, but we can expand our vision from "I am responsible to raise these kids alone" to "Who can help our family pursue God's mission for the world?"

A vision expansion is the first step: Do our kids have a small group leader at their Wednesday night church group? That sounds like someone who is "seeking out our kids and helping them apply faith to their daily life" to me. Do our kids have a single aunt or uncle (or honorary aunt or uncle) who loves Jesus and is in their lives already? Let's talk to them and perhaps say, "Hey, I am looking for low-key discipleship care for my kids. Could you just lean in, model Jesus, and be available to talk about his love for them?"

That's a lot like how it looks in our family: My sister, Angela, and her family live in our neighborhood and go to our church. They love Jesus, and she and I have a deep relationship that allows us to talk about and coach each other's kids in kind and collaborative ways. Our kids also have a single woman named Cassie whom I have known for ten years through a mentorship relationship. Cassie has earned trust with us to a point where she has become a big sister to our kids. It is not forced. She genuinely loves them, we love her, and to ask her to care for and mentor our kids in natural ways when she is around does not differ much from how we do life with her already. All I did was ask, "Hey, when the kids perhaps are not my biggest fans as they hit adolescence, can you please remind them that their parents try hard but Jesus is the best no matter what?" She laughed and agreed.

Our kids are also a part of church groups that seek to mentor our kids through the gospel. They have grandparents, coaches, and music teachers who love Jesus and speak about him well. Do they have five adults who are preaching to them every week? No. But they have roughly five adults who live the gospel out well, point our kids to Jesus, and embody what living married and single on mission can look like.

Change "When" to "If"

As we have already touched on, a simple and powerful way to keep our eyes on the mission of God while talking about marriage and singleness as equally valuable ways to live into that mission is to make a small verbal adjustment. When we're talking with our kids about their future, instead of saying, "When you get married," we can say, "If God calls you to marriage." This can begin when our kids are very young (zero to four). Little kids get so excited about princesses, fairy tales, and being moms or dads one day that it's easy to start making promises. We do this by saying things like, "You'll find your Prince Charming someday! When you get married, it will be like this . . . "

There is a slightly higher probability that our kids will marry than stay single. According to global statistics, 63.7 percent of women are married or in some type of union.[5] In the United States, 47 percent of adults have never married, and the remaining 53 percent are either currently married or have divorced or been widowed.[6] However, probabilities do not mean marriage is God's plan for our children. He may call them to be like the apostle Paul who saw singleness as a better way to serve God. Are we willing to submit to God that this might be his desire for our kids?

I mean, I get it: Many of us love the idea of our kids having squishy little versions of themselves (that we can say "goodbye" to at the end of the day). Our desire to have grandkids is in part a God-infused longing to fill the earth with himself through multiplication. But our kids do not need to bear children to do this. If God does not call our kids to marriage, and he does not call them to foster or adopt their own children as single people, they are still a part of the creation mandate to "have kids." Remember our buddy John rolling up with his own espresso in the gospel foundation conversation? He, a single guy, said of his spiritual children, "I could have no greater joy than to hear that my children are following the truth" (3 Jn 4). And Paul, another single guy, said of his spiritual child, Timothy, "I am writing to Timothy, my true son in the faith" (1 Tim 1:2). If our kids are following Jesus, they will have kids because they are a part of the multiplying mission of God. We just have to be willing to see our children's spiritual kids as valuable "grandkids," too.[7]

As our kids get older (ages five to nine), we can add more to our simple "It needs to be different" vision for marriage by highlighting discipleship. Recently, I was walking with Gwyn through some woods by Lake Michigan, remembering how my parents had brought me to that same forest when I was little. I almost said to Gwyn, ten, "My parents brought me here when I was young, and . . . [you'll bring your kids, too!]" Nope. I don't know that. Instead I said, "Gwyn, my parents brought me here when I was a kid, and maybe you'll bring your kids or those you disciple here, too." We need to normalize multiplication but cannot guarantee marriage and children for them.

Let's Talk Rainbow Flags and Discerning Age Appropriateness

It's time to talk about the rainbow flags. In the last chapter, I described how three-year-old Gwyn and I discussed same-sex marriage in the bathroom. After that occurrence, we did not regularly talk about things like same-sex marriage until the kids were a bit older and they started noticing shades of rainbow all around them.

It's not that I didn't want to have these conversations when they were zero to four, but the subject came up more naturally and our kids were more curious in the five to nine age range. Here is a general rule of thumb for when I start talking with my children about things.

WHEN ASKING MYSELF, "IS THIS AGE APPROPRIATE?" I CONSIDER:	
1. Am I listening to experts who offer guidance on when things are age appropriate to share?	• Discern "age appropriateness" based on experts we trust. • If there are no experts to help us answer, ask a wise friend or pastor or two. • If there are no wise friends, pray, wing it, and be willing to apologize or circle back if we learn later we handled it incorrectly. That's called real-life parenting.
2. Will what I share be graphic or explicit?	• If yes, do not share.[8]
3. Am I sharing in a way that plants unnecessary "what-ifs"?	• Our kids do not need to be invited to think they are going to struggle in a certain way. If it happens, it happens. We can walk that road when we get there, but we do not need to plant an idea. • An example of a conversation that may plant "what-ifs" is directly saying, without being asked, "You might struggle with your gender or sexuality." Or asking, "Do you ever struggle with your gender? Do you ever feel attracted to the same sex?" We don't have to tell our kids they might struggle in this way to signal that we will be safe to talk to about *any* version of sexual brokenness if they ever want to.
4. Am I anticipating my child's questions by bringing up topics before they encounter them in the world?	• I recommend bringing up topics six months to a year before we expect our children to learn about it from others. • This signals our willingness to help them in real time and solidifies us as the primary expert in their lives. • If we never teach our kids about sexuality and gender, their God-given curiosity can lead them to not-so-godly spaces: their friends, the playground, the internet.

WHEN ASKING MYSELF, "IS THIS AGE APPROPRIATE?" I CONSIDER:	
5. Am I bringing up topics in a way that honors God's passion for both truth and love?	• This will help our kids have winsome, truthful responses at the ready to engage their friends. • The way we speak about gender and sexuality now (or our avoidance of it) signals to our kids our level of ability to talk about it in the future. • When we speak with both love and truth about sexuality topics, then however our kids experience their versions of sexual or gender brokenness in the future, they will have formed strong predictions of how we will respond to them with both love and truth because we have been subtly telling them for years. • An example of a way to bring up topics with love and truth without making it pointed at our kids is, "Some people struggle with how they feel in their bodies or are attracted to the same gender, and they might tell you that. How should we respond?"
6. Am I keeping this specific topic rooted in the greater gospel narrative?	• Responding to sex and gender questions through a gospel lens siphons the legalism out of sexuality and places it in the greater gorgeous gospel that flourishes us. Kids (adults too) receive rules much better when they understand the "why" underneath them.[9]

"Mom, what does that mean?"

Juliette, five, pointed to a rainbow flag while we were driving to a doctor appointment. Some of our best conversations happen when we are all "trapped" in the car together. The boredom paired with a lack of intense "Now we are having a deep conversation" vibes seems to stir their curiosity and spark a desire to ask questions.

I ran her question through my "Is this age appropriate?" diagnostic:

1. I had not heard an expert give a best practice about this yet, and I did not know who to call, so I would do option three: pray and wing it.

2. I would not be sexually graphic.

3. I would not ask idea-planting "what if" questions.

4. I did not even have to bring up the topic. It was right there.

5. I would speak about the topic both lovingly and truthfully.

6. I would keep the response rooted in the greater gospel narrative.

Okeedokee, I could proceed. "That flag means that sometimes boys like-like each other or girls like-like each other and want to get married."

I could see Juliette's eyes go wide in the rearview mirror. "What? Boys heart-eyes each other?" In our home, "heart-eyes" is the phrase we use to describe someone liking someone romantically.

"Yes, some boys heart-eyes other boys and some girls heart-eyes other girls and want to marry each other."

Juliette is taken aback and says, "That's weird!"

Kids blurt out what's in their heads. And kids of this age are always looking for anomalies—things that don't fit. Men marrying each other and women marrying each other does not belong in her worldview—and (I say this tenderly) it shouldn't. However, I can coach her tone. We can hold to the truth, but we don't need to do so with a turned-up nose.

"Yes, I hear you, honey, but in our country, women can marry women and men can marry men, but we do not believe it is God's design. It's sin." She is quiet. "We do not believe it is God's design because . . . why?" I ask.

Gwyn, age seven, who has been listening quietly, jumps in. "Because . . . different," she says. She's heard versions of this conversation many times throughout her young life.

"Yes! Different!" I say. "When moms and dads love each other—even though we are so different from each other—we show you a picture of how much God loves you, even though God is so different from us. Two girls or two boys aren't different enough."

Satisfied with the answer, Juliette asks, "Can you turn on the radio?"

As our kids shift into the seven to twelve age range, I start to intentionally bring up "what if" scenarios about rainbow-flag-related things. One such "what if" encounter was inspired by pajama day at their public school. Gwyn, seven at the time, decided to bring in a pillow that had a picture of Jojo Siwa on it. Jojo is a former Dance Moms dancer turned Nickelodeon star who came out as gay in 2021. My girls did not know she was gay but simply liked her hair bows and effervescent attitude. As I looked at Gwyn's choice in pillow, I began to wonder what her peers might say. Kids can be cruel, and I wanted Gwyn to be ready to respond.

"Hey, girls?" I said to Gwyn and Juliette, who was five. I didn't know if this was too early for this conversation for Juliette, but as I briefly thought through my "age appropriate" questions, this seemed like the time. "Did you know that Jojo Siwa is dating a girl?"

They looked at me with wide eyes. "What? No way. Really?"

I nodded. "Yup. Some people like their friends that way, and then they date them." They had heard this before, but kids, like adults, often need to hear things many times before it sinks in.

"But that's not what we do!" the girls said.

"No, it's not," I agree. "Why? Why is marriage between moms and dads?" Here we go again.

"Because," Gwyn began, "they are different. When moms and dads love each other—even though they are different—they show us how much God loves us."

I smiled at her. "Yes!"

Justice Juju, as we call Juliette because of her fierce devotion to the truth, was still hopped up: "But we aren't supposed to date our friends!" she said strongly.

"You are right. We aren't," I agreed, knowing she was thinking only of dating same-gendered friends.

This is where the "what if" part of the conversation began. "But what if your friends do date their friends? Are we supposed to be mean to them?" I asked.

Juliette jumped in. "Yes!"

I swallowed a laugh. "No. We are to be kind to them always. We believe differently because we follow Jesus, but we love Jojo Siwa and anyone like her no matter what."

Gwyn and Juliette nodded. "Yeah," they said.

I knew I was pushing the window of their attention span to keep going, but I needed them to hear the next part. "Some of your teachers might teach something different at school," I said, thinking about our decision to send them to public school.[10] "They might talk about how girls and boys should date and marry their friends."

I continued, "We love our teachers, and we respect them, but if they talk about things like that at school, let's talk about it at home."

Juliette raised her eyebrows and said, "Yeah, because you are a better teacher than they are."

I chuckle and continue, "They are great at teaching you math and reading and friendships, but not all of them believe what we believe about God's design for marriage. If they bring that up, will you tell me? We can talk about what they say and see how it aligns with how we view the world, okay?"

They agree, and we move on with getting ready and leaving.

As parents, we will likely have many opportunities to talk about things like the rainbow flags as they come up, and we need to be ready. When we respond, we need to share not just the "no" of God's plan for sexuality but his beautiful "yes," because the "yes" is the reason for God's "no": He wants to show the world his love, and anything outside of his design does not display that picture accurately. Additionally, bringing up "what-ifs" as kids get older will, God willing, help them be ready to share the "yes" of God's beautiful path of flourishing to their friends gracefully and truthfully.

What We Watch and Read

And here we are: to TV shows. What do we say when an LGBTQ character comes on the screen? Do we turn the channel? Roll our eyes? Let kids watch it? This is a sensitive one for me. Almost every single person I know who identifies as LGBTQ or same-sex attracted and is surrendering and submitting their version of sexual or gender brokenness to Jesus has a painful personal story of watching a show or movie with their parents, friends, or siblings and an LGBTQ-identifying character comes on the screen. A family member or friend in the room moans, groans, and throws their hands in the air about "Ugh! Why? Why does everything have to be LGBTQXYZ? It wrecks the show!"

Even though this family is not rolling their eyes and raging about my friend who is secretly struggling, the friend internalizes it as, "I am bad. I am a disgrace. My sin struggle is not welcome at the foot of the cross next to theirs." If they were considering inviting their family into the journey with them, they decide in that painful moment (and in the hundreds of similar moments like it) not to do so. Why would they open up with a family member who seems bitter about this sin? The way we respond to these things matters. When we watch shows or read books, let's make sure to do our pre-work so we can approach them with a heart of grief-love like Jesus.

This world is broken. We need to grieve its fallen state, but let's not let unfiltered grief spew out onto whoever is in the room with us while we watch TV. The Bible tells us where to take our grief and anger over sin: It's called lament. The psalmists model how to take our unfiltered emotions to God and let God sift them through his fingers. As we share our grief to God, let's let him search our heart for places where we are judging another's speck in their eye when we have a plank in our own.

What do we do when an unmarried heterosexual couple has a "fade-to-black" sex scene in a show? Do we act the same way? Do we get as fiery when a movie celebrates greed, backstabbing, or injustice? This is not a call to make sure we are equally hating sinners; this is a call to ensure we see everyone as equally in need of a Savior—including us. We must grieve the world's brokenness to

God, work through forgiveness for our enemies, then learn to love our enemies before we engage culture (Ps 142:2; Col 3:13; Mt 5:44). This way we can be ready for whatever comes on the screen. With such a heart posture, this is how our family practically engages books and television shows.

Major component. When it comes to evaluating sexual sin, if heavily sexualized heterosexual romance, cheating, unbiblical remarriage, same-sex romance, or transgender-affirming themes are a major part of the book or show, we say, "We aren't going to watch this show" or "We aren't going to borrow this book."[11] When our kids ask why, if they are ages zero to four, and depending on how much we have talked about the positive vision of marriage, we will say something to the effect of, "They just talk about things that we don't believe." If they are ages five to eight and they have heard our positive vision for marriage talk several times, we will say, "You know the rainbow flag stuff we have talked about? They believe boys can marry each other or girls can marry each other, and we don't believe that." Regarding gender transitioning, we would say something like, "They believe people who feel uncomfortable with their boy bodies or girl bodies should transition their bodies from boy to girl or girl to boy. We believe that's a real struggle people have, but we don't think it's wise to push them toward transition. They need to ask God and the church for help—and we need to be there to support them." If unmarried heterosexual sex is a part of the show, we will say, "God wants marriage to reflect God's covenant or promise-love to us. They didn't covenant or promise before God to be together forever, so they are not showing the world a picture of God's love for them. We don't want to watch that."

Minor component normalized. If sexual relationships that don't honor God, romantic relationships that don't honor God, or strongly pro-transition themes are a minor part of the show or book but the producers are trying to normalize the themes even subtly, I likely won't have our kids watch it or read it—but I will pray about it. Stories have a way of capturing our hearts like nothing else, but sometimes the storylines are a good way to talk about the reality of such sins in the world.[12] This takes discernment.

Minor component neutral. If there is an LGBTQ character in the show or book, or a heterosexual couple had a baby outside marriage, but their choices are not a major part of the story, I may stop the show at some point and talk about what we believe about marriage, sex, and gender. If it is very minor, I may let the tape roll. The world is going to be the world, and we can choose to engage it or not.

It is just the facts of parenting that our kids are going to ask us questions about what they see in the world. It is our job as parents to be ready to answer those questions with peaceful, gospel-shaped, age-appropriate wisdom. In order to do that, we need to remember the purpose of life, the purpose of marriage and singleness, and then teach as the questions come or before our kids encounter the issues on their own so they are ready to, themselves, engage the world with peaceful, gospel-shaped, age-appropriate wisdom.

QUESTIONS TO CONSIDER

1. How did you feel about the exhortation to live into your marriage or singleness gospel picture well?

2. Do your kids have any potential mentors in their lives who could model marriage and singleness well and care for your kids through the teen years and beyond? How might you pray into this?

3. Have your kids asked you about the rainbow flag? What did you say?

4. What's your reaction to our approach to watching TV shows with kids?

5. GENDER

Lay the Foundation

> "How can we engage gender? I hear people yelling
> about it on both sides of the conversation, but I'm sitting
> here with my kids wondering how to raise them into
> healthy boys and girls outside of stereotyped boxes
> or a gender-neutral swamp. What can I do?"

THE KIDS AND I STOPPED at the grocery store for a few things
after school. The 4 p.m. hungries had set in, and every ultra-
processed snack called to my kids like a beacon. As we tossed Swiss
Rolls, Nutter Butters, and apples into the cart, I noticed one of the
grocery baggers who appeared to be a young woman in the process
of transitioning to male. She had a whisper of a full beard growing
and was wearing masculine clothes, and she seemed happy as she
loaded groceries for customers. I could tell Gwyn, nine at the time,
noticed her, too. Her head cocked to the side and her brain seemed
to be whirring, trying to figure out what she was looking at. This
was not her first experience with a transgender person, but it was
the first person she had seen in the process of transitioning. As we

loaded the groceries into the car a half-hour later, I wanted to follow up to see if Gwyn had questions about what she'd seen.

Our kids need help interpreting the wild world around them. If we don't help, confusing moments can become "unformulated experiences." Author and parenting expert Becky Kennedy defines an unformulated experience as "the feeling that something's not right, without a clear explanation of what's happening. Unformulated experience is terrifying to a child, because that 'something's not right' feeling free-floats around the body without an anchor of safety."[1]

The better option than letting kids interpret a confusing world around them is to step in with biblical wisdom and to literally put language to it. Renowned brain expert and psychiatrist Dan Siegel says, "What kids often need, especially when they experience strong emotions, is to have someone help them use their left brain to make sense of what's going on—to put things in order and to name these big and scary right-brain feelings so they can deal with them effectively. . . . In fact, research shows that merely assigning a name or label to what we feel literally calms down the activity of the emotional circuitry in the right hemisphere."[2] To help children calmly interpret the world around them, we need to step in and help their left brain regulate the emotion heavy, image-focused, story-driven right brain. According to Kennedy, when we offer "clear, direct, honest information" as "our child's loving, trusted adult," we help kids to calmly make sense of the world.[3]

So here I was, ready to offer clear, direct, honest information, and hopefully do it in the context of a unified, healthy relationship between Gwyn and me.

"Hey, Gwyn, did you see that girl bagging groceries with the facial hair?" Gwyn was helping me to load a bag of groceries into the car.

"That was a girl? Why did she have a beard?" she asked.

I wanted to help her put language to what she was seeing. "I'm guessing she was transitioning—you know, in the process of trying to change from a girl to a boy."

She looked at me first with understanding then confusion. "Okay . . . why are you telling me this?"

I shrugged, trying to play it cool. "I was just wondering if you noticed her." I wanted to help Gwyn interpret, but maybe she was fine. Or maybe she was hiding her questions to show me and her siblings that this was easy for her. I looked next at Ellis. He was five; could he hear this? Parenting is rarely ever one-on-one if we have more than one child. I thought about my age-appropriate questions: One: What do experts say? I didn't have any to ask. Two: Will I be explicit? No. Three: Am I going to plant unnecessary "what-ifs"? No. Four: Am I being anticipatory of what they will encounter in real life in the future? Yes. Five: Am I going to speak truth in love? Yes. And six: Will I root it in the gospel? Yes. Okay, that's enough positives to share.

So I said, "Sometimes people feel severe pain in their minds because of the way their bodies are. They might try to make the pain go away by changing their bodies, like the person who bagged our groceries. In our family, we believe that it's the way our bodies are made when we're born that makes us a boy or a girl. We do not believe transitioning is God's best. But I want you to know about this so that we can show lots of love to people who feel this pain and might believe different things than we do."

This was not the only conversation we would have, but it was a start: naming this individual's real pain while reminding our kids what it means to be a boy or a girl.

What Does It Mean to Be Transgender?

Transgender is an umbrella term to describe anyone who feels they have a disconnect between their biological sex (the "plumbing" of our bodies) and how they perceive their internal sense of gender (their internal feeling of being male or female). My separation of the two does not mean I agree that they *should* be separated or that we should have different words for sex and gender, but my doing this gives language to some people's experience within their sexed bodies.

It reminds me of when I am triggered. I experienced childhood sexual assault from a stranger as a kid, and even now when I am physically safe, my internal sense of self is on high alert, telling me I am not safe. There is a disconnect between my insides and my outsides. Is this how it should be? No. I should have integration at all times. But because of sin in the world and sin done to me, I experience this inner-outer disconnect more often than I would like. Is the struggle between my insides and outsides a sin? No. It's a struggle with a sin-laden world. What I choose to do to remedy that internal-external disconnect could become damaging or sinful (choosing to drink alcohol copiously, for example), but to wrestle with disconnect is not a sin in and of itself.

Similarly, I do not believe that our friends who wrestle with an internal and external disconnect between their bodies and their sense of who they are in those bodies are sinning in that struggle. I believe it can become damaging and sinful in how they cope with that challenge if they choose surgical, hormonal, or social transitioning means.

Within the umbrella category of "transgender," there are some who experience diagnosable "gender dysphoria." That is, "a marked incongruence between one's experienced or expressed gender and biological sex."[4] To be diagnosed with gender dysphoria, according to psychologists Mark Yarhouse and Julia Sadusky, someone needs to have "a strong desire to be of the other gender or an insistence that one is the other gender," along with several other markers as specified in the *Diagnostic and Statistical Manual of Mental Disorders-5 (DSM-5)*.[5]

Few people are diagnosed with gender dysphoria. According to *DSM-5*, only 0.005 percent to 0.014 percent of adult men and 0.002 percent to 0.003 percent of adult women have distressing incongruence between their perception of their biological sex and their bodies. However, many experts put that number more around 1 percent of the population.[6] In a 2023 Gallup poll, for example, 2.8 percent of Gen Z, 1.1 percent of millennials, 0.5 percent of Gen X, and 0.2 percent of baby boomers identified as transgender.[7]

If we focus on those Generation Z numbers, we can see an interesting pattern that leads many to scratch their heads in bewilderment. The Gender Identity Development Service (GIDS) in the UK notes there were only 138 child and adolescent referrals for gender treatment in 2010, but in 2021 and 2022 there were over 3,500 referrals. That's a 2,400 percent increase in one decade. What is more interesting to note is in 2019 and 2020, over 75 percent of adolescent referrals were for biological females.[8] This sharply contradicts the previously established precedent of gender dysphoria being significantly more common among biological males. In the United States we have also seen rise in gender dysphoria diagnoses; there were 15,000 diagnoses of gender dysphoria in kids ages six to seventeen in 2017, and in 2021 there were over 42,000. That's a 180 percent increase in five years.[9]

Why Are the Numbers so High?

When I share statistics like these during public speaking engagements, the audience can't help but ask, "Why?" Why is the next generation identifying as transgender and transitioning at a more frequent rate than those of preceding generations? Is it a giant trend of "rapid onset gender dysphoria" or something else?[10] Moreover, why is Gen Z identifying as LGBTQ more than any other generation (28 percent, compared with 10 percent of all adults)?[11]

Are they bored? Or do they have too much access to social media, so they pick a gender or sexual attraction to get attention? I think such broad reactions do not represent the tender heart of

God and will not help draw fellow broken-beloved people to him. Let's kindly hypothesize together about why these numbers are so high and see if we can learn something from Generation Z that will help us raise Generation Alpha, Beta, and beyond.

Hypothesis: Language. The first reason I believe we have such a rise in these gender-related statistics is that for the first time in history, we have language to describe the nuances of how we feel inside. We don't feel like we fit male or female gender stereotypes? We can choose the word "nonbinary" to describe our experience. We feel more female one day but more male the other? We might be "genderfluid." If we actually feel ambivalent about our gender and outside of the binary completely, then we can say we are "greygender."[12] The categories continue, and they help people put language to what they experience inside.

It's easy to scoff, dismissing it all as a bid for attention, but here's a comparison: I have gone to the doctor many times with several symptoms of illness. I knew something was wrong, but I couldn't name why. That inability to name what was going on made me feel anxious and unsettled. When the doctors tested me and said I had influenza A, pneumonia, or even asthma, there was a sense of relief. My right brain anxiety calmed with left-brain language.

Friends who wrestle with gender dissonance can feel a similar sense of "something is off." We know from research that as young people try to make sense of their experiences, they're often shaped by the language they find in the world around them. This is one piece of what Yarhouse (and originally Hacking) call the "looping effect."[13] Whereas older generations might have felt something different inside about their gender and not had the ability to Google and name it, Gen Z does, so there are, on paper, more transgender kids out there. Now, *should* we have all of this language? That's another conversation for the next chapter.

Hypothesis: Heart-starved. My second hypothesis is more heart-related. How did you feel about yourself in junior high and high school? How secure was your identity? (I hear some of you laughing, remembering what an awkward mess you were. Me too.) Now, let's throw cell phones into the mix and pummel ourselves with peer pressure to post about our perfectly curated life to a watching, critical world. No wonder anxiety and depression are on the rise for Generation Z. They were the adolescent guinea pigs who were largely given free-range access to smartphones between 2010 and 2016 right after smartphones were invented in 2007.[14] Generation Z now uses smartphones between six and eight hours per day.[15]

Jonathan Haidt, in his bestselling book *The Anxious Generation*, draws a convincing, causative line between the proliferation of teenage smartphone use and the skyrocketing of teenage anxiety and depression. Major depression has increased by 145 percent in teen girls and 161 percent in teen boys since 2010, and anxiety has increased by 139 percent for eighteen- to twenty-five-year-olds in the same period. From 1979 to 2010, only 5 percent of US high school seniors said they felt they had "no chance of a successful life." But in the early 2000s, the boys' numbers started to spike, and in 2010, the girls' began to jump as well.[16] From 1991 to 2011, US middle and high school students generally felt "satisfied with oneself," but that number began to plummet for both boys and girls from 2011 to 2015 and continues to drop.[17] Similarly, global feelings of alienation, or students feeling like they didn't belong, were generally static from 2000 to 2012 but jumped in 2012 when smartphones became ubiquitous.[18]

What do all of these statistics tell us other than kids are addicted to their phones and that they are sad and anxious? It tells me that in addition to the very normal questions all of us have about our identity in adolescence, the smartphone-wielding Generation Z had an extra layer of challenge during puberty to sort through their questions of identity and belonging. On the internet, we are "known" without really being known. We are "loved" without people seeing and loving all of us. We are "liked" but only if we play the algorithm game. The internet scratched the itch of their hearts but like a bug bite: They needed more, more, and more.[19] As believers we know that the needs of our heart—to be seen, to be known, to be loved, to belong—can be met only in Christ with the church supporting this process.

Do you know who can be quicker to help meet these identity and heart needs than the church? The LGBTQ community. "You belong—here is our flag. You are unique—here is your unique flag. You have a purpose—we are going to change the world. You are loved—you don't have to change anything about you unless you want to." All of this makes me wonder if normal adolescent questions of identity and belonging, paired with cell phones that exacerbate loneliness, paired with whispers of questions about sexuality or gender, paired with internet searches to put language to those questions, paired with watching pornography (which can turn a small curiosity into a neuropathway superhighway of desire[20]) equals more people being drawn to this group than any other generation.

Hypothesis: Prevalence of pornography. I can't finish my hypothesis without briefly turning my full attention to pornography. In chapters eleven and twelve, I will dive into the heart behind pornography use and how we can help our kids navigate it, but for now I need to just look at the landscape and its potential correlation to transitioning. People often ask me why girls, specifically, want to transition, and I cannot help but think of the pervasive evil of pornographic content. One study found that over 91 percent of men and 60 percent of women consume pornography (videos, pictures, or written forms) monthly.[21] Another says 58 percent of Americans have watched pornography at some point in their lives, with 27 percent watching it in the past month (44 percent of men and 11 percent of women admit to watching monthly).[22]

If we look specifically at teenagers, 73 percent have consumed pornography by the time they are seventeen, and of those who are regular consumers, 45 percent say it gives helpful information about sex. Another 45 percent say they watch "to find out what arouses and excites them."[23] Ten percent more LGBTQ teens, however (54 percent), say they watch pornography to figure out what arouses them.

With the new prevalence of AI (artificial intelligence)-generated pornography, a Home Security Heroes study found that 98 percent of "deepfake" videos (which use artificial intelligence to have real or fake people do whatever the AI writers want) were pornographic and 99 percent targeted women and girls.[24] An Internet Watch Foundation study found that 99.6 percent of AI-produced child sexual abuse images were of girls ages seven to thirteen.[25] All of this abusive, objectifying content does not leave the consumer unaffected. At a minimum, it leaves people anxious and depressed.[26] As Fight the New Drug has reported, "Research routinely shows that frequent porn consumers are more likely to objectify and dehumanize others sexually, more likely to express an intent to rape, less likely to intervene during a sexual assault, more likely to victim blame survivors of sexual violence, more likely to support violence against women, more likely to forward sexts without consent, and more likely to commit acts of sexual violence."[27] Even if people are not watching pornography themselves, to have such a large percentage of peers engaging with it changes the tone of a generation to normalize a spirit of violence and aggression.

The pervasive consumption of pornography is making it scarier to live vulnerably as a woman in this terrifying world. Women are about one-third physically weaker than men.[28] Although I do not struggle with my gender as my female friends who experience gender dysphoria do, I can see the draw to transition to male as a way to feel safer. This broken world is unbelievably evil, and I can sympathize with the desire to want to hide in a stronger male body.

Hypothesis: Naming our internal ache for eternity. My final hypothesis circles back to my first, about naming. Is Gen Z simply naming and putting concrete language around what we all feel inside our post-fall, pre-resurrected bodies? Author and professor Abigail Favale says, "Underneath every desire can be found a desire for something good. Even if that good desire becomes distorted or aimed at the wrong thing. Trans identities signal a longing for wholeness, for an integrated sense of self in which the body does reveal the person."[29] When our friends who struggle with gender talk about the ache they feel between how they perceive their sexed bodies and the body itself, I wonder if everyone can relate at some level.

Indeed, Paul says in Romans 8 that "all creation has been groaning," and human beings "also groan . . . for we long for our bodies to be released from sin and suffering" (Rom 8:22-23). Every human feels a level of discontent living in a body that is marred by sin. This universal struggle should not lead us to dismiss the unique struggles our transgender-identifying friends experience, but to have empathy when they say, "I feel dissonance between who I truly am and my experience inside." We can relate without negating the level to which they are experiencing the fall's effects on their embodied selves. We can also encourage them not to remedy the struggle with temporary (as in, they will not last into eternity) "fixes," but to look for what is going on underneath or adjacent to the struggle with gender.

"This desire [to heal body and soul] is fundamentally a good one," Favale says. "It reflects the truth of the human being as a unity of body and soul. The error comes in thinking that this unity has to be achieved through artifice, through violence against the body, rather than recognizing that we are integrated by our very nature. The lie *I have to force my body to reveal my true self*—supplants the truth: *the body I am is always already revealing my personhood.*"[30]

What Does the Bible Say About Our Embodied Selves?

So what does the Bible say about our embodied selves—or, we could just say, about ourselves? As Dietrich Bonhoeffer says, "A human being is a human body. A human being does not have a body—or have a soul; instead a human being 'is' a body and soul."[31] We are our bodies.

As we dive into what the Bible says about God's design for how we should view our male and female selves (even if we struggle with being male or female), please note this is a crash course in the most compelling arguments for me for God's good design.

In the beginning, out of the dust, God created man in his image. Theologian Kelly Kapic says of our dust-filled origin story, "The Genesis account of creation celebrates the good unity of the human person, and it traces our connection to the earth—we really are what you might call 'earthlings.' Our existence occurs not as beings who drop out of the sky but rise from the dust."[32] God did not create us as souls who are entombed in flesh, but we are intentionally created as matter plus souls.

From that dusty, embodied, earthy beginning, God forms the man and woman. Both male and female are marked with unique *imago Dei* dignity and given the mission of God to be fruitful, multiply, and fill the earth. "Sexual difference," Favale declares, "is not an extraneous or faulty feature of the cosmos, but an essential part of its goodness."[33] When Adam first sees Eve he says:

> At last! . . .
>> This one is bone from my bone,
>>> and flesh from my flesh!
>> She will be called "woman,"
>>> because she was taken from "man." (Gen 2:23)

The woman had not even spoken, let alone stepped into the kitchen to make Adam dinner. Nor did she pop on high heels and sashay to Target or start talking about her emotions. All she did was exist in her naked, bodily form and he knew she was like but unlike him. Favale says of this moment, "Genesis 2 emphasizes another vital principle: the body reveals the person. . . . Her body speaks the truth of her identity, and this truth is immediately recognized by the man, who is struck with joy and wonder at the revelation of a person with whom he can—at last—have true communion. Our bodies, then, serve a sacramental function, by revealing and communicating a spiritual reality."[34]

As we discuss God's creation of male and female, it's important to consider intersex people. These beloved individuals are born with genitalia or chromosomes that are gender-ambiguous and absolutely deserve love and care. Some people purport that because intersex people exist—and in high numbers—it means God allows for creative freedom for gender expression. They point to statistics such as 1.7 out of 100 births being intersex—which is almost the same number as people with red hair—as evidence for God's creativity when it comes to gender.[35] However, those numbers include women who have polycystic ovarian syndrome (PCOS) or men who have an extra X chromosome (Klinefelter syndrome) but still would be unquestionably identifiable as male. "The vast majority of individuals categorized as intersex are unambiguously male or female, even if the presentation of maleness or femaleness is atypical in some way," Favale says in *Genesis of Gender*. She posits that fewer than two out of ten thousand people have truly ambiguous genitalia and would meet her definition of intersex.[36] Regardless of how many intersex people exist, these people are not some new third sex that is neither male nor female. Instead, they have bodies that reflect some features of both *male* and *female*. And their bodies, like all of our bodies, can be offered up to God in obedience, precisely as they are—not as a third sex but as faithful bodies affected by the fall.

One thing I treasure about difficult conversations like this one on gender is that it forces us to take a mirror and hold it up to the dusty corners of our hearts, our families, and our churches and ask, "Why do we believe what we believe? Why do we teach this about girls or that about boys?" If we simply pass on old-timey gender stereotypes or the latest gender fluidity thinking, it may get our kids through a few years of life, but for them to truly advance the kingdom of God in their sexed bodies, they need ancient truth. That ancient truth is grounded in their bodies.

QUESTIONS TO CONSIDER

1. How would you handle a situation in which your kids notice a transgender person? If you have had this experience, what do you wish you had done differently? What would you do the same?

2. What stood out to you from the definition of transgender? What stood out to you from the percentages of transgender young people and those who desire to transition?

3. What did you think of my hypotheses about why there are so many people who desire to transition and who identify as LGBTQ? Did any stand out to you? Why?

4. What did you learn from the biblical arguments for God's good design for male and female?

6. GENDER

Walk the Foundation

Key teaching: "I love your version of boy or girl."

GWYN CAME UP THE STAIRS dressed in baggy pants, a football jersey, and a trucker hat that said, "Citizen of heaven." She looked adorable, and like what we might have called in the eighties and nineties a "tomboy"—or a girl who is confident to act more "boyish" in her behaviors or dress but is aware that she is a girl. Sometimes Gwyn comes out of her room in a skirt and chunky boots and asks me to do her makeup and hair. "Back in the nineteen hundreds" (as my kids say), we would have called her a "girly-girl." No matter how she dresses or acts, Gwyn is a girl.

"Oh, Gwyn," I said, looking at her football garb. "It's fun to try on different ways we want to show the world who we are, isn't it?"

She shrugged. Matt chimed in: "You are such a cool girl, Gwyn, no matter what you're wearing." Gwyn beamed.

Matt and I say these things to encourage Gwyn because we plain-old love her, and we want to affirm her in her femaleness apart from what she is wearing or how she acts. The world has other strong opinions that can be so stereotypical they make me cringe. It's helpful for us as parents to remove as many of the world's lies and stereotypes as we can by affirming our kids' version of girl or boy.

What does it mean to help our kids love their version of male or female? When I teach about God's design for human sexuality, I sometimes joke and say, "Which of you women feel like you're the ideal embodiment of womanhood?"

Everyone laughs. I'm not sure any woman feels like "the ideal woman." Then I ask, "Which of you men are the ideal embodiment of male?"

Sometimes a goofy man may raise his hand in jest, but the reality is the same: No one feels like they are the ideal woman or man. The only perfect human is Jesus. Male and female are created in God's image, but within our maleness and femaleness is diversity. Girls can be like the judge Deborah, who was a warrior and sensitive to God's voice (Judges 4–5). Boys can be like King David, who was both mighty in battle and wrote poetry (Psalm 23; 1 Sam 18:7).

Let's define some things: To be female, one has only X chromosomes (usually XX) and usually has corresponding sexual organs. I appreciate Abigail Favale's simple definition of woman as "the kind of human being whose body is organized around the potential to gestate new life."[1] If a woman experiences infertility issues, it does not make her less of a woman; she still has the potential to produce a baby. Celibate single women, too, are not less women because they are not making babies. They still have the potential or are naturally ordered toward giving birth as single women. Their giving up sex and procreation for the sake of the cross is a beautiful gospel picture of the worthiness of sacrificing for Jesus.

Likewise, a male is someone with a Y chromosome (usually XY), usually has corresponding sexual organs, and has the potential to naturally fertilize a female egg from his body. If a male's penis or other sexual organs do not have the ability to fertilize an egg, it does not make him less of a male—it means that part of his body isn't working the way male bodies are designed to work. Having a body with the natural potential to fertilize an egg makes someone a man. Single men, too, are not less men if they are not physically procreating from their bodies. Their giving up heirs serves as a beautiful picture of the worth-it-ness of following Jesus.

Raising Our Kids as Male and Female

How can we help our kids grow up as healthy boys and girls in this gender-hurting world? I believe a huge part of it is helping our kids belong—with their gender, with their families, and with the church. Why do I correlate belonging and helping our kids love their sexed bodies? I absolutely know that gender dysphoria consists of more than a desire to belong to a group, but, anecdotally, when I talk with my friends who wrestle with gender, they seem to experience a significant lack of belonging with others of their biological sex because they do not fit a stereotyped box. I am curious if even a small piece of the suffering of young people experiencing gender dissonance could be alleviated if we removed some of the stereotypes and celebrated their version of boy or girl in our male and female worlds.

When our kids experience small but regular ways of belonging in our homes, it prepares them for the adult-sized calling God has on their life to belong to the big mission of God. First off, let's talk about belonging with their gender. God chose the gender for our kids because he knew that the embodied way they would live their femaleness or maleness would show the world a unique vision of how God loves and relates to us. If we are made in God's image as male and female, then our very maleness and femaleness shows the world a unique picture of God's love for the world. Satan does not want our kids to own and love their version of male or female. He does not want them to feel they belong in their bodies as they live into the mission of God. He wants division. Fissure. And rejection of who God made because he hates God, our kids, and the world (Jn 10:10).

Because of what Matt and I observe in the world, and because we flat-out know Satan does not want our kids to love their gendered bodies because to do so would glorify and advance the mission of Satan's enemy, God, we seek to celebrate our kids' versions of female and male in several ways. One way is by inviting them to belong with us in the male and female world starting at age three or four—when they first start to notice their gender.[2] We regularly say, "You are such a cool boy," or "I love how God made you a girl."

Around those ages is when we also start to take our kids on gender-specific dates. Matt often takes Ellis disc golfing or to Lowe's, not to necessarily teach him "man things" but to be with and love Ellis man-to-man. Matt may overtly tell Ellis he belongs—"I just love having a guy day with you, buddy"—but simply being with Ellis while embodied in his masculine self says a lot. Similarly, I try to help our girls feel like they belong in girl world by intentionally making time for our daughters. When we hang out, I don't offer a list of what it means to be a girl; I simply love them through my being a woman. I may intentionally compliment their versions of female, but being together girl-to-girl is what speaks "you belong" the loudest.

Helping our kids feel a sense of belonging to their gender can also mean calming down on the clothing wars. When our kids were four to nine, I found myself fighting them on what to wear to church. I wanted them to look cute, but the more I talked with my gender-wrestling friends about the pre-church fights they'd had as kids (forced to wear dresses as girls or khakis as boys, which emphasized how "other" they felt), I realized the fight might not be worth it. Do we need to "dress up for Jesus"? Where is that verse? So instead of arguing for proper dress through a stereotyped lens, I now encourage changing out of soccer shorts into something nicer by saying, "You know, just like we don't wear swimsuits to school or a parka to the beach in July, there are clothes that are more appropriate for certain spaces. What could help you feel like your version of girl (or boy) while being appropriate for church?"

We also try to help our kids belong with their gender through less stereotyped play. If our four- to six-year-old son wanted to play with dolls, I would say, "That's fine, buddy! Man, you're such a good dad." I would never say he was a "good mom" for caring for baby dolls. Men are parents too. If he asked to paint his nails, I would likely let him, saying, "It's fun to paint, isn't it." If he was nearing schoolyard bullying age (seven to nine) I might say, "Just so you know, boys don't usually do that, but you're a boy and you do it, so it's just fine." I wouldn't harp about it, I would never make fun of him (ever), but I might warn him in case someone else started to laugh at him. If someone did happen to laugh, I hope my son would think, *Mom told me this could happen, but just because they're laughing doesn't make me a girl. I am my version of boy.* Girls tend to have a less hard time doing traditionally "boy" things, but they are not without cultural stereotypes.

I also catch girls and boys in the seven- to ten-year-old range playing games that include rhymes like, "Boys go to Jupiter to get more stupider," or the making-fun-of-girls equivalent. When my girls take part in this sort of meanness, I see Ellis's eyes widen with shame.

"Girls," I say to Gwyn and Juliette, "is that kind to Ellis, who is a boy?"

They quickly say, "Oh, not Ellis. He's smart."

This may seem like overkill, but they are sinning by calling boys dumb, and they're not telling Ellis he is good in how God made him as a boy. In this world, we cannot hear we are made "wonderfully" too often (Ps 139:14).

"Let's not say that," I say. "It's not loving to boys who God loves and thinks are smart."

The second place we want our kids to feel they belong is with our family. Part of the small-but-important ways our kids experience belonging to the mission of God is by experiencing belonging with families. This can look like the myriad ways we take time as a family to reestablish togetherness—daily during meals, weekly as we sabbath rest, and several times per year during vacations and staycations. During these times we say to one another, "You belong. You matter. You are a vital part of this family."

We also want our kids to know they are a part of the mission of God through belonging to the family of God. As parents, we need to find churches where we are not only growing as people through good teaching and healthy relationships, but where our kids are known, loved, and belong. Our girls currently do GEMS (Girls Everywhere Meeting the Savior, i.e., Reformed Girl Scouts or Reformed Awana), and they love it. I knew I would do everything I could to keep them in it when I overheard one of their small group leaders say, "Oh Gwyn, oh, Juliette, do you know you are such a delight? I am so glad you are here." I felt the Holy Spirit nudge me, saying, "Laurie, this is important and it does not happen everywhere. Pay attention." I did, and we have been going since.

As parents, we need our kids to experience sweet, life-giving, gospel-drenched Christian culture that speaks to their need to belong and invites them into belonging with the mission God.

"We Are All Broken"

The next way we try to help our kids love their version of boy or girl is to help them see that brokenness is normal. If they struggle with their gender, if they have a friend who wrestles with gender, or when they discover other ways they battle the effects of the fall, we want our kids to understand how normal and good it is to rely Jesus in these bodies marred by sin. As Paul says, "The sinful nature wants to do evil, which is just the opposite of what the Spirit wants. And the Spirit gives us desires that are the opposite of what the sinful nature desires. These two forces are constantly fighting each other, so you are not free to carry out your good intentions" (Gal 5:17). We want to and should pursue doing right but struggling with sin is normal.

Here's an example of how we teach that brokenness is normal for pre-resurrected humans. Juliette, six at the time, was supposed to be in bed. She had popped up like a gopher, come down the stairs, and asked for a snack. "Juliette, you need to go to bed," I said, but I gave her a healthy something-or-other and ushered her back up to bed.

"Am I a bad girl?" she asked.

"What? Juliette, no! You're loved. You are beloved because God made you and Jesus died for you." It seemed like Juliette's disobedience in coming down the stairs was reminding her of all of the other times she'd sinned that day and was eliciting a shame spiral. How relatable.

I did not want to remove any gentle conviction she was feeling, but I did want to stop the shame spiral. To hold both in tension, Juliette needed a solid foundation of eternal identity, and she needed to know that struggling with sin (her temporary identity) was normal. So after reminding her of who she was in Christ, I said, "Juliette, you struggle with sin. We all struggle with things." She sighed, turning away. "I struggle with making work my life and not Jesus. I can get mad at you guys and yell when I don't want to."

She seemed to like this line of thinking and looked at me with hope.

"What does Dad struggle with?" I asked, inviting her to take part in recognizing how normal it is to struggle with sin.

Juliette considered for a moment and said, "He worries about money."

I nodded, saying, "Yes, he struggles to trust God with our finances." Then we talked about what each of the other kids struggled with. It seemed to perk her up—not because we were putting others down to make ourselves feel better, but because suddenly the ground felt level again at the foot of the cross. Struggling with sin is the normal, pre-resurrected state for a Christian.

"We all struggle with things, Juliette." She was listening intently now. "But you cannot fight those struggles on your own. You cannot choose good things without God's help. Do you want to ask God to help you?"

She shook her head "no." I get it. It can be hard to be vulnerable in front of Mom and Jesus—even as a kid.

"Can I ask God to help you?"

She nodded slightly.

"Jesus, help Juliette. We can't choose you without your help, Holy Spirit. Will you help her?" She did not need to do all of the work of taking her brokenness to Jesus on her own. She simply needed a mom to walk with her to the cross.

Juliette brightened a bit after we prayed. I looked her in the eyes to model to Juliette how God sees her in the midst of any mess she may find herself in and said, "I adore you, Juliette—no matter what. Do you know that?"

She rolled her eyes, but I could tell that somewhere inside she felt good hearing it. "I know," she said. "You tell me every day."

Through miniature interactions like these, our kids can learn that struggling with sin is normal, it does not change our eternal identities, and we can and must take those struggles to God for help.

If a Loved One Transitions

Let's pivot slightly and move from helping our kids know who they are to helping them live that identity in Christ as they interact with real neighbors who might not just struggle with their sexed bodies but who choose to transition.

To begin, let's talk about what it means to "transition." There are three types of gender transitioning. Socially, someone changes their dress and perhaps their name and pronouns to align with how they feel inside. Hormonally, someone takes hormones that are more prominent in their desired gender to change things like vocal register, body hair, and weight distribution. (Biological males wanting to transition to female would take estrogen, for example, or biological females would take testosterone.[3]) The third way to transition is surgically, where people remove or add body parts to align with their desired gender.

Many parents have asked me, "Should we talk to our kids about friends or family who have transitioned or who are in the process of transitioning?"

If this is someone in your kids' life, I would say, "Yes." Parents need to go first in these conversations to make the gospel the anchoring lens through which their kids interpret their experience. And, to harken back to the analogy of how kids are antifragile like trees, they need both good soil (the belonging-identity work we are doing) and wind (interacting with the world) to grow strong roots. What better way to help our kids grow strong roots so they can push back the darkness and usher in the light than to talk lovingly and truthfully about real-life neighbors and friends who struggle with the effects of sin too?

We have had several situations in our family's life where close family friends have either transitioned or begun to socially transition. Because these friends were regularly in our kids' lives, we wanted to help set a gospel foundation underneath our kids so they could engage with them with grace and truth. In the following example, we wanted to help our kids hear both the truth that our friend "Eric" was going to socially transition to "Liz," and the gospel lens through which they could understand his transition and how to interact with him. We used our morning devotional time to talk about it.

"So, you know how our friend Eric is having a hard time wrestling with how he feels inside?" I began.

Ellis, four at the time, cocked his head and asked, "What's wrong?"

I swallowed and said, "He was born a boy, but he struggles with how he feels inside. He doesn't really feel like a boy." I wanted our kids to hear the truth about our friend: He had a particular struggle that we might not relate to. I named it without judgmentalism. Then, I wanted to take that particular struggle with sin's effects and bring it back to a place where our kids could relate: to the gospel reality of sin. "But we all struggle with things, don't we? I struggle with working too much and getting mad. Dad struggles with worrying. Gwyn, Juliette, and Ellis, you struggle with . . . "

The kids jumped in to name their struggles. This is a common conversation, and I believe it should be in Christian homes: We are loved. We are broken. Our brokenness does not change our beloved identity. Such truth-speaking helps make talking about specific sin struggles easier.

After helping our kids see that Eric's struggles were not the exact same as theirs but similar, because sin struggles are struggles, I wanted to show that the path of help for him was the same as for them. "Instead of Eric taking his struggle with his body to Jesus and saying, 'Jesus! Will you help me?' he is going *with* the struggle."

I motioned forward with my hand to show the path of God, and motioned toward the right to show the struggle, away from the path of God. The kids nodded, understanding it. We regularly make it a practice in our home to take our struggles to God. They could see this pathway was something Eric could do, too.

I wanted my kids to understand more of the pressure Eric had around him to not follow Jesus with this particular sin struggle— while at the same time not seeing him as a victim of his particular battle with the effects of the fall. "He also has friends who say, 'That's a good idea! You should not listen to Jesus. You should go with the struggle.' What should he do instead?"

Our kids offered their ideas. He should "Find new friends," or "Talk to his parents."

I nodded, saying, "He could do that." In this I was subtly telling our kids they could talk to us about whatever struggle they had—and that friends aren't always right. I wanted them to know this, but I was also aware one conversation would not teach it.

Then I asked a direct question specific to Eric's wrestling with the effects of the fall. I wanted our kids to clearly understand that the solution for him was not what the world preaches. "Is it actually possible for boys to become girls?"

All three kids said, "No!"

I was grateful they were learning the concept, but I wanted to ensure we talked about the grace part, too. So for our devotional, we read through Genesis 1 about how God created people male and female. Matt jumped in to ask our kids if this meant God ever put people in the wrong bodies.

"No," they said again.

He continued, "Do people really struggle sometimes with how they feel in their bodies?"

They shouted, "Yes!"

We have talked about this, but kids and adults need to hear things several times before it becomes a part of our foundational beliefs. He added, "Is it a sin to struggle?"

They paused on this one, not sure how to answer correctly. Matt jumped back in: "It is not a sin to struggle. We all struggle with things, remember? But it can be a sin to change our bodies to go with the struggle."

All three kids nodded again. To really help our kids embody gospel love and truth in their culture right now, Matt asked again: "Can boys become girls?"

They paused, thinking about it. "No . . . "

I nodded, adding, "No. Boys cannot become girls and girls cannot become boys. Boys cannot have babies—even if they change their bodies—and girls cannot be boys—even if they change their bodies."

All of this is great—in theory. Bring up the real situation, translate it for our kids in a way they can understand, and then hold it up to the greater gospel-grace picture. But we need one more step. How can we help our kids interact with real-life people? We needed to take the theory and make it practical. So I asked, "What should we say when we see him?"

One of our kids shouted, "We should tell him, 'You aren't a girl!'" (This is why we have pre-conversations.)

I swallowed and said, "Well, I don't think we should say that. How about we say, 'We love you!' God and his parents and others are going to walk with him and his gender."

I remembered his new name, "Liz." I needed to address that. Those closest to him were not going to use it, but I didn't know what to do yet. I could see the benefit of using the new name to perhaps open a door to talk deeper about the heart stuff going on in him. As he found and learned to rely on Jesus' strength, he could perhaps eventually come back to his given name and pronouns. But was that right? What should parents teach? Let's think together.

What Do We Do About Language?

In Holland, Michigan, there is a place called Tunnel Park. It's called that because a literal tunnel cuts through a dune and takes visitors from the parking lot on one side to the sand dunes and Lake Michigan on the other. On the parking lot side is a playground where kids and families play, a bit of sand, and people wearing summertime clothes. Families are on the other side of the tunnel, too, but the attire is beachy, and people are building sand castles and playing water games. The worlds seem similar but also like different cultures.

For the sake of analogy, let's pretend these are two different cultures. On the parking lot side, let's say that's where Christians who hold to a traditional view of marriage and gender live, and on the other side of the tunnel is where people who are affirming of same-sex marriage and all forms of gender transitioning live. (They are "affirming," which means they believe that God's design includes same-sex marriage and transitioning.)

As we are living on the traditional side, we start to notice our son, daughter, or family friend walking away from us down into the tunnel toward the affirming world. We notice they are walking away quickly, and we quietly ask, "Hey, son, hey, daughter, are you struggling? Can we talk about that?" We use their given name and their birth pronouns, and because they have not walked very far into the tunnel, they are still willing to wrestle and consider. They are open to talking. We have a great relationship, so there is no need to yell or run to get their attention; we can talk to each other respectfully.

But what if our son, daughter, or family friend follows the normal pattern for people who identify as LGBTQ and is silent about their struggles for years? When they finally share their journey with us, they are all the way through the tunnel and into the other culture.[4] "This is who I am!" they declare.

If we choose to stay where we are, we have to yell to get their attention, which will likely not produce a fruitful, gentle, honoring conversation (Col 4:6; 2 Tim 2:25). Instead of yelling, we consider how Jesus left the ninety-nine sheep of the flock to pursue the one sheep who strayed, and we start to move toward them (Mt 18:12). As we walk into the tunnel and toward the other culture, we hear the change in language, we see various shades of rainbow flags that represent their beliefs, and we notice the shift in attire.

If culture is, as Andy Crouch defines it, "what we make of the world" as represented through formal ideas, passed-down precognitive assumptions, and the social and physical dimensions of life (symbols, institutions, and practices), one could make an argument that the LGBTQ community is its own culture.[5] LGBTQ people have formulated their formal ideas (such as "love is love" and the elevation of chosen family), they are passing down assumptions about what it means to be an LGBTQ person, and they have social and physical symbols, institutions, and practices as seen their flags, nonprofit organizations, and activism.

How should Christians approach new cultures that do not believe as they do? I believe we should approach them like missionaries. Just as a missionary would never fly across the world without learning the language or customs of another culture, then jump off the plane and shout, "You need to know your true identity in Jesus!" scratching their heads as to why no one found such a new identity in Christ, Christians who hold a traditional view of marriage and gender should not coldheartedly shout a similar statement at their LGBTQ neighbors. At a minimum, we need to have an understanding of the language, customs, and beliefs of LGBTQ-affirming culture as we seek to lovingly invite them to a surrendered life with Christ.

This is how missionaries have engaged cultures for decades. If they were to reach a group of people for whom polygamy is common, for example, they would likely not begin by addressing polygamy. They would seek to get to know the culture, and with cultural respect help the native people understand God's love for them. In time they would disciple new believers to understand how God's love empowers humans to follow God's design for sexuality.

After all, this is how Jesus engaged us. He left heaven's culture for a Judeo-Palestinian one, taking on the cultural practices of footwashing, tithing, and speaking human language. He incarnated. "Incarnation is the theological term for the truth that the Son of God took human flesh, entered human culture and lived as we live (but without sin)," missiologist Duane Elmer says. "Similarly, missionaries are called to incarnate Christ in a new culture by understanding and adjusting to local realities and living out God's kingdom values."[6] However, Jesus did not simply conform to our culture and blindly adopt our practices; he created within our culture. He pushed back the darkness and ushered in the light. When Jesus washed the disciples' feet, he modeled true leadership by serving instead of being served (Jn 13:1-17). When Jesus talked about paying taxes, he highlighted the image stamped on the coin: "Give to Caesar what belongs to Caesar, and give to God what belongs to God" (Mk 12:17). In this he pointed out our image bearing as humans and encouraged people to give themselves fully to God.

Jesus also knew when to critique cultural customs and outright break them, such as when he talked with the Samaritan woman at the well (Jn 4:1-42). Jesus undoubtedly knew that good Jewish rabbis would never talk to women—especially Samaritan women—publicly. I am sure he also knew that in asking her for a drink, he was going against Jewish custom that said to eat or drink the food or water of a Samaritan was equal to "eating swine's flesh."[7] Jesus was so in step with the Father that he knew he needed to abandon cultural norms in that moment because she was ready to receive the truth of her identity. As a result of Jesus' cultural in-breaking, this woman became the first missionary (Jn 4:39).

Jesus also knew when to condemn culture. He flipped tables in the synagogue when the Jewish leaders were making it hard for the people to come to God (Jn 2:13-17). This is one of the passages people quote the most to me when I talk about engaging LGBTQ culture. People are quick to point to Jesus' anger. But please note that his anger was perfect and in absolute control. How long did it take him to weave together that whip? Someone in a blind rage could not have woven slowly and methodically. Also, Jesus' table-flipping anger was not focused on the sexual sinners of his day but on the religious, who were creating barriers to worship and monetizing the temple.

When it comes to engaging LGBTQ culture, we need to put on a missional lens and ask the Holy Spirit, "Is now the time to condemn, critique, cultivate, or create something new with you here?" No matter what we choose, our approach needs to be motivated by real love. After all, it was love that motivated God to enter our culture to save us (Jn 3:16).

With those thoughts in mind, I can see an argument for using preferred names and pronouns of transgender family and friends who have walked all the way through the tunnel and into LGBTQ-affirming culture. It might be hard to earn the relational equity required to talk about deeper matters of the heart when we disregard their language and entire way of living. However, I can also see an argument for not using the pronouns and chosen name if you have a strong conviction that to do so would be to agree with a lie, or if you feel God is calling you to break cultural customs like Jesus did—inviting the other person to live into who they truly are in Christ.

Options for Helping Our Kids Engage with Loved Ones

Personally, I cannot offer a one-size-fits-all path for us as we lead our kids. So I will share some options we can bring to God as parents, asking him if this is a time to adapt, transform, or break cultural customs. I trust God will show us.

Use the new name and pronouns. The conversation with our kids could sound like, "We are going to use his new name and use the pronouns 'she/her.' But do we believe that he is a girl? No. We do not. We are using this because we love him and want him to know and feel the love of Jesus even when he is not following Jesus with his gender." Depending on our kids' ages, however, holding this tension might be challenging.

Use no names or pronouns. "Hey, guys, we are going to try to just say, 'Hey!' instead of using their name or pronouns." This approach can potentially be offensive to our transgender loved ones and confuse our kids. I would recommend talking with our transgender loved one first and asking them if this is okay before we have them over and have them interact with our kids.

Ask the transgender loved one if it is okay if our kids use their old name. "We do not believe it is God's design to transition, but we love you. Can we use your former [often called 'dead'] name?" This, again, can be relationally tricky and takes enormous humility on the part of our transgender loved ones to let our kids do this.

Ask the transgender loved one if we can use a nickname for them. In Matt's therapy practice, he finds that an alternative name is often a helpful approach for parents of kids who are in the process of transitioning when the parents do not agree with the process. He asks the child if it is okay if they find an alternative to their new name to call them, such as a middle name, last name, or a special name everyone agrees on.

As a family, choose not to spend time with this loved one. For various reasons, it may not seem like the right thing for families to spend time with an individual. Someone may read verses such as 1 Corinthians 5:11—"you must not associate with anyone who claims to be a brother or sister but is sexually immoral or greedy, an idolater or slanderer, a drunkard or swindler" (NIV)—and determine it's best not to associate with them. If that is the case, we need to remember that this is talking about Christian people in ongoing, unrepentant sin. If we choose to do this with someone who is transitioning, let's ensure we are doing so in love and through conversation, and that we are doing it equally with everyone who claims to be a Christian and is living in unrepentant sin.

In our family we have taken different approaches with different relationships. Our decisions depended on where the person was on their journey and how close our relationship was. With one friend I asked, out of earshot of my kids, "Is it okay if we still call you by your birth name?" They graciously agreed.

Another family friend, Kat, was quite far down the tunnel but was taking some steps back. She was in a season of wondering, "Is this right? Maybe I should give God a try again." As we walked with her, we tried to use her preferred they/them pronouns, but our oldest kids were one and three years old, and this was above their pay grade. I apologized as they bounced between calling her "she" and "he." I even ended up calling her "she" more times than not. Eventually, I asked if it was okay to use she/her pronouns. She agreed.

When I later asked why she let me use she/her pronouns before she shifted back to them officially, she said, "I knew you knew me. When you said 'she,' it wasn't like you had a dress-shaped cookie cutter that you were stamping on me saying, 'You are a girl. Be a stereotype.' You understood my version of female and all the suffering that came with it." By the grace of God, Kat has now walked all the way back from LGBTQ-affirming culture to a historically Christian one, where she owns her version of female and is choosing a life of celibacy for Jesus. She is also discipling others on a similar journey.

That is a happy-ending story, but our family has also chosen to break relationships with other friends who claim faith while living in ongoing, unrepentant sin of many varieties. Are we always making the exact right choice? I am never going to say that. We pray, we seek God, and we step forward in humble faith—willing to change our approach as God convicts through his Word and his people. That's all any of us can do.

So what did we do in this scenario with Eric? Away from my kids, I asked for permission from Eric to use his given name and pronouns. He graciously let us because we had a close relationship. It seems to be true that the greater the depth of relationship, the greater amount of grace that can be offered back and forth in situations like these.

What If Our Kids Are Struggling?

What if our kids seem to be truly struggling with their bodies as male or female? How can we know if it's more than an expression of their version of boy or girl? Experts say that if our sons or daughters start praying for or wishing for opposite-sex body parts, or have intense anxiety about their bodies for six months or more, it is wise to ask for professional help.[8] As we are walking with them, however, we can rest in the reality that even though they are struggling more than the average child in this particular area, it does not change who they are. They are made by God, Jesus redeemed them, and they are struggling with living in a sin-drenched world and body—which is normal. God will give them grace to live in their broken bodies just as he gives grace to everyone. God's grace is sufficient, and his power actually works best in our weakness (2 Cor 12:8-10). This is true for our kids, for us as parents, and for the whole world.

▶ QUESTIONS TO CONSIDER

1. How have you thought about approaching LGBTQ people and conversations with them with a missional lens?

2. How do you engage the question of using pronouns and someone's preferred name?

3. What's your reaction to the Tunnel Park analogy?

4. What ideas do you have to help your kids feel like they belong with their gender, with your family, and with the family of God?

7. GOD'S DESIGN FOR SEX

Lay the Foundation

> "How do I talk with my kids about God's design for sex? When is it too early to talk? When is it too late? Do I need diagrams? How can I equip them and not scar them?"

WHEN I THINK ABOUT TALKING with my kids about sex, my heart starts to race, my overwhelmed prefrontal cortex wants to numb out, and I just want to go shopping or eat ice cream to alleviate my anxiety. So I'm the ideal candidate to talk about this. The good news is I have already started talking about sex, periods, and all the things with our ten- and eight-year-old girls, and our five-year-old son knows the very basics. I am also proud to say that I did not have a full-blown panic attack while talking with any of them and my shopping and ice cream eating habits have remained the same. The best news is the conversations seemed to go well with each of the kids, with only one child deadpan asking me, "Why are you telling me this? This is weird."

Why am I telling you about my own anxieties? Because I want you to know that if you dread talking to your kids about God's design for sex, you are not alone. Studies show that most parents believe they are the best ones to talk with their children about sex, but they do not feel they have the skills to do so. So they don't bring it up.[1] One study found that adolescent boys were not taught 75 percent of necessary sexual topics, ranging from body part development to masturbation, and girls were not taught 33 percent of necessary sexual topics.[2] "If many parents feel that they should communicate with their children about these topics—but few actually do, there is some sort of disconnect between attitude and behavior," the authors reflect.[3] I think they're right. Many of us wish we could outsource these conversations, but we know that what our kids learn from the internet, their peers, or the school system will be confusing at best and traumatizing at worst. So we sigh, accepting the fact that there is no one better to talk with our kids about the most personal parts of their life and bodies than those who are closest to them.

Before we bite the proverbial bullet and simply start teaching, however, let's look at why we are so hesitant to talk with them in the first place. I believe asking that question will help the conversations go better because we will talk with more confident peace.

Preparing to Talk: Why We Don't Want To

When talking with our kids about God's design for sex, a lot can come up for us as parents. Many of us have not been trained to ask our hearts, *Why am I hesitant? Why am I anxious?* We swallow our fear and pour information onto our kids, or we freeze and try to avoid the whole thing, or we say something about sex and gruffly add, "Don't do it," or we apologize the whole time for what we have to share. In other words, we go to a trauma response of fight, flight, freeze, or fawn (people-pleasing). Why do we do this? It could be because learning about sex felt—or was—traumatic for us.

For some of us, our first education about sex did not come through relationally rich conversations over a series of years but through sexual abuse. Truly, at least one in four girls and one in ten boys under the age of eighteen experience childhood sexual abuse.[4] Twenty percent of sexually abused children are abused prior to age eight, with most children abused between the ages of seven and thirteen.[5] If we have suffered sexual abuse as children, it undoubtedly affects the way we parent our kids and talk with our children about things like sex.[6]

For others of us, our first sexual learning experiences happened through the trauma of pornography—and I do mean trauma. Psychologist Julia Sadusky says of this reality, "While the word 'traumatic' is often overused, I mean it here in the literal sense. Pornography exposure often exceeds a child's capacity to cope and violates them in a profound way. It evokes many of the same emotions as sexual abuse, including powerlessness, helplessness, confusion, and shame."[7] For kids to stumble on their dad's stash of pornographic magazines, to type a curious question into Google and find graphic images, to have a peer show them something pornographic, or to have a predator intentionally display something to sexually stimulate a child is damaging to a child's soul. We adults would do well to face the feelings of shame that overwhelmed us when we first encountered the pornification of what God created as good.

Others of us learned about sex from our parents, but in less than helpful ways. In author and therapist Jay Stringer's research of nearly four thousand people, he found that 50 percent of people had mothers who did not talk about sex, 60 percent had fathers who did not talk about sex, only 8 percent had helpful talks with mom, and 5 percent had helpful sexual conversations with dad.[8] This is despite research showing that adolescents want to know more about sex and want to hear about it openly from their parents.[9]

Some of us were taught about God's design for sex, but it was packaged in fear and shame. In the 1980s through the early 2000s, many Christians were given talks about purity and holiness related to sex, but they were wrapped in a theology of "no" instead of a theology of "Here is God's beautiful path of flourishing, whether you're called to marriage or singleness." A fear-based theology is not of God and will not produce good fruit long term.

Some researchers found results of purity culture to be especially damaging to adult women's sex lives. Author Sheila Wray Gregoire says, "Purity culture worked. Girls who took Purity Pledges were much more likely to save sex for marriage than those who did not. And the younger the girl was when she took the pledge, the higher the odds were that she wouldn't 'do it' until she said, 'I do.' But on average, those same girls who took purity pledges before puberty had lower self-esteem in high school (and they still have lower self-esteem today), and they knew less about how sex and their bodies worked in general. They were also more likely to suffer from vaginismus, a sexual pain disorder long known to be more prevalent among conservative Christians."[10] I have friends whose personal experiences mirror Gregoire's findings. They suffered from sexual challenges in their marriages largely due to how they were taught about sex through a fear-based lens.

Still others of us learned about sex through hookup culture. Hookup culture, according to author Lisa Wade's long-term research of eighteen- to twenty-three-year-olds on religious and non religious campuses, is the practice of getting drunk or high and engaging in non-emotional sexual encounters with relative strangers on campus.[11] Hookup culture requires participants not to interact with their sexual partner the next day so as not to appear "needy." The result of such a culture is inevitably turmoil. "Half of first-year students express concern that they are not emotionally healthy, and one in ten say that they frequently feel depressed. . . . One in three students say that their intimate relationships have been 'traumatic' or 'very difficult to handle,' and 10 percent say that they've been sexually coerced or assaulted in the past year."[12] If God's design for sex is to display a picture of his intimate covenant love for the church, hookup culture is not that.

Still others of us had formative sexual learning experiences through same-sex sexual encounters. Perhaps these experiences took place in a college hookup culture, in a monogamous dating relationship, online through pornography, or through an abusive situation, but every situation affected our ability to process God's design for human sexuality and someday teach it to our kids.

To have these types of formative sexual encounters in our past and think we can teach our kids without being affected is wrong. Even if we push "mute" on our stories and robotically tell our kids about God's design for sex in marriage, our kids will still perceive our pain. "We think what children need most in sex education is information," author Kathy Bell says. "That's not true. . . . It is an involved and loving parent."[13] To be such a parent, we have to let God's light shine into our hearts, revealing places within us we have not grieved, forgiven, or repented (Ps 139:23-24). We do not have to be perfect, but we do need to let the Holy Spirit and trusted counselors help us process so we do not unnecessarily bleed onto our kids from unhealed wounds.

Over and over in our work of coaching (me) and counseling (Matt), we see how unprocessed parental sexual wounds affect kids. I remember meeting with a mother whose teenage son was engaging in sexual sin. I was encouraging her to place rules, yes, but to talk to him with empathy and relational gentleness instead of through a lens of anger and hostility. This mom was hearing none of what I was saying. She could see only her son's sin. As I prayed about what to do, I sensed the Holy Spirit saying to me, "Ask about her husband's pornography addiction." I did not want to cause more problems, but God kept nudging me gently.

"I am so sorry," I said calmly. "But I feel like I am supposed to ask you if you have any pornography issues in your marriage."

She became immediately quiet. "Yes. My husband."

I could almost see the icy bitterness fall from her words. I did not want to make the situation worse, but I kept going. "I am curious if you are so hurt by your husband's sexual sin that it is keeping you from loving your child in his sexual brokenness." She was quiet again. "That could be," she nodded. This was an abnormal moment where it seems God had given me divine insight into unprocessed pain that was bleeding onto other relationships in this family's life. Although our situations may differ a little or a lot from this, it is wise for us as parents to dig into our own sexual stories before, during, and after we talk with our kids about sex. We want to ensure we are leading them from our scars and not our wounds.[14]

Preparing to Talk: The Posture

Conversations about sex go best when parents focus on their posture or the attitude they take with their children in these discussions. *The Journal of Adolescent Research* published a qualitative study looking at conversations about sex among 112 parent-adolescent pairs. Although we traditionally think of adolescents as teenagers, in this study they were defined as between the ages of ten and nineteen. The researchers found that the posture of the parent needs to be receptive (able to listen to the child), informal (not taking oneself too seriously and not reading from a script), and composed ("I know what I am talking about; I am not anxious").[15] Such a posture can lessen the child's anxiety and decrease their avoidance of personal conversations about sex with the parent.

I found the idea of "informality" especially helpful. In reading through the transcripts of "successful" conversation in the study, I heard an easiness, humility, and sometimes humor in the parents. They did not think they had to say everything perfectly. It was interesting to note that the Christians in the study embodied such ease. "Unlike what one might think," the researchers in this secular study said, "children and parents who held very conservative religious beliefs and practices appeared to be quite comfortable talking about sex together."[16] Such an easiness in posture on the part of the parent calmed the child's anxiety and fostered a better perception on the part of the child, so the conversation "went well."

The researchers went on to clarify, "Adolescents' perception of their parents' lack of communication competence was associated with adolescents' self-reported anxiety, which predicted adolescents' avoidance during their discussions about sex." Translated: If parents are anxious and avoidant in these conversations, the child will be anxious and avoidant. It was extra interesting to note that it was not the parents' anxiety that mattered in these moments, but the child's *perception* of the parents' anxiety. This only emphasizes to me that as parents we have to work on our hearts and stories, because adolescents can pick up emotional nuances like no one else.

Preparing to Talk: The Quality of Relationship

The quality of the relationship between the parent and child is also critical in conversations about sex between parents and kids. "When it came down to actually talking about sex, adolescents who reported being closer and more satisfied with their relationship with their parent reported being less anxious and avoidant during the conversations," said the authors of the *Journal of Adolescent Research* study.[17] The closer and healthier the relationship between parent and child, the better the conversations about sex can go. Furthermore, a gentle posture does not just result in a better conversation, but it can result in more biblical actions. A 1990 study found that the teenage kids of parents with a friendly and attentive communication style engaged in less sexual promiscuity than children of parents who were dominant, contentious, and dramatic.[18]

To build healthy relationships between ourselves and our kids, we need to seek to develop trust, we need to pursue secure attachment, and we need to lead authoritatively. I will briefly cover each of these so we can have something to look back on regularly to know what we are aiming for relationally.

Building trust. The first relational dynamic parenting experts and psychiatrists encourage is trust. "Trust in relationships is . . . fundamental to the access of private information. If parents want their children to have permeable boundaries when it comes to discussions about sex, they must display characteristics central to this trait."[19] A study in the *Journal of Marriage and Family* found that when adolescents perceived their parents as trustworthy, they viewed them as higher in expertise and accessibility, which, in turn, resulted in more frequent discussions about sex.[20]

So how do we develop trust between ourselves and our kids? In our family, we say people "earn trust" with us when they behave in ways we expect (they are reliable), when they follow in the way of Jesus, and when they do these things over a long period of time. If someone says one thing and does another? They lose trust with us. If they tell a lie when the Bible says to tell the truth? They lose trust. If they follow through consistently and are walking in the way of Jesus? Then they earn trust. If they follow through consistently but do not love Jesus, there is some withholding of trust. If they behave in a way we expect, they follow Jesus, but we only met them yesterday—there is still a withholding of trust. As a parent, I seek to build trust between myself and my kids by doing what I say I will do, by following in the way of Jesus, and by doing it consistently over a long period of time. We do not do this perfectly, but it is something to aim for. Thank God we do not have to be perfect parents, but "good enough"—research confirms this.[21] And thank God Jesus' grace is enough for us and for our kids (2 Cor 12:9).

Attachment styles. The second parenting tool that's critical for healthy relationship formation between parents and kids is that of secure attachment. Pursuing healthy, secure attachment with our kids should be a goal not only so we can talk about sensitive issues with them, and not only because fifty years of research says it helps them develop secure relationships for their future,[22] but because we parents model God's parental love for our kids. When we help our kids feel secure with us, we are setting them up for a life of understanding the security they have with their Father, God.

There are four different attachment styles we have received from our parents and then offer to our kids:[23]

- *Secure attachment.* Secure attachment forms when parents respond to a child's physical and emotional needs consistently and kindly. Adults with secure attachment are able to form long-lasting relationships, can share their own emotions and receive others', and are able to more easily trust others.

- *Anxious attachment.* Anxious attachment is created within a child when a parent inconsistently responds to a baby's physical and emotional needs. The children learn they may or may not get comforted by their parents, so even when they encounter comfort, they may not be soothed. As adults, people with anxious attachment tend to be clingy and needy, struggle to trust others, and are concerned they will be abandoned.

- *Avoidant attachment.* Avoidant attachment forms when parents do not consistently care for a baby's emotional needs even when they may care for their physical ones. Adults who are avoidantly attached tend to be self-reliant and emotionally guarded. They can struggle to be vulnerable or to comfort those with whom they are in close relationship.

- *Disorganized attachment.* Disorganized attachment forms when children live through a traumatic or tumultuous childhood marked by irregular care or an incoherent relationship with the parent. Adults with a disorganized attachment style tend to crave close relationships but push them away quickly. They tend to more frequently have mental health and personality disorders.

If you're anything like me, reading that can bring on some anxiety. Our received attachment style affects how we parent, and we can't control what we received![24] However, secular and Christian researchers alike say our attachment style is not fixed.[25] We can grow and change—especially by the power of the Spirit. Additionally, we cannot ever be the perfectly attuned parent. Researchers have found that even in securely attached relationships, caregivers and babies are only in sync 30 percent of the time. The 70 percent we miss teaches our kids how to self-soothe and be resilient in a world that will not perfectly attune to them.[26]

"Repairing ruptures is the most essential thing in parenting," says UCLA neuropsychiatrist Dan Siegel.[27] Clinical psychologist Becky Kennedy adds, "When parents are willing to change, when they are willing to repair and reflect together, non-defensively, about moments in the past that felt bad to kids . . . the child's brain can rewire."[28] We aim for secure attachment, we seek to repair when we miss connection with our kids, and when we don't, we can be thankful that God is their perfect parent to whom they can always and forever securely attach.

Parenting styles. Authoritative parenting is another key concept that can help us as we prepare to explain sex to our kids. What is authoritative parenting? Let's look at it and how it compares to authoritarian and permissive parenting:[29]

- *Authoritative parenting.* Authoritative parents give their children clear guidelines and explain why they are leading the way they are. Children's voices are heard and taken into consideration, even if their suggestions are not followed. This style of parenting often results in a close, nurturing, warm relationship between parents and kids, as well as children who are confident, responsible, and able to self-regulate.

- *Authoritarian parenting.* Authoritarian parents often operate in a one-way mode of communication to their kids, dictating what they can do and what will happen if they do not follow the rules. There is little room for negotiation and children's voices are not taken into consideration. Children are often well-behaved because they fear consequences, but this can result in aggressiveness, poor self-esteem, and a poor relationship with their parents in the long term.

- *Permissive parenting.* Permissive parents are often warm and nurturing but have minimal expectations for their kids. Communication remains open between parents and children, but children tend to have to figure out life for themselves. This can lead to long-term unhealthy personal habits (eating and screen time, for example) and okay self-esteem, but it can also result in impulse issues, selfishness, and a lack of self-regulation.

I highlight these parenting styles because if researchers are correct that the relationship between parent and child is vital to how well conversations about sex go, we need to look more closely at how we engage our kids. Are we more authoritarian, with our kids obeying us now but perhaps hiding from us later? Are we permissive and kind, which may lead to impulse issues in our kids? Or are we authoritative—our kids know their voices matter, they know why the rules are there, and we pray and hope for genuinely healthy relationships and helpful conversations about sex now and in the future?

Saying that, I need to look at any shame spiraling that may be happening in us right now. Some of us may be thinking, *Well, it's done. I failed.* Nope. It's never too late. This is simply a heart check. Exactly zero parents on the planet are nailing parenting perfectly. Let's just notice where we lean in our parenting style and ask the Spirit and accountability friends to help us parent with grace, truth, and love like God parents us.

Preparing Our Minds: What Is God's Design for Sex?

As a woman who has experienced childhood sexual abuse at the hands of a male stranger and also whose default sexual attractions are toward women, it's safe to say I have had to work to understand God's design for sex in marriage. Everything I have shared in this chapter I have had to and am still walking through myself: Work on my sexual story? Yep. Consider my posture in how I talk about sex with my kids? Oh, yes. Continually work on how I relate to my kids through building trust, seeking to cultivate secure attachment (while focusing on the repair when I fail to attune), and beg God for help to be the authoritative parent instead of the permissive or authoritarian one? Absolutely. But more than all of these, what calms my anxious mind when it comes to talking with my kids about sex is understanding the theology of sex.

God designed sex to be a covenant renewal ceremony that produces fruit to the glory of God. Let's walk through each part of that definition. Human marriage is a covenant that represents the marriage between Christ and the church (Gen 2:24; Mt 19:5; Eph 5:31). The word *covenant* is key. In the Old Testament, the sign of the covenant was circumcision (Gen 12:9-13). In the New Testament, the sign of the covenant between Jesus and us is the bread and the wine—Communion (Mt 26:28). If marriage is a picture of God's covenant love to the world, what is the sign of that covenant love? It's sex.

When we stand before the church vowing fidelity to this other person, we are taking part in a covenant: a public, binding contract before God that provides a safe place in which to experience intimacy. But the covenant is not ratified until there is a consummation. Just as there was a bodily action in Jesus' covenant to us, ideally there needs to be a bodily ratification of our marriage vows.[30] Therefore we have the wedding night. But just as we do not engage in the Communion meal once, remembering and engaging Jesus' covenant to us one time, ideally we do not engage in sexual union with our spouses just once.

Every time a husband and wife come together in mind, heart, body, and spirit through the unifying act of sex, we say to our spouses, "I commit myself mind, heart, body, and spirit to you. I love you. You are still safe here in this covenant." Also, because sex is a metaphor of God's covenant love for us, when we engage in sexual intimacy, we say, "This is a glimmer of how much God wants to and will be one with you: mind, heart, body, spirit." Again, we hear wisdom from Tim Keller: "Sex is a covenant renewal ceremony for marriage, the physical reenactment of the inseparable oneness in all other areas—economic, legal, personal, psychological—created by the marriage covenant."[31]

Now, is this "covenant renewal ceremony" (a.k.a. sex) just a very boring, "Yes, let's read the terms of the agreement and henceforth proceed in coitus?" I mean, you can roll how you want to roll, but that's not how our relationship with God is supposed to be. Our marriages should not reflect a boring, one-note form of intimacy. Sex should be a culmination of the emotional, spiritual, social, financial, and physical oneness we are experiencing with our spouses throughout the rest of the relationship. My most intimate times with the Lord come out of enjoying being with him, laughing with him, studying him, being vulnerable with him, and listening to him. So, too, should our most intimate moments with our spouses.

My definition of sex, however, is a covenant renewal ceremony that results in bearing fruit. Fruit of union with God is love, joy, peace, patience, kindness, goodness, faithfulness, gentleness, and self-control, as well as the making of disciples (Gal 5:22-23; Mt 28:19). Sex with our spouses produces the fruit of emotional connectedness as well as another type of fruit: people. "The fact that sexual union is a covenant-making act profoundly affects our theology of children," says author and theologian Branson Parler. "Children are not merely a bundle of biology but are persons made in God's image. But there's another dimension to how we should think about children: They are the embodied, 'one flesh' sign and seal of the marriage covenant of their parents."[32]

Let's think about that for a moment: If God calls men and women to the one flesh covenant union of marriage, biological kids are the embodiment of that one flesh union. They are one-half of the genetics of their mom and one-half of their dad. This is a reason why divorce hurts children so deeply: It causes a fissure of their very one flesh existence.

Sex is one of the most tender subjects people encounter. It can be a gorgeous reflection of God's covenant love to us, and it can be a reminder of trauma we endured or sins we committed. It is my deep prayer that we lead the next generation to not only experience less sexual damage or sin, but, through understanding God's design for sex, gain a greater love for the gospel.

QUESTIONS TO CONSIDER

1. How deeply have you processed your sexual history? Do you feel you need to do more? Why or why not?

2. How do you approach your kids when it comes to talking about anything related to sex or the body? Does your posture feel receptive, informal, and composed? Or something else?

3. What would you say is the attachment style you received from your family of origin? How would you say your kids are attached to you now? How does that make you feel?

4. What do you think is your default parenting style? How might that affect intimate conversations with your kids?

8. GOD'S DESIGN FOR SEX

Walk the Foundation

> **Key teaching:** "To make a baby, God takes a seed from a dad and a seed from a mom, and God puts them together and makes a baby! Then God puts that baby inside the mom's tummy."

WE JUST NEVER KNOW when a question about sex is going to come up from our kids, do we? This time, it was my four-year-old, Ellis, while we were driving his older sisters to school.

"How did you have babies, Mom?"

My heart started racing. I took a deep breath as I remembered that my posture and relationship with my kids are more important than getting every word right. *You're okay, Krieg.* Then I thought about the gospel, sighing in the reality that sex is not sexy in the way the world says it is—it is a part of the gospel narrative. Age-appropriately sharing God's design for sex with our kids will not corrupt them; it will teach them more layers of how God designed the world to show them a picture of himself.

But first I needed to know if Ellis was actually asking about sex or about something else. I have a tendency to make something bigger than it is. Once, when Gwyn asked about the United States' Thanksgiving, I found myself sharing with her about the genocide of Native American people. She was four. I didn't need to make that sort of pedagogical leap again.

"Are you wondering where babies come from? Or how they come out?" I sensed Ellis was asking more about their location during birth than how they got in there. Bless God, that was his question.

"Yeah. How did babies come out of you?"

As I thought about where to begin, I mentally sorted through Ellis's informal, God's-design-for-sex-and-bodies curriculum Matt and I had taught so far. Ellis knew body parts.

"Remember the other day how I said boys have penises and girls don't?"

He tilted his head, thinking. Gratefully, Ellis did not turn red or giggle, even though his capacity for shame had begun around nineteen months, along with the majority of humanity.[1] I silently hoped his lack of shame was because in our house we try not to laugh at private parts or act embarrassed of them; instead we try to honor them as good and normal.

Ellis seemed to remember the body parts conversation we'd had the other day and many times before that.

"Yeah. Girls have vanginas . . ." he began.

Close enough for me, but not for Justice Juliette: "Vaginas!" she corrected.

"Right, so babies come out from the mama's vagina," I said, looking at Ellis in the rearview mirror to see if he seemed emotionally okay. I scanned the girls, too, who seemed to be listening intently.

Gwyn, nine at the time, piped up. "I don't want to do that."

My eyes went wide. Was she talking about not wanting to have sex or about having babies? *Don't make the leap, Laurie!*

Remember Thanksgiving! Gwyn clarified her question before I needed to.

"What if I get married and I don't want to have kids?" she asked.

I was relieved but realized that if she'd said she didn't want to have sex, I could have simply responded, "Well, you don't have to get married. God might call you to singleness." Such a response would have been biblically true and age appropriate for everyone in the car.

But Gwyn was saying she didn't know if she wanted to have kids. What did I say to that? This was becoming more of a big-picture theological question than a conversation about the mechanics of childbirth.

"Well, that's between you and God, but I do think that everyone—whether you are married or single—is supposed to 'have kids.'"

I turned the radio down, deciding now was the time to talk about God's design for babies. It wasn't the first time. It would not be the last.

"God wants everyone to have kids because he wants us to tell other people about him. He wants us to make disciples, whether that's with the kids we have from our bodies, or through adoption, or through mentoring.[2] Do you know how I have walked with Kat? And Cassie?"

These are two women I have mentored for many years. The kids nodded, knowing each of them well.

"They are people I have helped to know God. I have 'discipled' them. That's what God wants us to do whether we are married and have kids or are single and have mentor-kids."[3]

Juliette jumped in with understanding. "Oh, I get it. He wants us to 'have babies'—but it might not be babies from our bodies."

I nodded, shocked they seemed to get this heady concept.

Gwyn got it, too. "So, we all 'have babies' or 'make disciples.'"

My heart started racing again—happily this time. "Yes! God is all about procreation. He is all about making babies. Look around us!"

It was springtime. The trees were in their full pink, purple, and bright green glory, and the birds chirped happily, seeming to underline my point. "Birds have babies. Trees have babies."

Juliette chimed in: "Trees have acorns that they drop and make babies!"

My theologically nerdy little heart was about to burst as I thought of God's mandate to humanity to "be fruitful and multiply." God wants the whole earth filled with his glory, and one way he does that is through procreation.

"Yes! God loves us and wants to fill the earth with his love. He wants to spread his love through procreation."

As I waited for the next deep thought or question, Juliette asked, "Can we listen to the radio now?"

I laughed. "Yeah, we can." I turned up their favorite tune.

I share this not as a script but to offer a window into how families can talk naturally about sex and having kids without it being all, "Now let's talk about sexual intercourse." The advice to talk about sex with your kids through 100 one-minute conversations instead of one 100-minute conversation is becoming increasingly prevalent, and I think it's a great exhortation to teach kids in small-but-important ways they can learn.[4] Our conversation in the car was one of the one-minute conversations. Did I get into the nitty gritty of sex? No. But did I help to cast a biblical vision for it? Yes. *Boom.* One of the 100 minute-long conversations: done. But we do need to talk about the nitty gritty at some point. When do we do that? And how? Let's walk it out.

When Should We Talk About Sex?

When I first heard that parents should start talking with their kids about sex around seven to ten years of age, I was aghast.[5] I thought of my precious seven-year-old at home and could not envision tainting her innocence with such knowledge. However, as I read trusted experts in the field—secular and Christian alike—I found over and over that seven to ten was the ideal age for learning.[6] This is often when the body begins to prepare for puberty, and the initial talk about sex should be focused on puberty.[7] For girls, we often associate puberty with the first day of their period, but it actually begins two to three years earlier when they begin developing breast buds, around ages seven to thirteen.[8] For boys, puberty begins between ages nine and fourteen.[9]

However, as a teacher in this field and a real mom who wants to limit the amount of time her kids have to spend in future therapy, I needed more convincing. The onset of puberty did not seem a strong enough reason to talk about something so sacred and easily distorted as sex. So I researched further, beginning with relational changes that occur in the seven-to-ten-year-old age range. By five or six, children's focus increasingly shifts from family-oriented to peer-oriented, perhaps inviting them to ask their peers about their sexed bodies instead of their parents.[10]

Additionally, the gender of friendships changes. For example, one study found that for 36 percent of three- to four-year-olds, the gender of best friends doesn't matter, but that percentage drops to 23 percent in five- to six-year-olds. By the time kids are seven or eight, the majority of best friendships are exclusively same-sex.[11] In these ages, kids are forming cohorts of same-sex friends and are often beginning to experience crushes on the other gender.[12] Okay, perhaps there was something waking up in my kids that would be wise to address before puberty began.

One last encouraging kick in the tail for me was reading therapist Sam Jolman's ebook *How to Give a Sex Talk*, where he writes about the goodness of curiosity and how, according to researcher Emily Nagoski, sexual desire can mimic curiosity.[13] Kids may not be sexual before puberty, but they do live in sexed bodies—and in that seven-to-ten-year-old age range, they are increasingly aware of it and making relational decisions based on it. It could be a normal, innocent thing for a child that age to follow their curiosity to Google searches and best friends, who likely would not provide godly answers. The Google searches could lead to pornography, which is the antithesis of God's design for sacred, covenantal, honoring sex. I do not want sincere curiosity to lead my kids to Google, friends, or unholy lessons about sex.

These factors led me to undig my stubborn heels, sigh, and say, "Okay, fine. It is time." But which day is the right day? Experts recommend choosing a specific age and circumstance for sharing based on our children.[14] Are they very mature for their age and already asking questions? Maybe we talk to them at age seven. Are they sensitive and shy about emotions and would they perhaps prefer to wait to hear about this until later? Then maybe we wait until age eight, nine, or ten. Is their school introducing things next week that could confuse them? Then today might be the day. The important thing is to get to know our children and consider how they think about the world, how they relate to their friends, and how they relate to us. Then adjust our timing and posture to their style of learning, perhaps to their neurodivergent needs, and start talking with Holy Spirit-infused wisdom and grace somewhere in that seven-to-ten-ish window.

How Do We Talk About Sex?

After all that talk about addressing sex specifics in the seven-to-ten age range, I'm now going to focus on how to talk about sex in small ways from ages zero to twelve. There are conversations we can have before "the big one" about sexual intercourse in the seven-to-ten age range, and conversations we should have after. The more we can have a basic curriculum of "God's design for sex and gender" in our minds, the more we will actually use it with our kids. That's a win all around. My focus here is to dive into the gospel of "why" and to share conversations we can have before, during, and after sex-basics conversations. In appendix A, I offer a sample sex-basics conversation for you to adopt, adapt, or use as a reference. You'll also find recommended resources for teaching sex ed specifics in the Next Step Resources section.

Ages zero to three: Teach body parts. Every inch of recent research I have read on how to care for young kids in their developing sexuality says this: One of the most important things parents can do to help prevent childhood sexual abuse and remove shame from sexuality is to teach kids to use medically accurate, specific body part terms at a young age. If kids know the correct terms for penis, scrotum, vagina, vulva, and breast, for example, it signals to potential predators that they have been trained and will not be easy targets. And if, God forbid, something does happen to our children, being able to use clear language about what happened to them will help them get the help they need and work to convict predators and get them off the streets.[15] (We will talk more in depth about this in chapter ten on preventing childhood sexual abuse.)

To use specific medical language also tells our kids, "These are not shameful parts of you. They are good." When parents and caregivers talk about private parts like the good, normal body parts they are, this can set them up for a healthier relationship to their sexed bodies and a healthier potential for having sex if God calls them to marriage in the future.

However, even as I acknowledge that it's necessary to use anatomical terms and adopt a "this-is-normal" attitude in order to remove shame and protect from predation, I still cringe a little bit when children's books or sex education experts talk about private parts with what sounds like a shrug: "You have an elbow, you have an eyebrow, you have a penis."[16] I am concerned we are overdoing it a bit with such a nonchalant view, perhaps making room for predation on the other side of the pendulum: If our privates are just like any other body part, why protect and cover them at all?

God has the answer. Our private parts matter and need extra care not because they are shameful, but because they are the only parts of our bodies that can generate new life created in God's image. Our elbows cannot generate new life. Our eyebrows can make us look silly when they move, but they cannot generate new *imago Dei* life. Dogs can produce adorable new life, but not life that is created in God's image. Only human people have the capacity to allow God to form new lives that are made in his image.

It is in the most intimate place of us that God plants new life when we choose him. And it is a choosing. God does not force himself on us. He invites, and we choose to respond (see Jn 6:66-69; Mt 16:24). Where we choose God is not visible to the outside world or even on an x-ray. The heart—"the desire-producer that makes us tick," "the affective center of our being"—is mentioned 1,006 times in the Bible, and it is never talking about the blood-pumping organ in our chests.[17] This invisible core of us is not hidden because it is shameful; it is hidden because it is sacred. It is there where God births new life in us (1 Pet 1:23; 1 Cor 3:6-7). We are told to guard this area of us (Prov 4:23). Do we share the results of new birth through Christ in us publicly? Yes, through our baptisms and testimonies. Do we often have birth coaches in the process? Yes, they are called disciple makers, mentors, or parents. But the implanting of the seed of Christ in our hearts is not initially public. It intimately happens in the quiet places of our invisible hearts.

Similarly, if sex is a representation of God's covenant love to us, it must take place in a private, secret, and honorable place (Ps 139:15). Do we share the results publicly? (Hello, birth announcements! Yes!) Do we have birth coaches? (I would have never survived without mine.) But the creation process is private. Honorable. Worshipful.[18] So, too, must we treat the parts of our bodies that produce new life (our vaginas and penises, plus breasts, which sustain freshly born babies in the first hours of their lives)—with honor and protection.

The significance of teaching body parts and keeping private parts covered is a bit over the heads of kids age zero to four, but I think it's important for parents to know why we do it. We do not just follow pediatric scripts—even if they're helpful—without understanding the bigger picture. I believe doing so helps us have a better lens to assess the experts' ideas, inviting us to choose whether we accept them (because they fit into the gospel narrative), adjust them, or look for others.

One more note on naming private parts with specific language: We don't use the words *penis* and *vagina* in every sentence we say to our kids about private parts. We also use *private parts*. We never use pet names (like predators can), but we use *private parts* because it's an easy way to address the parts of the body that are covered by swimsuits without naming every single biological part of their bodies every single time.

Ages four to six: Teach sex basics. With the increased development of language and awareness of the world around them, kids in the three- to five-year-old age range start to notice pregnancy and babies, and they ask questions about how babies got in a woman's womb. My go-to answer is, "God takes a part from a mom and a part from a dad, puts it in the mom's belly, and makes a baby." One of my sisters prefers the language of seeds. "God takes a seed from a dad and a seed from a mom, and God puts them together and makes a baby! Then God puts that baby inside of the mom's tummy."

My friends who are adoptive parents have said something quite beautiful:

God made the world so that a man and woman can come together and plant a seed to make a baby grow. This is kind of like how a plant can grow when you take a seed and plant it in the soil. The seeds come from inside a man and a woman, but babies don't grow in the soil, do they? No. Babies grow inside a tummy mommy (or birth mom), just like you did. One day seeds come up from the soil and turn into a plant, like when you came out as a baby from inside your tummy mommy. Every baby like you that comes from a tummy mommy is special, but not all tummy mommy and birth daddies can give a baby what they need to grow—even if they really love that baby. And babies need help to grow, just like plants need good soil, water, and sunlight to grow. So some babies are adopted into new families, just like how God chose you to be adopted into our family! And we are so glad God chose you to be adopted in our forever family! God even adopts people into his family when we choose to follow Jesus. His family is our true forever family![19]

When asked how babies come out, I will say at this age, "Girls have three holes in their privates: One for tinkle, one for poop, and one for babies coming out. Isn't that interesting?" Now, why do I say "interesting" instead of, "Your three private holes are the most amazing thing on the planet!" as some people do to try to get their kids excited about God's design? Because I have noticed my kids' expressions when I tell them about vaginas or sex or anything related. Their expressions do not always read, "Boy, that's amazing! I sure love how God designed babies to be created!" Usually their look says something like, "Cool. Weird. Mostly weird."

To ignore their feelings of "That's weird" and push to, "You have to love procreation because it's God's design!" will not help kids process the weirdness. We need to empathize while holding the truth that it is a good part of God's design. Empathy is one of the most significant emotional gifts parents can offer their children.

Psychiatrist Dan Seigel defines empathy as "feeling felt."[20] Author and psychologist Becky Kennedy expands on this definition:

> When a child receives empathy—in fact, when any of us receives empathy—it makes them feel like someone is on their team, almost as if that person is taking on some of their emotional burden. When someone greets us with empathy ("Ugh, that feels so hard!"), we have that experience that Daniel Siegel described as "feeling felt." Our bodies also sense that someone else is present in our emotional experience, which makes the experience more manageable—thereby building our ability to regulate the feelings.[21]

Empathizing while maintaining "I'm in control here of this conversation," seems like a winning way to talk about sex with our kids.

In this four-to-six range we should start forming family rules about bodies, and we should also start talking about relational boundaries. (More on that in the next chapters.)

Ages seven to ten: Teach sex specifics and puberty prep. I hear Mufasa's voice from *The Lion King* in my head saying, "It is time." With both of my girls, I waited until the second half of eight years old to talk about God's design for sex. I focused most of the conversation around preparing for puberty. When I think about what I needed before the challenging teenage years, it was not details about the male scrotum. It was, *Can someone give me the basics of sex so I understand?* And, even more important, *Will someone be available to walk me through this whole period thing?*

Let's be honest: It is a jarring experience to realize that you are going to be bleeding out of your private part every month for the next forty years. Sure, sex is somewhere out there in the future (maybe), but what I mostly wondered was, *Will a trusted woman care for my soul and body during what seems like a turbulent time?* So I told Gwyn, "No matter what, I will be there for you," and I watched her body visibly relax. Humans can handle almost anything if they know they have a safe, trusted parent and capital-G (for God) Guide leading them.

Here is how Matt and I talk more specifically about the mechanics of sex with our kids. First of all, we pray to know when the right time is to have the initial talk. I honestly wish we had prayed more about this subject earlier in our kids' lives. We kind of just stumbled into it. But when they were eight-ish years old we prayed, and then we picked a day—based on a Holy Spirit nudge, something they said, something on TV, or something that just felt right. Then the parent of the same gender took the child to a safe place where we'd had serious talks with our kids before. The location is not a big deal, as long as it is private, safe, and reflective of the honor with which we care for the tender parts of their hearts and bodies.[22]

Some people make a big statement by taking their kids to a special location for this talk, but I get a little uncomfortable with the idea. If a goal of parenting in this space is to develop trust with our kids so we can have 100 informal, one-minute conversations about sex and sexuality, to make a big deal of this conversation could add a layer of pressure instead of specialness. This is up to the parents' judgment, of course, but I would suggest treating this conversation like the one about body parts: How can we normalize this conversation while honoring the topic as sacred? For us, this means staying in our home and using rooms where we have other serious conversations (normalizing). However, we lock the door, silence our phones, and focus for as long as it takes (treating it as sacred).

I will say I do love the idea of coming-of-age rituals and celebrations (which is what I think parents are hoping for when they have this conversation in a special location). We plan to celebrate our kids' becoming young men and women around the age of thirteen with a special trip somewhere. The purpose of these trips will not be to overload them with information (as we hope to have had hundreds of mini-conversations for information sharing before then), but to celebrate and mark in time the transition from child to young woman or man.

Then, we talk. What do we say? How do we say it? Feel free to jump to appendix A to read through our approach, then I will meet you back here.

After we talked with our girls about sex, I must say I did not leave thinking, *I nailed that.* I felt insecure—like I might have said ten wrong things—but then I remembered, *This is not just one conversation. We can keep circling back.* I have circled back with each of my girls about every six months in a private conversation like the first one, and in smaller ways in our everyday life, like the conversation at the start of this chapter. When we circle back, I may address male puberty, planning for periods, specifics of what happens inside a mom's body during pregnancy, or whatever questions they have. I may also restate what happens during sex. I have been surprised at how much they forget from each conversation. This could be because it's stressful, because it's confusing, or simply because they are kids. It only emphasizes the need to have more than one conversation. Every time we have another talk, we add to their understanding, deepen our relationship with them, and form pathways for more conversations about sex and sexuality for hopefully the rest of their lives.

Ages eleven and twelve: Follow up, follow through, and create stability. During this stage, we aim to have more free-flowing (yet still private) conversations with our kids about puberty and sex and prepare them to make good choices about screens (see chapters eleven and twelve). We primarily focus on being "with" them for all of it as it happens and seek to follow through on our part of the relationship. Remember the formula for trust? "Doing what we say we will do" plus "walking in the way of Jesus" plus "over a long period of time" equals "trust earned." I said I would go to get deodorant with them. Did I follow through? I said I would help get their backpacks ready with pads. Did I? I said I would follow up on wet dreams. Did I? We need to follow through if we want to be a source of safety to talk about sex, marriage, gender, and all the things in the years to come.

Relationships between us and our kids and between our kids and others can pivot in this season. Louann Brizendine, a neuropsychiatrist and the author of *The Female Brain* and *The Male Brain*, notes how young men produce twenty to twenty-five times more testosterone than in pre-adolescence. "If testosterone were beer," she says, "a 9-year-old boy would be getting the equivalent of a cup a day. But a 15-year-old would be getting the equivalent of nearly two gallons a day."[23] Such a hormone flood can lead to risky choices (sometimes sexual in nature) for young men.[24] Girls do not have the exact same flood, but their estrogen increases dramatically in this season, often leading to irregular emotions.[25] Once-confident girls can become anxious, depressed, and insecure.[26] Navigating these emotions can be tricky, requiring that we learn to manage our own emotions while teaching them healthy coping.

God's design for sex is a beautiful thing when it is placed in the greater gospel narrative. Helping our kids understand its beauty in age-appropriate, small-but-important ways can build the relationship not only between us and them, but between them and God.

QUESTIONS TO CONSIDER

1. How was the sex talk for you as a young person? How old were you when you had it (if you had it at all)?

2. How have you handled (or would you handle) the question, "How does a baby get in there?" when your kids are age zero to four?

3. What did you think about the timing we suggested in this chapter for sharing more specific details about sex with your kids?

4. What is your next step in walking with your kids in talking with them about God's design for sex?

9. HONOR OUR BODIES

Lay the Foundation

> "The statistics about kids being sexually abused make me shiver with anxiety. I know I cannot bubble wrap them from the evils of this world, but what can I do to protect them from potential sexual harm? Also, what is normal when it comes to kids and touch/play, and what is something else?"

WHEN MATT AND I FOUND OUT we were pregnant with our first child, we were absolutely elated. We had been trying for a year, and I didn't know if biological kids would be a part of our story. But then God blessed us with Gwyneth. At twenty weeks in utero, our friends threw us a big gender reveal party. We let them find out the gender from our doctor, and they surprised us with a box of hidden pink balloons at the party: "It's a girl!"

I cried happily until creeping terror laced its fingers around my heart. It's vulnerable to be a girl in this world. It's terrifying to be the parent of a girl in this world. It's frightening to be the parent of a girl or a boy in this world.

Some of us know the statistics. As mentioned earlier, at least one in four girls and one in ten boys under the age of eighteen experience childhood sexual abuse, and 20 percent are abused before age eight.[1] In a survey by the Centers for Disease Control of over fifteen thousand women and twelve thousand men across the United States, one in four women and one in twenty-six men reported experiencing complete or attempted rape. Nearly half of female rape victims and over half of male rape victims report first being abused before age eighteen.[2]

I'm going to focus now on "unwanted sexual contact" (having sexual body parts groped, grabbed, fondled without penetration, or kissed in a sexual way), as those numbers are some of the largest and can be overlooked because they do not include penetration. However, as someone who was molested by a stranger when I was eleven, I can attest that "just" experiencing unwanted sexual contact has the potential to destroy a life. It nearly did that to me.

Let's shine some light on that darkness, shall we?

Nearly one in two women (48 percent) in the United States report experiencing unwanted sexual contact at some point in their life, along with nearly one in four men (23 percent).[3] Of women who experienced unwanted sexual contact, the top three perpetrators were an acquaintance (60 percent), a family member (23 percent), or a stranger (22 percent). For men who experience unwanted sexual contact, the top three perpetrators were an acquaintance (62 percent), a stranger (22 percent), and someone they met during a brief encounter—a blind date or taxi ride, for example (11 percent). Although statistically every other woman will experience unwanted sexual contact in her life, one in four will experience it before she is eighteen. Similarly, if one in four men experience unwanted sexual contact in their life, one in ten will experience it before he is eighteen.

Who is ready to weep on the floor?

This is why I shiver with anxiety and, frankly, did not want to write this chapter. If you or someone you love has experienced childhood sexual abuse, you also don't want to read this chapter. We know the cost of childhood sexual abuse on us or on our friends. "Evil delights in sexual abuse because the return on investment is maximized. It takes but seconds to abuse, but the consequences can ruin the glory of a person for a lifetime," writes sexual abuse expert Dan Allender.[4] He is right. Seconds of perpetration can transform into years of suffering. However, as someone who was abused and has come through the healing journey scarred but no longer bleeding, I can say that redemption is possible.

Then we have kids. We bring them into this stupid, broken, evil world, and the temptation to hide them in bubble wrap is a siren song we want to hear. Being on the front lines of the sexuality conversation, I have to fight not to run away and shelter my kids from the evil I see about every other week. But as parents we don't have the option to either (a) shrug and let our kids run wild and free, or (b) bubble wrap them. There is a middle road. Today we are going to try to find that middle road between bubble-wrapping our kids and letting them run free.

Why Should We Protect Our Kids' Bodies?

Why should we protect our kids' bodies? That seems like an unnecessary question. Duh. Because they're kids! We are the parents, and we should have an animal instinct within us to protect them from harm. Sure. But not all parents have that instinct. There are studies and stories that highlight a growing, insidious, predatory tendency for parents to turn against their kids for financial or lustful gain.[5]

Even without that sad reality, knowing the greater gospel "why" of God's design for protecting our kids motivates me to protect them like little else. Specifically, understanding the greater gospel vision for bodies helps us better protect our kids because:

- It can calm our anxious brain down. God is in control, he knows about our sin problem, he sent a Redeemer, and one day he will conquer evil. This gospel preaches this from start to finish.
- Specific how-to's are more effective if they are focused on promoting the beauty of the gospel instead of making rules around sin.
- Our kids will be more receptive if we explain why we relate to other kids' bodies in the ways we do rather than just saying, "Because I said so." We are parenting, not parroting.

So let's go back to the gospel train. God created us good. We—not just our spirits but our embodied selves—were created in God's image (Gen 1:27). When we look into each other's faces, we see a reflection of God. That fact alone should give us pause when thinking about how we interact with another person. We are interacting with an eternal creature who was made in the image of the Creator. God also gave us jobs to do in our embodied selves (Gen 1:28), and Jesus emphasized and expanded on that task in Matthew 28. In perfectly loving union with God and each other, we are to push back the darkness and usher in the light until everyone everywhere is living in joyful submission to King Jesus for our good and God's glory. Sin made that task impossible. Jesus made it possible. In the end, God will redeem all those who trust in Jesus.

Our whole lives are about King Jesus. Everything we do is to promote his glory on earth as it is in heaven. Abusing an image bearer of a holy God does not fall into that category. Dishonoring another does not fall into the wisdom of God's design for the world. Duh again, right? Jesus said specifically, "If anyone causes one of these little ones . . . to stumble, it would be better for them to have a large millstone hung around their neck and to be drowned in the depths of the sea" (Mt 18:6 NIV). We must be passionate about protecting kids from harm.

Reading 1 Corinthians 6 gets me excited about honoring my body and that of my kids. Here, Paul is in the midst of reprimanding the Corinthian church for not only tolerating sexual sin but celebrating it (see 1 Cor 5:1-2). Paul says, "You say, 'Food was made for the stomach, and the stomach for food.' . . . But you can't say that our bodies were made for sexual immorality" (1 Cor 6:13). I would think Paul would finish his argument with, "Our bodies were made for sexual *morality*." But that is not the case. He says, "They were made for the Lord, and the Lord cares about our bodies." Our bodies were not made for *not sinning*; they were made for the *Lord*. Our embodied selves were made to worship and enjoy God.

Furthermore, Paul says our bodies are temples of the Holy Spirit. "Run from sexual sin! No other sin so clearly affects the body as this one does. For sexual immorality is a sin against your own body. Don't you realize that your body is the temple of the Holy Spirit, who lives in you and was given to you by God?" (1 Cor 6:18-19). Our bodies aren't just a house for our souls. We *are* our bodies. In addition, if we know and trust Jesus as our Savior, we are temples of the Holy Spirit! Good grief, that makes me not want to make bad choices with my body. The Holy Spirit is inside of me.

Finally, Paul says, "You do not belong to yourself, for God bought you with a high price. So you must honor God with your body" (1 Cor 6:19-20). What is the "high price" with which we were bought? Jesus' life. My eyes are wide right now as I consider that. Jesus, the Son of God, laid down his life for us. "So you must honor God with your body," Paul concludes. Yes. I will.

Now I am excited and even more passionate to protect my kids' bodies from harm. They are *imago Dei* and made to take part in God's beautiful mission for the world. If our kids know and trust Jesus as their Savior, they have the Holy Spirit indwelling them. God lives inside our kids. And, Jesus gave his life to save them.

These reasons motivate me to protect my kids with greater strength and ferocity than anxiety ever could. When fear motivates me to protect my children, I get short bursts of energy, but then I want to take a nap or get angry to feel strong again. When I look at my kids' bodies through God's lens, I peacefully yet ferociously want to ensure every inch of them is honored to the glory of God.[6]

How Can We Help Our Kids Honor Each Other's Bodies?

By now, I hopefully don't need to convince anyone to protect kids' bodies. It's instinctive to most of us, and after a brief dip in the theological pool of 1 Corinthians 6, we get the need: They are *imago Dei* and therefore made with a purpose, Jesus died for them, and if they trust Jesus as their Savior, they are temples of the Holy Spirit. Even if they do not trust Jesus yet, they are still invaluable humans worthy of protection and honor.

But I don't want my kids to just *not be sinned against*. I want my kids to see bodies the way God sees them—while they're in our home, and after they leave. I want them to expect honor and offer it wherever God leads them.

So how does God see our bodies, and how does he want us to treat each other?

Jesus exhorted us with the greatest commands to "love the LORD your God with all your heart, all your soul, all your mind, and all your strength," and to "love your neighbor as yourself" (Mk 12:30-31). Remember how the Bible could be summed up in five words: God wants to marry us? As the church, we are collectively called "the bride" or "Christ's body" (Rev 21:9; 1 Cor 12:27). Together, we are one body. In Romans 12:4-5 Paul says, "Just as our bodies have many parts and each part has a special function, so it is with Christ's body. We are many parts of one body, and we all belong to each other" (Rom 12:4-5). This means each of us who are a part of God's church have a different part to play in the unified whole of the body. We need each other:

If the whole body were an eye, how would you hear? Or if your whole body were an ear, how would you smell anything?

But our bodies have many parts, and God has put each part just where he wants it. (1 Cor 12:17-18)

I love this. As I picture God intentionally making each of our kids, it makes me wonder what role they will play in advancing the kingdom of God. How will they individually push back the darkness and usher in the light for the good of the body and the glory of God?

Then Paul tells us in Romans 12:10, "Be devoted to one another in love. Honor one another above yourselves" (NIV). Another way we could say this verse is, "Be tender and affectionate to one another as if to a cherished family member, honoring and valuing the reputation of another over yourself."[7] I'm laughing to myself now because our kids do not always treat their literal family members as "cherished."

For example, our kids do not honor each other's bodies when one of them peeks in on a sibling using the toilet and laughs. The child in the bathroom immediately screeches and likely feels shame, and I yell from somewhere in the house, "Hey! Are you honoring your brother or sister in what you just did?"

The accused puts their head down and says, "No."

I walk up to them and look them kindly but seriously in the eye. I don't want to heap unnecessary toxic shame on them, but I do want them to feel godly conviction. So I say, "Please say sorry to them when they come out." They do.

If our kids are not respecting, esteeming, and valuing the reputation of their sibling, then they are not respecting another body part in the body of Christ, which hurts the whole. I recently gave this example to my kids to help them understand the need to honor each other. "Let's say in the body of Christ, you, Gwyn, are the hand, and Ellis is the stomach. When you hurt or dishonor him, it's like you're punching yourself in the stomach." They looked at me with wide eyes and then laughed, but the analogy is pretty perfect. Paul says of this body of Christ, "If one part suffers, all the parts suffer with it" (1 Cor 12:26). When we dishonor another, it's like we are punching ourselves.

How Can We Model Honoring Each Other's Bodies?

Jesus never taught what he did not live. So, too, with us. If we want to help our kids honor each other's bodies, it begins with our behavior. Are we honoring their bodies like we expect them to do for each other?

For me, this begins by making sure I am not subtly making fun of them when they have to do toilet-related functions. For us, this also means not playfully popping them on the backside. Maybe in some homes or cultures a booty-pop is only playful and innocent, but in our home culture, it can feel like walking the line of dishonoring body parts that have a sacredness to them. It's normal for parents to joke and wrestle with their kids, and by no means do I want to make this a legalistic standard. However, at minimum we are wise to at least consider whether laughing at our kids' toilet-related bodily functions or bopping them on the booty is "being tender and affectionate to one another as if to a cherished family member, honoring and valuing the reputation of another over yourself." If it doesn't seem like honoring behavior, we can choose instead to shut the bathroom door for them when they forget, and we can hug and wrestle with them instead of slapping them playfully on the butt.

Another way I practice honoring bodies is by treasuring our aging, imperfect bodies. Research has found that when moms made self-critical comments of their own appearance and diet, their daughters reported lower body esteem, lower body satisfaction, and more problematic attitudes about eating than girls whose mothers had not made self-critical comments.[8] Because I have known the research on modeling self-honoring language for a few years, when my kids look at my wrinkles and say I look old or mention how wobbly my calves are, I say, "Thanks. I like how I look. I like myself." Do I feel a bit sad inside and tell them to talk more kindly? I sure do. But I want them to hear me honoring myself even in the face of critique, because that's what I hope they do with their own bodies.

We can also model honoring bodies by teaching them to respect someone else's "no" when it comes to touch. I am by nature not a very touchy person (being sexually abused as a kid did not help this fact), but because I know kids need plenty of touch throughout the day to facilitate bonding, reduce stress, alleviate fear, and even protect against illness, I work hard to say "yes" to my kids' petitions for hugs and snuggles even when I don't want to.[9] Sometimes saying "yes" is effective parenting—but not always. We touch-exhausted parents can also teach the power of "no" by sometimes saying, "No, thank you" to their desires to snuggle. When my internal "touch tank" is nearing full, I have learned to say, "Hey, bud, you get one more minute of cuddle time." If I wait until my touch tank is overflowing, I might yell at them out of overstimulation. Preparing them before I reach that mode honors them, honors me, and hopefully models that they can do the same with their relationships now and in the future.

Additionally, we can model honoring bodies through how we use social media. I am concerned about what all our photo taking and posting for the world to see is doing to our kids' sense of value in their embodied self. How are we respecting, esteeming, and valuing the reputation of our kids as *imago Dei*, temples of the Holy Spirit, and parts of the body of Christ when we take their picture without their consent, throw a cute, sometimes sarcastic, or even poking-fun-at-them-behind-their-back caption on it, and post it for friends or strangers to see? If we were to rewind the tape on our own lives and imagine our parents doing that to us as children, it might make us squirm. We thought they were delighting to be with us by taking our picture, but it wasn't really for themselves. It was for the unknown audience we had no idea existed on this ethereal thing called "the internet." Strangers and friends with whom we have no relationship comment about us. Our parents say things about us, but we have no idea. What would that have done to our sense of "I matter"? Might we feel used? For likes? For comments? For laughs? For a life lesson we didn't consent to teach?

Probably most of us parents post and share pictures out of pure motives—to invite friends and family to see into our lives, perhaps even for the glory of God. However, before we choose to share, I think we need to consider four things:

1. Before posting, let's ask ourselves, "Why am I posting this? For what reason?" If it's for selfish reasons, let's skip it.

2. Let's ask our kids if they are okay with the photo and caption and tell them who will see it. If they don't approve, don't post it. That's what I'm doing with the family stories in this book as well as any photos I post of my kids.

3. Let's think about how much time our kids have not being "on." Psychologist Julia Sadusky says, "I want children to expect moments when they don't need to perform for others and when they know that their bodies won't be on public display."[10] Do our kids have enough "off" times?

4. Let's consider the concerning implications around artificial intelligence (AI).

At this current moment, AI is freely data mining pictures of kids to develop its database. Anything you or I have publicly posted of our kids' faces is up for grabs. Zach Edwards, a senior threat analyst at Silent Push and an adviser at the nonprofit Internet Safety Labs, explains that all social platforms are ingesting public content. "Facebook, Twitter, any of the social networks, if you make a piece of content public, terms of service basically allow them to parse it for their own means," Edwards says.[11] Even more concerning is the new prevalence of AI-generated pornography. With one good picture of someone's face, AI can generate a 60-second porn film within thirty seconds.[12]

This is not just happening to famous people. It is happening to regular girls in regular high schools. Francesca Mani, a fourteen-year-old high school sophomore, was called to the office one day where she learned that a classmate had used a "nudify" program to take a clothed picture of her and turn it into a fake naked image. She was not the only one, according to a piece in *The New York Times*: "Fighting tears, feeling violated and humiliated, Francesca stumbled back to class. In the hallway, she said, she passed another group of girls crying for the same reason—and a cluster of boys mocking them."[13] God will lead us to what we need to do about social media, but I cannot talk about protecting our kids' bodies without giving us the facts to consider.

What Can We Do with Our Fear?

Parenting in this world is scary, and we need somewhere to take our anxious, angry, and helpless emotions. We can know God's design for us to honor bodies and we can practice what we preach, but without dealing with internal grief and anger about this world, I think we are going to struggle to teach our kids without raging or running.

There is a practice that has helped me live in this wild world without such emotional dysregulation. It has kept my heart soft and my armor strong. I didn't invent it. God did. It's called lament, and I sometimes define it as "venting to Someone who can actually do something about our pain." My former mental health therapist, Carolyn, taught me about lament when I was intensely wrestling with sexuality and faith after college.[14] Before she shared the concept with me, I did not know I could take all of my suffering, fears, and anger to God. I did not know he would not be disgusted and run, that he was "close to the brokenhearted" (Ps 34:18). Lament showed me I could—and should—bring all of my suffering to him.

We have an entire book of the Bible called Lamentations. The first four chapters are an acrostic that walks the reader through the Hebrew alphabet. In this I believe God is saying to us, "You need to grieve the brokenness in life from A to Z." Smack dab in the middle of this A-to-Z grief, however, the writer of Lamentations says, "Great is his faithfulness; / his mercies begin afresh each morning" (Lam 3:23). The hope in the midst of lament reminds me of author Ann Voskamp and her definition of lament: "Lament is not meaningless rage, but a rage that finds meaning in His outrageous love. Lament is an outrage . . . that still trusts in God's good outcome."[15] We grieve, but not as those without hope.

David, the tenderhearted warrior-king, a man after God's own heart (Acts 13:22), wrote many laments. One-third of the Psalms are psalms of lament and imprecation (or calling down God's justice on our enemies).[16] My favorite story about Jesus lamenting happens at the tomb of Lazarus. Jesus' friend had died, and he was greatly affected by the moment:

> When Jesus saw [Mary] weeping and saw the other people wailing with her, a deep anger welled up within him, and he was deeply troubled. "Where have you put him?" he asked them.
>
> They told him, "Lord, come and see." Then Jesus wept. (John 11:33-35)

With this translation, we can hear Jesus' grief, but it doesn't go far enough. "Every translation ancient and modern is afraid of what the text says," Tim Keller says. That "deep anger" is better translated "to quake with rage," and "deeply moved" should be "to roar or snort with anger like a lion or a bull." Keller fixes it for us: "The best translation would be, 'Bellowing with anger, he came to the tomb.'"[17] Why did Jesus do that? Why, if he had all power and all wisdom, and he knew he was going to raise his friend Lazarus from the dead, would Jesus get so angry? I believe it is because he was not just facing Lazarus's death; he was looking at death itself and saying, "This is not the way it was supposed to be!" And then he wept.

We also need to look at the world—at its abuse, its same-sex sexual relationships, its gender struggles, its porn addiction, and its AI evil—and we need to bellow alongside Jesus, "This is not the way it's supposed to be!" Instead of shouting it on the internet, shoving it in the faces of our LGBTQ-identifying family members, or bitterly arguing with our siblings who live with their opposite-sex partners before marriage, we need to yell it to God. Jesus' anger is perfectly righteous. I doubt if our first-response emotions ever are. Before we say anything, we need to sift our unfiltered emotions between the fingers of God's sovereign, holy, ever-present-help-in-trouble hands.

When I bring my laments to God, I often write down how the people I am angry at have sinned against me. I name each sin and picture Jesus dying for each one. Then I confess how I have sinned against them. Even if they did 99 percent of the issue and I did 1 percent (bitterness, gossip), Jesus had to equally die for that, too. I name my sin and picture giving it to Jesus, who died for my sin just as much as he died for theirs.

This process humbles me. I am humbled further when I ask God for love for my enemies. God not only invites us to grieve to him; he commands us to forgive and love our enemies. When I am struggling to love someone, I ask God for a picture of how he sees them. Usually I can picture their fear, their childhood, or their grief. It fills me with God's compassion. Only after I go through grief, forgiveness, and love can I move toward action. That action may be creating a strong boundary, pursuing a conversation, writing something online, or even writing a book! No matter what, the words will flow from a heart motivated by love—even if anger is still a part of it. That is righteous anger coming from a heart that has grieved, forgiven, and is full of the love of God. That is a heart that is heard.

That sounds hard. It is. It also is the primary reason I have been able to stay in the sexuality conversation with a soft heart and thick skin for over ten years. It is also how I can stay in the challenging middle road of teaching my kids bite-sized truth about God's design for the world without giving in to the world's theology or hiding us all in a cabin in the woods. It is also how I can live in this world with its abuse and not want to raze it to the ground.

Before I close, a word to those of you who have been sexually abused. I am looking over at you through the terrain of my own scarred-but-healing heart. I cannot overstate the importance of doing your own soul work before, during, and even after you walk through the intense parenting years, especially as you relate to your kids' sexuality. If you do not work through "that one thing that maybe was a thing, but I'm not sure it affected me," I promise you, it will affect your parenting. It already is. Start by asking people who love you if they think you could use some help, whether through therapy, a support group, or something else. For the sake of your kids, do something.

And last, a word to parents whose kids have been abused: just remember this—God plants seeds in garbage. I say this often to my kids when they wonder why there is suffering in the world: "I don't know exactly why this happened, but I do know that God plants seeds in garbage. He will rid the world of all evil one day, and he can make good things happen in the midst of terrible." If Jesus were applying for a job, the top of his application would read "Redeemer." He is the only one who can take horrific things done to us or to our kids and transform beauty from ashes, hope for despair, mourning into joyful songs of praise (Is 61:3). There will always be scars, but there will not always be despair.

QUESTIONS TO CONSIDER

1. How does understanding honoring bodies affect your desire to protect your kids?

2. How are you modeling what it means to honor God with your own body?

3. How do you post about your kids online? Do you feel like your posting is honoring to them? What might you want to change?

4. What do you feel drawn to lament regarding how our world does not honor each other's bodies?

10. HONOR OUR BODIES

Walk the Foundation

> **Key teaching:** "Let's honor each other's bodies."

STRAPPING OUR OLDEST INTO THE CAR SEAT for the first time after giving birth to her the day before was a shocking experience. "Wait, what? You're letting us take this tiny human home?" I wanted to ask the hospital staff.

Within hours, we had shifted from a top priority of "Get this baby out of the womb" to "Do everything we can to keep this baby safe." Matt drove with his hands on the wheel strictly on 10 a.m. and 2 p.m., and I sat next to the baby, triple checking her seatbelts and ensuring she was breathing every ten seconds. In that moment, we were most concerned about car seats, but give us a few weeks when we thought about hiring a babysitter or going to church, and we would add sexual abuse to our growing list of fears. We could drive carefully to try to prevent crashes, but what could we do to try to prevent childhood sexual abuse?

It's time to get practical.

How can we protect our kids? Gut-wrenchingly, there is no guaranteed way to shield them. Satan is all about stealing, killing, and destroying, and what a way to pummel a life by hurting them deeply while they are young. Truly, victims of childhood sexual abuse can struggle lifelong with interpersonal relationships, major mental health issues, and physical health issues, and they can have a distorted view of God.[1] But even as we recognize this reality, let's also grip hope that God plants seeds in garbage. With that in mind, let's practically lean in to try to protect our kids from sexual harm.

Protecting and Honoring Littlest Bodies (Ages Zero to Four)

It often begins with diapers, doesn't it? So many diapers. Let's start with how we can protect our kids when they are tiny.

Naming body parts. In the youngest ages, the best way to begin to protect and show honor to our kids' bodies is to name their body parts—all of them—while we change those diapers. Noses, eyebrows, elbows, and private parts—with specific names of penis, vagina, and breasts.

Why does knowing body parts help prevent abuse? We've discussed some of this already, but let's take another look:

1. It signals to the child that it is a shame-free body part that can be talked about.[2]

2. A child's accurate knowledge of private parts signals to a potential groomer that the child would be bad prey because kids who have been taught these names clearly have one or more adults who are attentively involved in their lives and teaching them about what these parts are and what they're for.[3]

3. It is common for groomers to use nicknames for private parts. If a child suddenly starts using nicknames for private parts when they have been taught otherwise, that will signal to caregivers that something is off.[4]

4. If a child knows accurate names, they can tell professionals with specificity what happened to them, and it can help prosecutors get offenders behind bars.[5]

Psychologist Julia Sadusky says of the reality that child abuse decreases with naming body parts, "When I learned that [it is the top preventer of abuse,] it blew my mind. It made me think, 'If we could get all Christians on the same page that we are going to do this, sexual abuse in childhood in our generation could go down markedly.'"[6] Let it be so, Lord.

Vetting church nurseries, babysitters, and childcare. As our kids get a little older, we may find we want to go to church. Or to work. Or on a date, for crying out loud. We want to leave our precious little ones with caregivers, but we know the statistics. Just a cursory Google search spits out that the Southern Baptist Convention maintains a list of seven hundred names of church leaders and volunteers who have allegedly abused victims (many of whom were children); and in the Catholic church in the United States, over one thousand children were abused by three hundred priests (with cases peaking between 1960 and 1985).[7]

As mentioned in the last chapter, one in four women and one in ten men experience unwanted sexual experiences as children, and the top perpetrators for both boys and girls are acquaintances—or someone they know a little bit.[8] We want to be able to send our kids to nursery at church, we want to find a good daycare, and we want to be able to trust a recommended babysitter, but the statistics are spooky. How can we know? We can't, but there are some good questions we can ask.

Let's start with church. Even though it's awkward, one of the first questions Matt and I ask if we're visiting a church is, "What is your background check policy?" If they don't do checks, we don't put our kids in that nursery, and we will not attend that church. (We think every church should do this as a bare minimum.) Next, we have learned to ask, "What is your process like for bringing volunteers in to serve?" Ideally, I want to hear about an interview process that not only looks for responsible, loving Christians but that also vets for things like ongoing, unrepentant sexual sin. Examples would be porn addiction, couples living together, and promiscuity of all types. Why do I say that? Because people who are glorifying sexual sin are not walking in the way of Jesus. Therefore I do not trust them.

Additionally, Satan may easily draw them into ever-darker sin if they are already saying "that dark is light and light is dark" (Is 5:20). I do not believe Satan has "sin categories" into which he kindly assigns people. He wants to steal, kill, and destroy however he can (Jn 10:10). Why not destroy a few kids, a church, and the offender in the process? I could see this happening, for example, if someone was not actively fighting a pornography addiction but instead diving into it, needing to watch more and more to chase the dopamine hit.[9] If nearly 50 percent of people who watch pornography end up watching things they were previously disgusted by,[10] that could lead them toward the increasingly popular teen-themed porn.[11] This is a scary reality. At least one study found that 85 percent of subjects who watched child sexual abuse materials (formerly known as "child porn") acted on it with real humans—mostly with children.[12] Such potential for progression of sin is why Matt and I say that if someone is not actively fighting their ongoing sexual sin, we can love you, but you may not change our child's diaper.

The next question we ask is about sexual abuse training related to changing diapers and bathroom time. How often and when are our kids alone with adults? Why? How do they engage things like changing diapers or bathroom time? Ideally, we want to hear that there is a two-person, non-relative (not moms and daughters or husband and wife) policy for changing diapers and going with kids to the bathroom at all times. Such policies can protect the volunteer in case a child says something happened that did not, and it protects the child from one-on-one, potentially hidden harm that could occur if there is only one helper. I do recognize that in small- to medium-sized churches this sort of situation is not always possible, but I want to hear intentional care behind the policy regardless.

Although Matt and I have not had to put our kids into daycare or a similar childcare situation, we have utilized gym childcare facilities, and we appreciate guidelines like the following for either daycare or gym childcare:[13]

- Ask about a child protection policy. What is their plan to keep your kids safe? If there is no plan, do not use that facility.
- Ensure the policy includes limited one-on-one interactions with your child.
- Ask about how volunteers are screened. Good hiring practices include detailed applications, personal and professional references, a criminal background check, and a thorough interview. Do they regularly run background checks on their staff and volunteers?
- Because older kids can be perpetrators against younger children, ask about how ages are separated, ensure there are different areas for different ages, and make sure adults are always present for all ages.
- Ensure there are clear procedures for reporting suspicions or incidents of abuse. Nonprofits focused on helping to prevent childhood sexual abuse recommend pushing to provide mandatory reporting and child sexual abuse training.

For babysitters, we try to hire trusted family members or ones recommended by others. I know this isn't always possible. In those cases, we can run our own background checks, ask for and call references, and even have dinner with a potential sitter several times before hiring them. We can watch how they interact with our kids in the room, ask about their own bathroom policy, and ask how they change diapers. (I would listen for a respectful, careful, honor-filled approach—not mocking, flippant, or even judging my questions.) Finally, I do not hire people who do not know Jesus to watch my kids in my home. Maybe that is extreme, but I can love people who do not know Jesus, I can care for and about them, I can even have them teach my kids at their public school. But when my kids are going to bed, they need the comfort of prayer, a song, and someone to tell them truth about God before going to sleep.

As my kids get older, in the three-to-eight range, and new baby-sitters rotate in and out, we ask how our kids feel about the new babysitter the next day. We ask, "Did you feel comfortable with them?" and "Did they respect our family rules?" I do not want to plant ideas in their head, but I hope asking such questions will invite disclosure if something does happen. If it sounds like the bathroom or diaper-changing situation was fine but my kids didn't like them for some inexplicable reason (beyond the fact that they prefer me and Matt over a babysitter), I don't invite the sitter back. I also don't hire them again if the vibes are off for me. I have learned to trust my own gut and my kids' instincts. Even if we are wrong in our assessment, I would rather be safe than sorry.

I will also add that in the two-to-three age range, I have a sense of urgency to get our kids potty-trained. This is for obvious reasons (goodbye, diapers!), but also because it helps relieve my anxiety with babysitters and at church. If my kids are trained, I can say to any caregiver, "They know how to go to the bathroom. They don't need help." I can breathe more easily knowing my kid will shut and lock the door on their own.

Not forcing hugs. When our oldest, Gwyn, was three years old, we started to ask, "Do you want a hug or a kiss?" and allowed her to choose if she did or did not. We had learned through books like *God Made All of Me* by Justin and Lindsey Holcomb that it was wise not to force hugs with us, grandparents, friends, or anyone else.[14] At first this seemed shocking. *Kids can say "no"?* But as I looked at our daughter, I reconsidered. If Gwyn learned that her "No touch, please," would be honored in our home when she was young, she would expect friends and significant others to honor her "No touch, please," when she was a teenager and beyond. If it was not honored, she would speak up.

Steph Lee, a spokesperson for the American Academy of Pediatrics, agrees, saying, "Learning how to say 'no' helps empower children to speak up when there is unwanted physical touch in any situation."[15] Teaching "no" to touch can help prevent sexual assault in childhood and adulthood. Additionally, giving our kids the ability to say "no" to touch helps them see themselves as valuable, because even their tiny voices are adhered to and honored. Finally (and I love this one), allowing our kids the option to say "yes" or "no" to touch—even to parents—encourages them to be more attuned to their bodies, because they have to think, *Do I want this touch or not?* In an age where much of our life is disembodied due to screens, this is a tremendous gift we can give our kids.

Practically, this can get awkward and robotic if we ask to hug our kids every time we want to. Here's how it works in real life with us: We reach for and hug our kids often. We kiss them on the head and cheek a lot. However, if they pull back or seem distracted, I ask, "Do you want a hug? Can I hug you?" If they say "no," I don't pressure them. If I did, how would that prime their decision-making ability for the future? *I can be pressured into doing things with my body I don't want to.* That is not the lesson I want my kids to learn.

Also, if our kids deny our request for a hug, it's okay for us to be sad, but we should not be devastated. Such a response teaches codependency, or a feeling of "I have to manage your emotions, parent, in order for me to be okay."[16] Codependent parenting is a one-way ticket to extra therapy for kids when they grow up.

Truly, kids of codependent parents can struggle with many things, including decision-making and relationship-forming in the future.[17] Another way to describe codependence is "relational idolatry"—or putting someone above God (Mt 22:37; 1 Jn 5:21). This idolatry always leads to suffering, because we were meant to worship God, not people. Kids can be a blessing to parents, but they do not complete us. God does.

A final note on awkwardness: When guests or family members come over, we don't stop everything if they reach for a hug and our kids reach back. We don't shout, "Stop! Do you want to hug?" However, if our kids are hesitant for whatever reason, we do jump in and ask, "Do you want to hug, high-five, or wave?" This makes the moment less awkward for the adult and gives our kids the agency to choose.

The doctor. Even at the young age of zero to four, I want my kids to know what healthy and unhealthy touch is. So as soon as they begin to understand language, I tell them what is going to happen before we go to the doctor. "The doctor is going to check your head, your ears, your tummy, and your private parts—your vagina or your penis. But remember our family rule? Only trusted people who mom and dad say are trustworthy are allowed to see or check your private parts. I say the doctor is allowed to check your private parts because he is helping us keep you clean and safe and strong." I also add, "And I will not leave. I will be there the whole time." Bonus points for finding a doctor who will also say this to our kids before checking their private parts. We have a Christian doctor who uses similar lines every time, and it blesses my mama heart while honoring my kids' bodies to the glory of God.

Protecting and Honoring Little Bodies (Ages Four to Six)

As our kids get older, they need more structure around relating to friends. This is where family rules can be very helpful.

Family rules. The idea is to develop a literal list of rules about body safety that our family knows and repeats regularly. For example, the authors of the book *30 Days of Sex Talks* share rules such as, "Nobody should be hurting you," and "Nobody should take photos of your private parts." This is wise, Jesus-following advice, even though the book is not "Christian."[18] Other ideas for rules from Christian resources include, "We do not keep secrets," and "We do not go in where someone is changing or showering."[19] The one on secrets is important, as predators can try to coerce kids into keeping their behavior a secret between them. Parents can say things like, "We have surprises but not secrets in our home. A surprise is a good thing like a birthday present. Secrets are bad things that make us feel sad or hurt."

Although we have been developing family rules since our kids were young, after reading the experts, I have tried to intentionally use language like, "This is a Krieg family rule." That way, if our kids run into others who do not follow our rules, they can "blame" it on their parents and save face. "Sorry, I have to keep the door open when we play because it's our family rule." I'm happy to have my kids be annoyed at Matt's and my rules if it means keeping them safe inside and outside our home. Whatever parents choose to do, being intentional and repeating the rules and why we believe them is a wise approach.

Here are our family rules to keep bodies safe. As always, you are welcome to adapt them to fit your family's priorities:

- Private parts are to be kept clean and safe.
- We do not show, ask to see, or touch someone else's private parts.
- If someone tries to touch us or see our private parts, we tell Mom or Dad or someone on our approved list (teachers, babysitters) right away.

- Only people Mom and Dad say are allowed to see our private parts can see them (for example, doctors or babysitters).

- We do not have to hug or kiss or be hugged or kissed by anyone if we do not want to. We get to choose.

- We honor everyone's bodies the way we want to be honored.

- We do not laugh at or slap each other's private parts because it is not honoring to them.

- We shut the bathroom door when we are going to the bathroom and shut the door when we are changing our clothes—not because the body is bad but because it deserves dignity and respect.

- We keep doors open when we are playing with friends in bedrooms or playrooms.

- Love can look like "no." (I will explain this at the end of the chapter.)

What if our kids touch their own private parts regularly? Kids can touch their own private parts for many reasons. They have a scratch, they need to clean themselves, they're bored, or they notice that when they play with their clitoris or penis it feels good. Even babies have been seen to touch their private parts for pleasure, or what we call "masturbate," in utero.[20] This action is not related to lust at this age but simply something they notice about their bodies that feels good.

As kids grow older, some continue to touch their private parts for pleasure. The authors of one literature review report that about 25 percent of boys and 15 percent of girls ages two to five regularly touch themselves or masturbate in public, and 60 percent of boys and 43 percent of girls do so in private. By the time they are ten to twelve years old, however, those numbers have dropped to 1 percent of boys and 2 percent of girls regularly touching themselves in public, and 8 percent of boys and 11 percent of girls doing so in private.[21]

Some kids engage in this behavior in excessive ways. A cross-sectional study of six hundred children found that almost 11 percent of those children engaged in "pathological" or excessive masturbation (defined as masturbating "most of the time" each day). The most common emotional states associated with the desire to touch themselves were boredom (23 percent) and agitation (12 percent). It was interesting to me that in over 75 percent of cases, pathological masturbation co-occurred with psychiatric disorders such as anxiety or ADHD.[22] Kids are looking for something to do with their hands, and this feels good to them.

However, excessively touching of oneself for pleasure can be a sign of distress in our children. If they are masturbating excessively (or "most of the time"), that could indicate that something has happened to them—such as abuse. A parent would also likely see sexualized behavior alongside this self-stimulation. The American Psychological Association says caregivers may see "sexualized play with dolls, putting objects into anuses or vaginas, seductive behavior, requesting sexual stimulation from adults or other children, and age-inappropriate sexual knowledge."[23] Kids can also engage in self-pleasure because of a lack of parental physical affection.[24]

So if self-stimulation for pleasure is relatively normal and kids tend to grow out of it, should we parents talk to them about it? If our kids are ages zero to two, I likely would not. They are just figuring out their bodies. I would say, "You have a good body!" and redirect their hands if they are leaning toward excessive touch. If they are ages three to twelve and I notice this behavior happening in public, I would say something. With kids these ages, we must address an issue like this with tenderness and curiosity instead of fear or panic. For example, I might ask, "Are you okay? Are you feeling itchy? It seems like you are touching your [penis or vagina] a lot." I would ask this quietly and draw attention to it subtly so as not to shame them and because they might not even notice what they are doing. They might be struggling with a piece of clothing, have an infection, or need to use the bathroom. If they aren't struggling with any of those things, I would likely remind them, "Hey, we only touch our privates to keep them clean and safe." Because I know the research, I might also ask "Are you feeling bored? Frustrated?" Even if they say "no," I would try to distract them to another of their hands to calm their boredom or frustration. Therapists can be good resources to help agitated and bored kids find healthier outlets for their energy.

If I noticed excessive self-touch at home, I would first acknowledge that it's normal and feels good. "Hey, buddy, I notice that you sometimes touch your [penis or vagina]. What does that feel like to you? That can feel good, can't it?" Because I also want to be the first resource for my kids about their bodies, I would perhaps take another opportunity to say something about their private parts. "Your body is good, and that includes your private parts. But we are supposed to keep our bodies clean and safe. When you touch your [penis or vagina], it has germs on it from tinkling and pooping, and that gets on your hand, and that doesn't keep you clean, does it?"

Depending on whether we have talked about sex yet or not, I might add, "Hey, did you know that you have a part of you— [your clitoris or nerves on your penis]—that feels good when you touch it? But that's supposed to feel good in marriage (if God calls you to it). Not now."[25] Words like *clitoris* or *nerves on your penis* may seem intense for a child to hear. But unless our kids have experienced abuse, those words are not sexualized. They are biological. We are giving our kids knowledge and signaling to them that we are the experts on this; we are not afraid of their bodies and can help them steward their sexuality for their good and God's glory. We are also helping set a framework for conversations about self-stimulation as they enter teen years, when lust may begin to play a role in masturbation.

Finally, after addressing what our sexual body parts are for, we can help our kids brainstorm where to take their boredom or anxiety. "What is another way we could relax or rest ourselves that feels good?" In questions like these, we are helping our kids to name the emotion underneath the action and to find healthier outlets for their habit.

What if we catch them playing a game that includes private parts? It's normal for kids to be curious about each other's bodies and play games like "doctor" with each other. How should we respond? The first thing is to try not to overreact. If our personal stories include abuse or a loved one being abused, this is likely going to take some work. But it may help us to realize this is normal. It is likely not an abusive situation but a curious and silly one. Private parts are silly. Kids are curious. And games reenacting doctor visits are common. So we should stay curious and calm and ask questions before assuming abuse has occurred.

If the play happened with another family, we need to pull our child(ren) aside into another room to remove any extra shame and ask, "Hey, guys, what were you playing?" Then listen to what happened, taking note of normal, somewhat abnormal, and very abnormal behavior (listed below). "Private parts are kind of silly, aren't they? And it's normal to be curious about them. But do you remember our family rules? We don't show, ask to see, touch someone else, or let someone else touch our private parts. Those parts are private, which means we don't show others. What is another game we could play instead?" We need to be gentle, inviting our kids to remember that we are safe people with whom they can talk about these sensitive topics—even in moments like these that catch many of us off guard.

Now, what if in their retelling of what happened, we hear things that sound a bit intense? How can we know what is normal and abnormal behavior? The American Academy of Pediatrics says that normal, common behaviors include occasionally touching genitalia in public or private, viewing or touching a peer's or new sibling's private parts, showing genitals to peers, standing too close to people, and trying to see adults naked.[26] When children do these things, signs of normalcy and health are that they can be distracted to another activity and the behavior is not excessive (doing it most of each day).

Less common, more abnormal behaviors include rubbing body parts on others, inserting tongues in mouths while kissing, trying to touch adult private parts, and crudely mimicking sexual acts. A sign of concern would be that the child is not easily distracted from these behaviors and that they seem persistent and consistent.

Finally, very uncommon and very abnormal behaviors that are cause for even greater concern are asking peers to engage in specific, coercive sexual acts, inserting objects into genitals, imitating intercourse, touching animal genitals, coercive sexual experimentation, and engaging in sexual behaviors with others that are distressing to them.[27] It would also be very disconcerting for a child who is roughly four years older than another child (in years, maturity, mental capacity, or strength) to pressure a younger child to engage in sexual acts.[28] These "very uncommon" behaviors become very concerning if a child continually returns to them even when told not to. What can a parent do in situations where disconcerting behavior may have occurred? See appendix B for guidelines.

Protecting and Honoring Older Kids (Ages Seven to Twelve)

Now let's explore how we can help protect our older children from abuse and teach them to honor their own and others' bodies.

What about sleepovers? As our kids get older, the sleepover question is bound to come up. Do we do let them go to sleepovers? Do we host sleepovers? Do we make a rule that we just "don't do sleepovers"? There is no consensus from the experts, and this is where I sigh. If I'm being honest, Matt and I still go back and forth on the best practice for our home when it comes to sleepovers. Our reasoning is based on anecdotal evidence because of stories we hear from clients, but it's also statistical because of the number of people who experience sexual harm. And it is also personal. Neither of us was sexually abused during a sleepover, but my own preteen sleepovers were often exhausting, gossipy, and mean.

Our kids are currently five, eight, and ten, and we have had sleepovers with cousins, left our kids overnight with babysitters, and hosted some school friends at our house for a sleepover. We have yet to let them sleep over at a friend's house. If we did, I would want to know the parents well. I would want to spend some time in their home, seeing how they live and if it aligns with our beliefs. If it's hard to determine, I would likely call the parents and ask some questions recommended by Kelly Newcom:[29]

- Will you be home the entire time?
- Who else will be home? Friends, siblings, relatives, neighbors?
- What types of media do you allow? What is internet access like?
- Where and how will they be sleeping?
- Are there any alcohol, cigarettes, drugs, or pornography they could have access to?

But remember, parents can lie. Kids can lie. And at the end of the day, it's a risk. This is why we have allowed sleepovers at others' houses only when we have very high trust with our family members, and we have allowed people to sleep over in our home only when we have medium to high trust in them.

Trust jar. How can we measure trust? In our home we use a metaphorical container called a "trust jar." We talk about the trust jar a lot in our house, having adapted the concept from author Brené Brown. When Brown was helping her third-grade daughter understand the intangible concept of trust, she explained to her, "Trust is like a marble jar. For every moment of trust earned, one marble goes into the jar. You only share your important stories with friends who have filled up their marble jars."[30] I liked this idea so much that I quickly taught it to my kids to help them discern safe from unsafe people, or trustworthy from untrustworthy.

"When people behave in ways we expect (they are reliable—they do what they say they will do), when they walk in the way of Jesus (they live out God's definition of love (1 Cor. 13) and live into the fruit of the spirit (Gal. 5:22-23)), and when they do both for a long time, they earn a marble in the jar of your relationship," I explained to my kids. They nodded. "When they don't behave in ways we expect and they do not walk in the way of Jesus (like they lie or act unkindly or disrespectfully), they lose a marble—maybe several marbles." They seemed to get it.

To expand on this metaphor, I brought up someone they trust a lot: Cassie, their single pal who's more like a big sister than a babysitter and former housemate. She is someone we trust with our kids overnight. "How many marbles do you think Cassie has in her jar?"

"Like, all of them!" they said.

I nodded. "Yeah! We trust her a lot. But when I first met her, even though she was doing what she said she would do, and was walking in the way of Jesus, I had not known her for a long time. So she only had a few marbles."

They were aghast. "What? Really?"

"Yes, it takes time to trust people," I explained. "But now we have known her for a long time, and she keeps walking with Jesus (imperfectly, of course), and she still is reliable. So she has a full trust jar."

This is how we approach things like sleepovers and play dates; we evaluate our level of trust with our kids' friends and families. Even if their friends are not Christians (many of them are not), we still want them to "walk in the way of Jesus." There is a level of common grace offered to nonbelievers, and Romans 2:15 says Gentiles can follow God's law as it is "written on their hearts." The hope is that we parents can help lead their friends' parents to Christ one day, but in the meantime, as we do life with nonbelievers and take responsibility for our kids' safety, we look for trustworthy, Christlike characteristics before saying "yes" to playdates or sleepovers.

The best way to discern trustworthiness and keep a close eye on our kids' body safety is to try to become the hangout house. As I am writing this in our downstairs office, Matt just texted me a picture of what is a very common scene in our home: Our two girls are doing crafts at the paint-splattered kitchen table, there are three extra neighborhood and school friends with them, and there are snacks everywhere. We are a primary hangout house for our kids' friends, and I could not love it more. (Our snack budget may always be aching, but who cares.) We want our kids and their friends to feel safe here and consider it a privilege to facilitate that safety. The more our kids and their friends can feel at home in our homes, the more they form foundational friendship habits of what can become healthy, God-honoring, body-honoring play.

Signs of unhealthy friendships. As our kids get older, parents should focus more on helping them cultivate healthy friendships, because protecting our kids' body boundaries does not begin and end with bodies. The nature of relationships is just that—they are relational. I have been in relationships (sexual ones) that did not begin with a raw animal attraction to the other person. They began with crossing relational and emotional boundaries first. I was not a child when these relationships developed, but I want our children to be prepared for a future where they could end up in places they might not have intended because of a lack of emotional boundaries. For that reason, we teach our kids not only body safety but relational safety.

"What are signs of a friendship turning unhealthy?" I have asked my girls this question at least once every few months since they turned eight and ten. They can rattle off the list to me easily at this point:

- You put the individual above God (or they put you before God).
- You filter your thoughts through theirs ("What would they say about . . . ?").
- You can't say "no" easily.
- Your friendship is not often inclusive of others.

I could title this list "Codependent Friendships." Codependency (or relational idolatry, as we called it earlier) has the ability to break through our relational "no's" and then our physical "no's" like few things can. If I had a dollar for every person who has come to me and said, "This person was just a friend, but we quickly became codependent [putting the other before God], obsessive [because that's the nature of relational idolatry], and exclusive [you're not able to say "no" without backlash and other friends are not welcomed]. Then we ended up sleeping together!" I would have several hundred dollars. We need to help our kids understand their "no" matters not only physically but relationally and emotionally. We need to help them discern signs of emotional and relational boundary pushing and health.

This starts with us as parents. Do we let our kids say "no" to our emotional or relational pursuit? Sometimes my anxiety prompts me to ask questions I don't necessarily need the answers to. "You had a bad dream? Do you want to tell me about it?" I ask. Sometimes they don't. Can I respect that no? "Oh, you had a hard day. Do you want to share more?" Sometimes they don't. Can I listen to their "no"? God can give us parents wisdom on when to push further, but it is wise for us to remember that we need to respect our kids' physical *and* emotional "no's."

Love can look like "no." In that same vein, we regularly tell our kids, "Love can look like 'no.'" I began teaching this when I realized that the biblical truths "Love your neighbor" and "Love your enemy" can be confusing to kids, because it can seem like we are to hug every bully who just punched us (Mk 12:31; Mt 5:38, 44). So when our kids mention a friend who has consistently hurt them, I say, "It seems like they have dumped a lot of marbles out of the trust jar." They nod in agreement. "Love can look like 'no,'" I offer, perhaps pointing to 1 Corinthians 13:6: "[Love] rejoices whenever the truth wins out." I continue, "We can love our enemies by speaking the truth to them in kindness." Love can look like "no."

Parenting in this wild world is—well, wild. With God's help and wisdom, we can help curb the abuse statistics for our kids and our neighbors.

QUESTIONS TO CONSIDER

1. How have you approached body safety with your young kids? Is there anything you would like to add or adjust in your family's body safety plan?

2. What do you think about the idea of family rules for body safety?

3. How does the trust jar idea sit with you? How do you help your kids discern between trustworthy and untrustworthy people?

4. How did it feel for you to walk through this chapter? Why do you think that is?

11. HONOR GOD WITH OUR MINDS

Lay the Foundation

"Pornography feels so insidious and unavoidable. How do I prepare my kids before they see it? (And will they definitely encounter it?) The internet is evil in a thousand other ways, too. And screens by themselves! What can we actually do?"

MATT'S SPECIALTY as a clinical mental health therapist is sexuality. Most of his clients have a history of affairs, marriage issues, sexual or gender identity issues, or pornography addiction. Matt is never lacking in clients. He has had a rotating waiting list for his clinical services since 2020.

The focus of Matt's practice arose from his own story. When he was eleven, he stumbled on a pornographic calendar. This led to his friends printing images of porn and giving them to Matt at school, which led to Matt learning how to use the newly invented internet, which led to an on-again-off-again battle with pornography that lasted to age thirty. The rescue for Matt was not more accountability (although that was a help); it was understanding the heart of the issue.

Matt now takes what he learned both in life and graduate school about getting to the issue below the issue and uses it to help clients with their own challenges. For example, if he is meeting with a teenager and his or her parents to discuss pornography addiction, Matt turns the focus to both the child's and the parents' views of sex in general.

He has explained it to me after a long day with clients, "One of the most simultaneously helpful and awkward things I can ask both parents and teens is, 'How do you view sex in general? With what mindset do you approach sex?' The child looks at the parent like, 'Are we allowed to talk about this?'" I chuckle, picturing how uncomfortable that must be.

With Matt's prompting, the parent and the child share what they believe about sex.

"It ends up being both an eye-opening and empathy-building conversation." He pauses, taking a bite of his inevitably late dinner after seeing evening clients. "At first, the parent is confused and scared about the child's sexual brokenness. But after talking through their core beliefs about sex, they often find they have a similar mindset. They see sex as something (and someone) to consume, or they're trying to be passive by going to sex instead of dealing with their life pain, or they're seeking the next novel thing to entertain them, or they're trying to control how they get their heart needs met through sex (or porn). The once-judgmental parent has empathy, because they see that their view of sex is almost the same."

I nod, understanding through my own sexually broken lens. I used to be judgmental of people who wrestled with pornography until I looked in the mirror and saw I was no better.

The Holy Spirit held that mirror to my heart after Matt confessed his own secret pornography addiction six years into our marriage. After days of conversation and ongoing repentance on Matt's part, it was time for me to extend grace. I remember sitting on the floor in our condo, looking out at the sunshiny day but feeling like our home was frigid. Matt sat next to me on the couch, his head in his hands. He was repentant, but I was having a hard time caring. Matt had been consuming porn and lying to me about it every time I asked for six years. I was understandably angry. I should have been. The judgmentalism, however—my looking down on him rather than calling out Matt's sin through eye-to-eye, Christian-to-Christian biblical judgment—was not necessary.[1] We are called to judge other Christians, not to be judgmental.

The Holy Spirit pinpricked my heart, putting a finger on my own version of sexual brokenness. *Laurie, why did you run to women for relationship? Why do you still sometimes struggle with lust for them?* My eyes went wide as I thought about the answer, my pride exposed. I thought my sexual sin was holier than Matt's. I had gone to women because I felt empty inside and wanted to control how I got those needs met. I went to women to be seen, known, loved, and find belonging—but those were real people, not sex-trafficking-promoting porn. *Ask Matt why he ran to pornography*, I sensed the Holy Spirit prompting. I wanted to roll my eyes, but I refrained.

"Matt, why did you go to pornography?" I asked. "Why did you watch it?"

Because Matt was freshly sober from addictively engaging porn, it was challenging for him to access his heart. (Truly it takes at least two to four weeks to begin to lose withdrawal symptoms and even begin to become more self-aware.)[2] God graciously helped Matt answer my question: "I wanted to be seen, known, loved, and find belonging. Porn made me feel that way for brief moments in time." Matt's answer revealed that although we ran to different things, the reason we ran was the same: heart needs.

There is always a story attached to pornography. The story tells the user through the screen, "I choose you. You belong." The story paired with a dopamine-oxytocin brain blast from orgasm makes it feel like someone is filling the emptiness inside—briefly.[3] But because it is a screen and because it is outside God's design for sex, porn only fuels addiction. Porn scratches the itch of our heart to be seen, known, and loved while leaving the consumer always needing more. I can relate to this out of my own sexual brokenness, which was also outside of God's design for flourishing in the world.

The Hole in Our Hearts

God made us eternal creatures with what can feel like a black hole in our hearts. It is easy to take our craving to be seen, known, loved, and find belonging to the world for fulfillment. *Porn, give us purpose*, we beg. Therapist Jay Stringer found in his research that men are seven times more likely to escalate pornography use if they lack purpose in their lives.[4] But it isn't just porn we turn toward to feel good about ourselves. Girlfriend, boyfriend, children, money, power, social media likes, home renovations, Target runs, this pan of brownies, Netflix marathoning—*please help us feel seen, soothed, safe, and secure*, we scream. But it can't.

"You have made us for yourself, O Lord, and our heart is restless until it rests in you," Saint Augustine said.[5] God made us out of his great love, and only in taking our restless, empty hearts to him can we fulfill the reason we were created: "For everything comes from him and exists by his power and is intended for his glory" (Rom 11:36). I used to be confused about this "give glory to God" business. It felt like God was a self-seeking worship hoarder. But we do not worship God because he needs it; we worship God because *we* need it. God deserves worship, but we need to worship. We were made to worship something, and we will: money, sex, power, our kids, shopping, that pop star, our next new couch . . .

but it is only in worshiping God that we will be satiated. It is only in loving the Lord our God with all our heart, soul, mind, and strength that we will find our true rest and purpose. It is simply how we were created.

So how do we worship? After saying everything "exists by his power and is intended for his glory" at the end of Romans 11, the next thing Paul says in chapter 12 is, "Therefore, I urge you, brothers and sisters, in view of God's mercy, to offer your bodies as a living sacrifice, holy and pleasing to God—this is your true and proper worship" (Rom 12:1-2 NIV). We worship by surrendering to God. We worship not just on Sunday mornings by singing a few songs during church, but by giving God our bodies as living sacrifices.

Let's key in on the phrase "holy and pleasing to God." Thankfully, Jesus took the punishment for our sins past, present, and future on the cross so we can go to the Father with his holiness covering us (Heb 10:14). But it is not God's will for us to take our "ticket to heaven" and keep sinning (see Rom 6). Paul says in Romans 12:2, "Do not conform to the pattern of this world but be transformed by the renewing of your mind" (NIV). God wants us to walk in the way of Jesus. He wants to empower us to be "transformed into his image with ever-increasing glory" (2 Cor 3:18 NIV).

Some of us are stuck in the patterns of this world. Some of us are not renewing our minds and therefore not being transformed into the image of Christ. We may have our ticket to heaven, but look under the hood and our heart looks like hell. I do not use that word lightly.

The Porn Epidemic

I have been writing and researching this book for hundreds of hours, reading disturbing stories and study findings I never want to think about again. And I have concluded that more than any other issue in the area of sexuality, I am absolutely most concerned about the insidious evil of pornography.

Certainly I believe porn is fueling some of the child abuse and sexuality and gender questions, but I am absolutely convinced that, more than anything else, pornography consumption is quietly decaying the church from the inside out—and the worst thing is some of us don't even care.

If you could see me now, my jaw is clenched and I am having to hold myself in the chair to keep writing, because I want to throw myself on the floor and weep for mercy for the church. In September of 2024, Barna and Pure Desire Ministries released a study on pornography use. They found that 54 percent of practicing Christians watch porn sometimes, whereas 68 percent of all U.S. adults occasionally watch it.[6] That number is not as distressing to me as these next statistics: More than three in five Christians (62 percent) believe they can have a healthy sex life and watch porn, and almost half of Christians who view porn (49 percent) are comfortable with how much they use it.[7] Comfortable. As in, "Meh. It's fine." Biola professor and Think Biblically podcast host Sean McDowell says, "It's just not a big deal to them. . . . There's no sense of urgency whatsoever. I think this is an example where people are taking their cues far more from the culture and the ideas around us than Scripture and their Christian worldview."[8] In other words, when it comes to pornography use in the church, the majority of us (54 percent) are not renewing our minds; we are conforming to the world.

As I process why I am so angry about these numbers, I find myself most disturbed by the lack of concern. First of all, it's sad. It's as if we're looking at the cross of Christ—where the Son of God died a bloody, horrific, torturous death and went to hell and back for us—and saying, "Thanks, Jesus. I don't care what my sin cost you. It doesn't affect me, so thanks!" The second reason it grieves me is that how dare we try to lead our kids in the sexuality space when we ourselves are not actively struggling against sexual sin but shrugging at it?

Why worry about a speck in your friend's eye when you have a log in your own? How can you think of saying to your friend, "Let me help you get rid of that speck in your eye," when you can't see past the log in your own eye? Hypocrite! First get rid of the log in your own eye; then you will see well enough to deal with the speck in your friend's eye. (Mt 7:3-5)

In this Jesus is not saying, "Oh, everybody sins. Let's all just love each other in the midst of our sinfulness." He is saying, "Get rid of the log, hypocrite! Then you will be able to see to judge your fellow Christian fairly and without pride or hypocrisy." If Christians are not actively seeking to rid ourselves of the sexual logs in our eyes, we will not be able to judge our neighbors rightly, let alone lead our kids with an ounce of integrity.

The third reason these statistics grieve me so deeply is that porn does affect us. An unbelievable number of studies show again and again that porn affects users and those around them. In the Barna and Pure Desire study alone, porn users admitted they frequently felt anxious, critical of themselves, easily overwhelmed, and depressed.[9]

Not only does pornography consumption cause mental health issues, it causes relational problems.[10] It distorts views of sex and causes sexual dysfunction.[11] It can also lead to dopamine desensitization, which means the user needs to either consume more or watch more extreme forms of porn, such as those involving violence or sexual abuse of children.[12] In one 2016 study, researchers found that over time, 50 percent of porn consumers began watching material that at one time disinterested or disgusted them.[13] This escalation is especially distressing if people turn to increasingly popular forms of pornography featuring the abuse of teenagers or children.[14] Not only is this illegal, but it leads to other illegal acts. At least one study found that 85 percent of men who watched child sexual abuse materials took their screen use to the physical realm and acted on it, with each offender targeting an average of 13.56 victims.[15] Porn also fuels sexually violent behavior. At least one in three, up to as many as nine out of ten, porn scenes show sexual violence and encourage violent behavior.[16] And it promotes sex trafficking. Even in the creation of "mainstream" pornography, trafficking occurs more than people think and with minors.[17] One report found the average age of kids who had been trafficked and were forced into porn production was 12.8 years old.[18]

Let's pivot to teenagers' porn use as this is the next oldest ages for our kids. I, for one, want to know the potential damage to help curb my kids' interactions with it for as long as possible, and to remind me that this is not *just a screen problem*. Porn leads to life problems. As mentioned earlier, first encounters with pornography are traumatic for any human being. There is no way for someone to prepare their minds for what they will see. What adds to this trauma is that when a young heart sees the evil, the scenes wake up a child or teenager's good sexual desires and their good needs to be seen, known, and loved. Our sexuality and our needs are meant to draw us closer to God, but pornography isolates us and shames us. What can help alleviate the feelings of shame and loneliness—even for a few seconds—is more pornography. Many teenagers find themselves trapped in this cycle.

The Barna and Pure Desire study found that 39 percent of Gen Z adults view porn daily or weekly, more than half of younger millennials and Gen Z adults (ages eighteen to thirty-seven) have sent a nude image of themselves to another person, and three out of four have received one.[19] Common Sense Media executed a demographically representative U.S. survey of more than thirteen hundred teenagers (ages thirteen to seventeen) in September 2022.[20] It found that the average age of first exposure is twelve years old. By the time teenagers are seventeen, almost three in four (73 percent) have seen pornography, over half of teens (54 percent) see pornography by age thirteen, and one in five (15 percent) see it by age ten.[21] Did you know that many teens are seeing porn in school? This survey found that an average of 30 percent of students see porn in all types of school systems, with the highest percentage seeing it on private or religious school campuses (41 percent), the next highest in public schools (20 percent), and the lowest in homeschool settings (11 percent).[22]

This survey also showed that LGBTQ-identifying teens consume pornography at a higher rate than non-LGBTQ-identifying teens. They intentionally watch pornography more often than their cisgender (those who align with their biological sex) and heterosexual counterparts (66 percent versus 44 percent), more of them have been exposed to it (89 percent versus 70 percent), and they watch it to "find out what arouses and excites them" more than their cisgender-heterosexual counterparts (54 percent versus 45 percent).[23] The study authors commented, "It suggests that pornography may play a larger role in exploration for LGBTQ+ teens than for other teens."[24]

The second thing I will highlight from this study is the power of parents to help kids as they interact in a world where pornography is so pervasive. When parents do not talk with their kids about sex, the kids tend to seek it out and learn about sex through pornography.[25] Of teens who were not taught about sex at all, about one in three (30 percent) said they learned "a lot" to "everything I know" about sex from pornography.[26] Again, this is disturbing due to the violent, sometimes child-featuring content on even mainstream porn sites. The Common Sense Media survey specifically highlights studies featuring teens, showing that porn use increases anxiety and depression, interpersonal relationship problems, and sexual aggression (choking, name-calling) in teenagers.[27]

However, parents should be encouraged that teenagers want to talk to their parents about sex, and 47 percent of parents, caregivers, or other trusted adults have done so.[28] Teens also want to be able to talk about porn. They simply "don't know how to initiate the conversation" (39 percent) or "did not know who to talk to" (34 percent).[29] When teenagers did talk with trusted adults about porn, however, most were encouraged by the conversations. Specifically, among teens who have had these conversations about internet pornography, almost three in four (71 percent) said the conversation "made [them] feel like there are helpful resources other than pornography to explore [their] sexuality."[30] Yes and amen: We as parents can be a more helpful, godly resource about sexuality than porn.

The Four Mindsets

Porn is everywhere. Some Christians are addicted to it, and others will suffer because of it even if it doesn't become compulsive. Kids are watching it in school because their friends show it to them. Many videos are violent, featuring minors and promoting trafficking. It is easy to feel hopeless. What should we parents do before the chances of our kids seeing it as teenagers increase? For starters, let's remember that the kingdom of heaven is forcefully advancing. God is still on his throne, and he will not relent when it comes to pursuing us.

But we also need to get our heads on straight when it comes to "renewing our minds." We need to talk more specifically about the questions Matt asks in therapy and shift our mindsets regarding our approach to sex. If we start to think about what we are thinking about, and if we bring unhealthy thinking into the light before God, we will begin to renew our minds for the glory of God and the good of his world. Let's look at four ways we can shift our mindset regarding how we view sex.[31]

Consuming or providing. The world approaches sex consumeristically. "What can you give to me? How can you make me feel good about myself?" Pornography feeds on this mindset. Its goal is to help the user feel good no matter what it costs their relationships, their future, or the people in the video.

In contrast, God provides for his creation (Mt 6:31-33). If sex is a covenant renewal ceremony that produces fruit to the glory of God, are we seeking to provide for our spouses when it comes to sex? If we are not married and engaging in sexual intercourse outside of marriage, then by engaging in sexual promiscuity, we are taking something out of God's design that does not belong to us and living like a consumer. How can single people instead use their longing for sexual union to drive them to worship, saying, "God, you are worthy of giving up everything"?

Passive or present. If we are looking at pornography or numbing out through selfish sex with our spouses, we are being passive to our real life and engaging in a fake or numbing life. God is an ever-present help in trouble (Ps 46:1). We need to learn to be present to our real lives because that is the world we live in—even if it means being present to our pain. If we are married, the best way to have sex with our spouse is to be aware of ourselves, our spouse, and God's presence with us. If we are not married, how can we learn to be present and loving to ourselves as sexual beings even while abstaining from sexual intimacy?

Novelty-seeking or faithful. The world is always looking for the next dopamine blast, the next Instagram reel, the next house renovation, and the next "hit" of joy. It is constantly seeking what's novel. God is faithful (2 Thess 3:3). He never gets bored with us. He never needs us to perform or do something fancy for him. If God has called us to marriage, then in our covenant, we model God's faithfulness by not looking for the next hit of dopamine with our spouse (or through pornography or an affair) but by deepening the faithful bond we already have. If we are not married, to refrain from sexual sin is to remain faithful to God and to model his beautiful fidelity to the church.

Controlling or trusting. The world wants to control how we get our heart needs met—our needs to be seen, soothed, safe, and secure. The world says our destiny is in our own hands, when really, there is very little over which we have control. Even porn, as good as it feels for a few minutes, leaves us depressed and self-hateful. We truly have no control over the satisfaction of our hearts.

But God hopes in humanity (1 Cor 13:7). He entrusts us with his mission. Even though we have failed him many times, he always forgives, takes us back, and invites us to advance his kingdom with him again. When we approach sex, are we trying to control the situation so we get our heart needs met in this space? Or are we trusting our spouse so that, whether we get the outcome we want or not, we're hopeful and trusting with our entire relationship, willing to work through our hurdles together? If we are not married, are we trusting God to fulfill the needs of our heart through ways other than sexual release?

With which mindset do we approach sex and sexuality?

As we look to lead our kids in a world where pornography is pervasive, let's remember that we are not without hope. When Jesus was launching the early church, he did not bring his disciples to an isolated corner of the desert and say, "This is good. Start the church here." He brought them to Caesarea Philippi, a place where animal-human orgies occurred regularly. There, he said, "I say to you that you are Peter (which means 'rock'), and upon this rock I will build my church, and all the powers of hell will not conquer it" (Mt 16:18). God's plans for us, for our kids, and for the church will not be overcome by pornography, by ancient sexual evil, or by hell itself. Jesus wins.

> **QUESTIONS TO CONSIDER**

1. How do you feel about the reality that pornography is everywhere in the world?

2. Which pornography statistic bothered you the most?

3. What has your relationship been like to pornography?

4. As you consider the four mindsets, which one resonates as you think about sex or other idols in your life (money, power, things, your kids, pumpkin spice lattes)?

12. HONOR GOD WITH OUR MINDS

Walk the Foundation

> **Key teaching:** *"If you see a picture of a private part online, shut the screen and come and get me. You will not get in trouble."*

IT'S BEEN INTERESTING to write a parenting book about sex, puberty, and gender while parenting little kids of my own. There have been days when I sit at the kitchen table with twenty to thirty books around me, and they are not just any books: They are too-graphic children's picture books explaining puberty, helpful books explaining body safety, googly-eyed preteen books proclaiming the "joys of becoming a young woman," porn-prevention books, and giant theology books on sex and marriage.

But kids are curious. As I was putting Juliette to bed recently, I noticed her reading a book I had not thumbed through yet or checked out on a site for parents and caregivers.[1]

"Hey, buddy, what are you reading?" She told me the name of an innocuous graphic novel. "Is there anything inappropriate in there?"

She shook her head. "No."

This is a common conversation for us. We talk about what might be inappropriate in our home often (things like violence, heterosexual romance above their age range, or overt LGBTQ affirmation).

She stopped reading and looked at me with huge eyes. "But one of your books was!"

I froze. "What? What did you see?"

She was ready to tell all. "Your kids' books by your laptop! I was walking down there getting a drink, and I saw the kids' book and opened it and read it. It was so bad, Mom." She shuddered.

I quickly rolled back the clock to see if I had told them explicitly not to read that particular stack. Shoot. I hadn't. *Great, Laurie. You're trying to teach parents how to keep their kids from inappropriate sexual stuff, and in the actual writing of that book, you go and traumatize your kid with an inappropriate book.* I had not read the book she mentioned and was inwardly quaking at what she might have seen. Before I rushed to see just how unsuitable it was, I focused on healing Juliette's heart and mind first. The content wasn't as important as how Juliette felt about the content.

"Oh, Juliette. Thank you so much for telling me."

This is always where parents need to begin—thanking their kids for telling them something that must be challenging to say. Honesty is hard, and bringing darkness into the light is difficult. We need to acknowledge that.

I continued by bringing my own error into the light: "I am so sorry. I had not read that one. Will you forgive me for not telling you not to read that stack?"

I always try to apologize to my kids whenever I can—even for an innocent mistake—to show them how normal it is. Making mistakes or sinning is not the end of the world. Jesus took care of it all on the cross. Confession and owning mistakes is a normal, healthy part of the Christian walk.

Juliette nodded at my apology but still gave me the side-eye.

So I explained. "I am trying to help parents talk to their kids about sex and stuff, but sometimes people don't do it the way our family does."

She nodded enthusiastically. "You can say that again." At eight years old, Juliette had recently heard the more in-depth sex talk from me, so she had me as her anchoring reference to compare the inappropriate book to. Although I was not glad she saw it, I was quietly grateful I was her anchor—not that book.

"Juliette, can I pray with you?"

I did not want to make this event more than it was, but I did want to teach Juliette we can invite the light of the Holy Spirit into any darkness. If (or, statistically speaking, when) Juliette sees porn one day, she does not have to think, *Oh no! I can't tell my mom. I can't tell God!* Psalm 139 tells us:

> I can never escape from your Spirit!
> I can never get away from your presence! . . .
> I could ask the darkness to hide me
> and the light around me to become night—
> but even in darkness I cannot hide from you.
> To you the night shines as bright as day.
> Darkness and light are the same to you.
> (Psalm 139:7, 11-12)

We do not need to be afraid of our kids seeing evil. Do we try to protect them from it? Yes. Can God redeem and restore our kids even if and when they see it? Also yes.

So without making this an overt conversation about the dangers of pornography, I subtly taught Juliette what to do if and when she encounters it. She did the right thing by telling me. I did the right thing by working to protect her from it in the future. And we both did the right thing by talking about it and framing the content of the book as a distortion of the light.

Although Juliette did not see pornography, the explicitly sexual content of the inappropriate children's book seemed to be intruding on her brain, and I did not want her to feel like a powerless victim of what she'd seen—now or in the future.[2] Psychologist Julia Sadusky says seeing sexually vulgar scenes can hinder a child's development as an adult. "I have walked with clients who, through early exposure to pornography, began having intrusive sexual thoughts that later manifested in obsessive compulsive disorder. For many years, they could not figure out why they couldn't get distressing content out of their heads. It seemed to be their brain's way of saying, 'Something intruded when you were young,' and their brain was right. Facing this reality was essential for their healing."[3]

After talking with Juliette about how what she saw differed from God's design, I asked if she wanted me to pray for her.

"Sometimes, when I see stuff like that, I like to pray over my brain to get those thoughts out. Do you want to pray?"

She nodded.

So I prayed, "Jesus, please cover Juliette's mind, her heart, and her body. I pray the cross of Christ between those pictures and her brain, and I pray that every time they try to pop into her head, they bounce off the cross and do not sink into Juliette's mind."

Now, is that prayer magical? No. But God is powerful, and Jesus on the cross took on all past, present, and future sin and shame forever. Praying reminds us of that reality and our authority as children of the Most High God (1 Pet 2:24). We do not have to be pushed around by the visual assaults of the world, but we can be transformed by the renewing of our minds. What better way to refresh and renew our minds than by remembering the cross?

After praying, Juliette looked more peaceful. "I'm sorry again, buddy," I said. "If it keeps popping into your head, feel free to tell me. I am happy to hear you and pray with you over and over."

I say this whenever our kids stumble across something inappropriate. I never want them to think they have to hide what they have seen or wrestle with it on their own. I may even circle back to ask if she's still thinking about it a day or two later. I will not obsessively return to it—I don't want to encourage her to think about it—but I will casually ask at least once more.

How We Intentionally Talk About Pornography at Each Age

How do we help our kids know what is right and wrong when it comes to inappropriate content, and how can we help them learn to tell us when they see something like pornography? Let's look at each stage.

Ages zero to three. When our kids are between zero and three, we don't teach much directly about pornography beyond, "That is not appropriate for you at this age." If they want to watch something or stumble across something that borders on inappropriate, they can ask questions, but even explaining the reality of naked body parts online feels too intense and intangible, so we just say, "It's not appropriate. You just need to trust me, bud."

When Gwyn was three years old, I was shocked to see that as we watched an innocent Daniel Tiger song together on YouTube, the next automatic-play video was Barbie pornography. Why would someone create such vile videos? Unfortunately, that question did not help me process the reality that cartoon pornography exists. So instead of giving the creator a piece of my mind, I shut the iPad and Matt and I set more intense boundaries on all screen use.

Ages four to eight. It is in the four- to eight-year-old age range that we introduce the idea of people taking pictures of others' private parts and putting them on the internet. We can bring up the conversation whenever it seems like it's time. Pray, and dive in with something like, "Did you guys know that some people put pictures of private parts online?"

The first time I told our kids this, they were aghast. "They take pictures and put them on the internet for *everyone to see?*" they shouted.

Their emotion was spot-on. We should always be so grieved and surprised. After telling our kids in this age-appropriate way that pornography exists (without yet using the actual word), we need to empathize, restate that it's wrong, and then tell them what they should do if and when they encounter it.

"Yes, it is evil and sad. But if you guys are ever online and see something like that, shut the computer or turn off the tablet, come and find me or Dad (or a trusted caregiver), and tell us what happened."

Our kids need to hear this plan repeatedly. In this four- to eight-year-old range, I say something about private part pictures at least once every six months or so. But I always add this final part: "You will not get in trouble." I even ask them immediately afterward to ensure they understand: "If you see a naked private part online like a penis, vagina, or breasts, what do you do?"

They tell me the plan.

"And will you get in trouble?"

They have learned to say an emphatic, "No!"

It is crucial for our kids to understand that it is not their fault if they stumble onto sinful content. The odd thing about sexual sin is it can cause a mixture of confusing emotions within us. It can repel us, it can arouse us, it can make us curious, it can confuse us, and it can shame us. Instead of teaching kids to parse out every emotion at these young ages, encourage them to know the action steps: "Shut the screen, tell a trusted adult, and you will not get in trouble—no matter how you feel about what you saw."

Ages nine to twelve. In the older-kid range we start to introduce the word *pornography*. We wait at least until age nine because it's such an aggressive term. *Pornography* is not a good thing that gets distorted like the words *vagina* or *penis* (which can be taught to our kids with proper language from birth). Porn is bad through-and-through. But if parents have not said the word *pornography* aloud, this is the time to do it. If 15 percent of kids are first exposed to porn under ten years old, and the average age of exposure is twelve years old, this is the time to be direct.[4] Parents can bring up the topic similarly to when we brought it up when our kids were younger: Just pray and do it. "You know, when people put pictures of private parts online or even videos of people having sex on the internet, it's called 'pornography.' Have you heard that word before?" Then, we can do the same as what we did when our kids were younger: Empathize, talk about how it's evil, and remind them of the plan.

In these ages, we can elaborate further when we talk about how pornography is evil. We don't have to simply say, "Pornography is wrong," we can say why it's wrong in the context of the gospel. "Do you remember what marriage is? It shows the world a picture of how much God loves them. Sex in marriage is supposed to be a very personal way the mom and the dad tell each other how much God loves them. But it's supposed to be sacred, private, and in the safety of a promise. It's not supposed to be on display for all to see."

Some kids in this age range may be able to understand the metaphor of how when moms and dads unite through sex and produce the fruit of babies, it shows a picture of how God temples within us when we say "yes" to Jesus (and we are reborn and able to produce more fruit by the power of the Holy Spirit). But that metaphor may be over many of our kids' heads. No matter what, talking about pornography in this gospel-positive way sets our kids up for greater understanding about the gospel vision of sex as they grow older.

What if Our Kids Encounter Pornography?

In the nine to twelve age range, we can continue to repeat the plan for what to do when they encounter pornography, but this is also a season of life when many kids see and perhaps begin consuming porn. They can pivot from stumbling across sinful images to seeking it out. How can we respond if they don't follow the family rules of finding us and instead linger or go looking for it? What if we discover they have been regularly consuming it when we check our computer's history months or years later? If this happens in this age range, we need to gently approach our child. Even though we likely feel a swarm of triggers and emotions, they are probably feeling more—and they don't have the adult brain to process it all. Porn can elicit feelings of repulsion, arousal, curiosity, confusion, and shame. We need to approach those feelings with tender questions and empathy.

"Oh, honey, it can be confusing to see all of that, can't it? How do you feel?" In these moments, it's vital we remember that sexuality is good. Our kids' sexuality is broken but a good pointer to their need for God. It is pornography's distortion of sex that is bad.

We must also remember that our kids are not monsters—they are normal, human sinners. They were captivated by a distortion of something good and drawn into it. We need to reassure our kids that we love them the exact same as we did before and we will never leave them, and then we need to help them process what they saw.

"How did it make you feel?" we ask. Then, we try to meet them emotionally, putting ourselves in their shoes: We stumble across porn. We feel drawn in. We feel a mix of shame and arousal, and then we start hiding. What might we need to hear? I would want to hear empathy, truth, and boundaries for my future flourishing. It might sound like, "I am so sorry you've been navigating this alone. It's so sad that people put this online and seeing it must be so hard. But this is not the way God has designed sex. It's a private thing to be done in the promise of marriage to tell the husband or wife, 'God loves you so much.' This is not that."

Then we need to set rules and boundaries—not to destroy our kids, but to help promote their flourishing. I would ask my kids to help think about how we can partner to help them avoid this content in the future. If they don't know, we can share our ideas and invite them into helping them succeed.

Next, we try to determine their part in the activity. Did they lie intentionally about it? Or were they just panicked, so they blurted something untruthful? Was this their seventh time engaging? Their fiftieth? Their first? Parents should not be sin hunters but freedom seekers. I would work to see if there is any part in engaging that was sinful, not in order to punish my kids but to help free them through godly conviction and repentance. This is a very tricky space, and I would advise reaching out to trusted people for help discerning.

Finally, I would bring our kids to a posture of tenderhearted prayer. I would pray over them and invite them to tell God how they feel—confessing any sin as needed. We need to be sure to curb any confessions of our kids saying, "I am the worst." Toxic, self-hateful shame has a way of sneaking in easily when people engage sexual sin. Conviction of sin is good; confession of worthlessness is actually further sin. We are not worthless if we sin; we are normal, post-fall humans in need of a Savior.

Let's Talk About Screen Rules

Although this is not directly related to pornography prevention, a family's relationship to screens affects access to the internet, which is riddled with soft porn that can be found on social media and more intense forms that can be accessed with a little more effort. I'll share our family's plan for screens, and as always, you are welcome to adapt to your needs.

When our kids are ages zero to three, we limit screen use as a whole.[5] We let them watch bits here and there as it serves our family or provides educational value. We also put protective blockers of pornography and violence on all devices. When our kids were this age, Matt and I started to police our own screen use so we could practice what we preached about screens to our kids.

Studies say parents' screen use is a good indicator for how kids will use screens.[6] In our family, we want our kids to see screens as tools and engage with accountability, honesty, and a lack of hiddenness. Therefore we try not to have screens behind closed doors such as bedrooms or bathrooms. Sin loves hiddenness, so we try to eliminate screens from private spaces for parents and kids. Granted, Matt and I do have laptops we use for work that are used in a closed office, but even there, Matt and I share an account so we can see what each other looks at any time.

Between ages four and eight, we still limit screen time, and we have our kids ask us before they watch a new show or series. We then look up the content to ensure the content is appropriate for them.[7] Around nine years old, we allow our kids to get a text-only watch, and we control who texts them.[8] We do this to help them begin to develop a healthy (while still highly monitored) relationship to screens, and because sometimes we need to get ahold of our kids. The watch may turn into a dumb phone (no internet) when they are around thirteen. We plan to allow our kids to have a smartphone around fourteen or fifteen when they begin high school. They can consider getting parent-approved social media apps when they are sixteen—we want our kids to learn to navigate the quagmire of social media before they go to college or begin a career at eighteen. Before age sixteen, we do not let our kids use social media at all (including YouTube), unless we are showing them something or have approved a brief engagement.[9]

Research has guided these decisions. During the tender puberty years of ten to fourteen, kids' minds are growing rapidly, and they are especially susceptible to cultural influences around them. If teenagers are, on average, on their phones six to eight hours per day, the primary culture they are consuming and assimilating into is internet culture.[10] We do not want internet culture to be the primary shaper of our kids' identity during those years (or before), so we are waiting until fourteen to fifteen to let them have a smartphone. Otherwise, they likely will fall into the astronomical statistics surrounding the correlative relationship between adolescence, smartphone use, and major anxiety and depression.[11] We do not want to make adolescence harder, so we are focusing on helping our kids form real, in-person relationships with their peers.

As with all of their technology, when our kids get a smartphone around fourteen or fifteen, we will own the phone so we can take it away if needed. As they learn to use it, we will work hard to continue to build on our relationship of trust and talk through what they encounter online. At age eighteen, we pray they have built enough grounding in the gospel and with us to handle the internet outside of our home in college or while beginning a career.

Cultivating a Providing Versus Consuming Mindset

As we discussed earlier, a consuming mindset takes and absorbs people and things for selfish reasons. A providing mindset gives and creates for and with another person. Caring for our kids' sexuality does not begin and end with shielding them from pornography. It begins with helping them learn to steward their lives and hearts toward God. Our views of sex are a reflection of how we view the world. When Matt has someone in his office with a porn problem, he knows it is not just a porn problem but a mindset issue. Porn users scroll through videos thinking, *Which video (and person in that video) will make me feel good about me?* That's a consuming mindset. They likely view sex that way, too, as well as the world at large: *How can you make me feel good about me?* Matt knows this before he asks a porn addict a single question.

Our mindsets are not glasses we take off and on. The more we engage in evil behavior like consumeristic sex, consumeristic porn, or a consumeristic view of the world, the more those glasses become our eyeballs: We see everyone and everything as something to consume.

So let's start forming a worldview from the lens of how God sees us: not as people to consume but as beloved bearers of his image for whom he wants to provide. How can we cultivate that in our kids so that when they awaken to their own sexuality, it flows from a providing instead of consuming worldview? When I think about cultivating such a mindset, I go back to the gospel.

"What is the purpose of your life, dear one?" I ask my kids.

"To give glory to God. To make his name great," they ideally say—with some prompting.

I continue, "And how do we do that?"

"We push back the darkness and usher in the light—we advance the kingdom of God."

Having that gospel vision as the drumbeat we live by will shape the culture of our homes and create a providing instead of consuming mindset.

One way to help our kids develop a providing instead of consuming mindset is to teach them to do regular household chores. Encouraging our kids to take part in the work of the household not only emphasizes that their lives are about God and advancing the kingdom (which requires work), but longitudinal studies show they make for more compassionate, competent, and socially confident kids.[12] This makes sense because they get used to seeing hard tasks and thinking, *I can do that.* After reading studies that told us this truth, we have been pushing our kids to do more consistent chores. When they complain, I often say, "Well, I want you to be empathetic and have a good job in the future, so sorry, kid. This is what we do." Or I say something more gospel-focused: "God has called you to a good task to advance his kingdom, and this is a good starting place to learn to do it with him." Or I just say, "Well, then, no money for LEGO." I mean, that's real-life parenting.

Another way we can cultivate a providing mindset in our kids when it comes to screens is to watch shows as a family. This not only decreases the sneaky-fun curiosity of having a screen to ourselves, but it makes us have to compromise and to think of the other. When we have to come up with an idea for a movie to watch that at least mildly pleases everyone, it forces us to find common ground with a brother, sister, or parent. Since we instituted this "watch together when we can" rule, it has fostered some fun family laughs and togetherness—even around a screen.

Cultivating a Present Instead of Passive Mindset

With a passive mindset, a person does everything possible to avoid the pain (and therefore the joy) of now. With a present mindset, an individual is alert and awake to the pain—and the joy—of the moment.

When Matt was detoxing from his porn addiction, the first thing he noticed was that he was not just addicted to porn; he was addicted to screens. As he decreased screen use in his life, he soon realized he had been running to screens because he was running from pain in his life. "I did not know how to cope with my own self-hatred and anxiety," Matt says.

Bingo. Studies show it is common for people to run to things like porn to soothe their internal anxiety, depression, and stressful experiences.[13] The problem with turning to porn to soothe mental and emotional pain is that it actually makes mental health issues worse.[14] If we want to teach our kids not to run to porn, social media, video games, food, money, sex, or power to soothe their internal conflicts, we need to first teach them how to stay present to the life they are really living.

To teach this, we have to model it. Many of us, when we feel bored, sad, scared, or depressed, hit the "escape" buttons on our lives hundreds of times per day by reaching for our many things—most often our phones. Because of this, we live "forever elsewhere," says MIT professor Sherry Turkle.[15] If we want our kids to be present to their lives, we need to be present first.[16] In a cross-sectional three-year study of ten thousand adolescents and their parents, researchers found that when parents used their phones around their kids, children had higher total screen time usage and early adolescents engaged more with problematic (bordering on or outright obsessive/addictive) use of social media, video games, and mobile devices. Additionally, the researchers found that when parents rewarded or took away screen time for good or bad behaviors, this only increased screen time for kids as a whole. However, limiting screen use completely (establishing one flat rule rather than adjusting for good and bad behavior) led to decreased total screen time and less problematic social media and mobile phone use.[17]

Studies like these encourage Matt and me to leave our phones plugged in at an out-of-reach charging station as often as possible. As discussed earlier, we also work to not bring our phones into any bedroom or bathroom to remove temptation to look at inappropriate things or simply escape.

Teaching presence is not just about removing phones; it's about learning to remain connected in the midst of suffering. That's fun, isn't it? Who wants to suffer? No one. But it's a reality of life that our kids will experience hardship, hopefully in small ways now, and likely bigger ways as they grow older. Can we teach our kids to feel disappointment, name the emotion, and grieve it in real time? Or do we throw an iPad at them? I am nodding in solidarity right now because there have been times I have done just that—and sometimes we truly need to: at the doctor's office, during a work call, or after giving birth, for crying out loud, or, "Please toddler, just let me breastfeed your brother in peace!" However, research shows that regularly giving kids screens to help them "calm down" can hinder their ability to emotionally regulate in the future.[18] Many of us know this instinctively. We don't need studies. But studies can encourage us to put on our big-parent pants and say, "Okay, let's learn how to suffer together."

Recently, for example, our kids were all struggling with their days ahead. Both of the girls had orthodontist appointments where they would be getting braces, and Ellis was anxious because he would not have the girls with him at school while they were at the orthodontist. For our five-minute family devotions that day, I said, "Okay, everyone, let's go around the room and tell Jesus where we need him. Let's tell him how we are struggling." In the moment, I wanted to remove my kids' pain, but as I thought long term, I wanted them to learn how to suffer well with Jesus. Each of us went around the room and told God our fears. Afterward, I reminded them, "You guys? When you feel scared, you can squeeze your hand like this and remember that God holds you by your right hand." I squeezed my hand as I quoted Isaiah 41:13, which says, "I hold you by your right hand. . . . Don't be afraid. I am here to help you." They all squeezed their right hand to remember.

This moment was short. It was powerful. It reminded us all that we have an ever-present help in trouble to help us be present to our real lives.

Cultivating A Faithful Instead of Novelty-Seeking Mindset

Reminder: A novelty-seeking mindset consistently tires of what was once new and seeks more. A faithful mindset consistently hopes for the best and stays for better or worse.

Novelty is the elixir of our screen-addicted world. Our brains were wired to seek and learn what is new. We see it in babies. As a result, some people think "learning apps" are good for them, but in general, the consensus is that screens for small children are not great.[19] Part of the reason is that babies learn new things very quickly. Toddlers, for example, rapidly learn how to use an app that can read a book to them. But then the novelty wears off. They get used to the process of clicking, "turning pages," and moving on. Then they need the next novelty hit.[20] But giving a toddler the next app does not teach them how to faithfully endure real life. Real life is sometimes boring. It's the mom getting up with her aching back and going to the closet to fetch the book and slowly getting back down to read. (I'm not just describing myself here, am I?)

It's easy to judge toddlers, but we adults are worse. We passively learn to love the dopamine hit we get when we see a new comment on Instagram, a notification of stocks going up, or a text back from someone we love. "Tech companies understand what causes dopamine surges in the brain and they lace their products with 'hijacking techniques' that lure us in and create 'compulsion loops,'" says *New York Times* columnist David Brooks.[21] Adults are addicted to novelty, too.

One way to model faithfulness to our kids is through our marital vocations, whether we are married or single. Are we working hard to show our kids the faithful, steadfast love of God for us in how we love and pursue our spouses through the mundane parts of life? Are we working hard to show our kids the faithful, steadfast love of God in how we love our brothers and sisters in Christ when it's not a mountain-top experience? If not, we need to do whatever it takes to joyfully and faithfully live into the marital vocation into which God has called us.

Cultivating a Trusting Instead of Controlling Mindset

A controlling mindset schemes to get another's support without trust. A trusting mindset leans on God and others for support.

It is the absolute default of humanity to scheme to get what we need on our own. We have been doing this since the Garden of Eden: "God, I don't trust you to give me what I need or to care for me, so I will listen to this serpent and take what I need on my own." With social media, love of money, love of power, pornography, or obsession with fashion, we can do the same thing, saying, "I feel empty. I will go to this thing to get what I need. I will control how I get my support."

I see this reality play out frequently with my kids with money and their longing for stuff. As we have been teaching them to do more chores and giving them money for their work, some of them let that money flow through their fingers like water. They immediately want to shop. They don't even care what they buy; it just needs to be something. I have to laugh a little because it feels like I'm in the middle of a Christian radio drama with my kids.

"Honey, I see that you're feeling anxious right now and you just want to buy something to make yourself feel better inside. Is that true?"

They often say outright, "Yes!"

I follow up with, "Okay, are you willing to take that emptiness to God and let him fill you? Can you trust him to care for your needs inside? Only he can satisfy that ache."

Usually in the bright lights of Target, the words I say might as well be in another language. But if I can wrangle them out the door without spending every cent in their wallets, we can detox at home and talk more about trusting God to fill our emptiness.

As silly as this sounds, as parents we truly do need to help our kids begin to name their emptiness (such as anxiety or a lack of feeling secure) and the temptation they face (buying every toy in Target) and help them learn to redirect their emptiness toward Christ. This is a lifelong lesson—one many of us adults still face (even in Target!). The more we can help our kids name their ache, name the temptation, and consider the idea that Jesus is the ultimate "Need-Meeter," the more we'll help our kids learn to trust Christ instead of controlling how to get their needs met through stuff.

Reflecting on the Mindsets

In Matt's work with his clients, he often starts the mindsets conversation by asking, "What is God's mindset toward you?" Is God a consumer of people? No, God is a provider, constantly sustaining his beloved creation (Phil 4:19). Is God passive? No, God is active. He is present in our lives and closer than our very breath (Ps 46:1). Is God novelty-seeking, tossing us aside when he is bored of us? No, God is absolutely faithful. (2 Thess 3:3). Is God controlling? Yes and no. While God is in control, he doesn't pick us up, set us off to the side, and tell us to get out of the way while he finishes advancing his kingdom "the right way." He trusts us to be an integral part of his ongoing story (Mt 28:19). As Christians, we are called to be "little Christs," which speaks less about what we avoid and more about how we view and interact with the world he created.

Leading our kids in a porn-saturated world does not begin and end with porn blockers on our devices or other ways to help our kids avoid this evil. It begins with cultivating a heart and mind that knows a God who provides, is present, is faithful, and trusts humanity to work as his representatives full of the Holy Spirit to advance his kingdom. This is how we can walk on a foundation of wisdom.

QUESTIONS TO CONSIDER

1. Do you have rules for screens in your family? What are they?

2. What is your plan for your kids encountering pornography? Have they heard this plan? How often?

3. Have your kids stumbled across pornography? How did you handle it? How might you handle it in the future?

4. Which mindset stood out to you as one you need to work on? How might you teach that to your kids?

CONCLUSION

WELL, HERE WE ARE: the beginning of the end. I pray as we look underneath our feet we see new foundations of wisdom about the gospel, about marriage and singleness, about gender, sex, and body safety, and about porn prevention.

Together we learned that God created the world good, sin distorted it, Jesus rescued and is rescuing us, and one day the world will be redeemed. Our purpose is to push back the darkness and usher in the light, until everyone everywhere is living in joyful submission to King Jesus for God's glory and our good.

Marriage and singleness are ways we can live out God's mission. We show the world through our marriage and singleness a picture of eternity where we will be married to Christ and in faithful relationship to our brothers and sisters in Christ. Marriage has to be between one man and one woman for life because we are different. We can say to our kids, "When moms and dads love each other—even though they are so different from each other—they show you a picture of how much God loves you—even though he is so different from us."

In our sexed bodies we live out God's mission to push back the darkness and usher in the light. We can tell our kids that we live out that mission as "your version of boy or girl—which is good." As men and women, we do not live out our maleness and femaleness in the exact same ways, but we all do so in our good, sexed bodies.

Sex is supposed to worship God. In marriage, it is a covenant renewal ceremony that produces fruit to the glory of God. When we talk to our kids about it, we can say, "God takes a seed from a dad and a seed from a mom, and God puts them together and makes a baby! Then God puts that baby inside of the mom's tummy."

To keep our kids safe and to help them honor each other's bodies, we can remind them in small and big ways that "you have a good body." We tell them this through protecting them and honoring them as bearers of the image of a holy God, and if they know and trust Jesus, they are temples of the Holy Spirit and fellow parts of the body of Christ.

When it comes to helping our kids stay away from pornography, we say, "If you see a picture of a private part online, shut the screen and come and get me. You will not get in trouble." But even if our kids see pornography, all is not lost. We can walk with them. There is always redemption and healing, and we can continually work on shaping all of our mindsets so that our lives are oriented toward Christ instead of worshiping things and people.

We teach this gospel lens because we want our kids to walk wisely. We want them to walk in the way of Jesus. Not only do we want that, but that is the heart of Christ for us and for our kids: No matter how we experience sexual brokenness within us or around us, we have the tools we need to walk in the way of Jesus—no matter what.

But we can't do this work on our own. So let's end with a prayer, yeah?

God, we love you. Thank you for your love for us. Our kids are actually your kids. We are your kids. Lead us. Remind us of your wisdom right when we need it. Empower us so that no matter how we experience sexual brokenness within us or around us, we are able to walk in wisdom no matter what. Thank you for your grace when we don't. We love you. Amen.

Now, let's go: Let's build these foundations in our homes and walk them out.

ACKNOWLEDGMENTS

THERE IS ABSOLUTELY NO WAY I could have written this book on my own. I had an army of people praying for me, encouraging me, and offering practical support throughout the journey.

First, thank you to my agent, Austin Wilson, for believing in this book so much that you started shopping it around while it was incomplete because I was finishing my master's.

To my editor, Kelli Trujillo: You prayed to acquire a book like this—and God dropped the (unfinished!) proposal right into your lap. Thank you not only for editing and praying over it, but also for sending me cards, texts, and emails of encouragement along the way.

To my faithful group of prayer-warrior women—Renee Allsbrook, Suzie Palmer, Molly Rottschafer, Michele Wells, Cassie Davito, Courtney Bytwerk, and Kelli O'Dell: Thank you for praying me through.

To my email prayer team and supporters: Thank you for partnering with the Holy Spirit to help bring this book to life.

To my spiritual director, Sarah Behm: Thank you for leading me to Jesus and his strength over and over.

To my early readers and editors—Michele Wells, Suzie Palmer, Andrew Klum, Greg Coles, Julia Sadusky, and Jon Sherrill: Thank you for your time, insight, and encouragement.

Dan Allender, I'll never forget how you asked to be an early reader of the book. Your humility and the way you lift others up inspires me to do the same.

To my sisters by blood and/or in the Lord, Angela Bowles and Kerri Chamberlain: It's a joy to do life with you both. Thank you for always being just a phone call away—whether to talk goofy with me or listen to my voice memos about whatever part of this book I was 1,000 percent passionate about that day.

To my parents, Marcia and Randy Hekman, and Matt's dad, Steve: Thank you for passing the baton farther than you received it. You've given us a beautiful legacy. (We miss you, Patty Krieg! Thank you for cheering us on from heaven.)

And to Matt: Thank you for letting me pick your brain, hear your heart, and share both your stories and mine—so this book could become the fruit of both our parenting journeys. You're my favorite. It's such a gift to stumbly figure out this parenting thing together.

And to our kids—Gwyn, Juliette, and Ellis: You are the best kids in the universe. We can't believe we get to be your mom and dad. It's our prayer that you take what we teach you here and offer something even richer to the next generation. Keep pushing back the darkness and ushering in the light!

And most importantly, to Jesus: Thank you for the burden to write this. We lay this book at your feet. Let it reach the moms, dads, and caregivers you had in mind when you invited us to write it. And, thanks for parenting us so well.

NEXT STEP RESOURCES

WE RECOMMEND READING THIS BOOK alongside The Center for Faith, Sexuality & Gender's *Christian Sexuality: Raising Kids* video series. Matt and I lead it alongside experts like Dan Allender, Jackie and Preston Perry, John Mark Comer, Curt Thompson, and more. You can find it at centerforfaith.com or at courses.christian-sexuality.com/courses/raising-kids. We also recommend the following resources.

The Gospel

For Parents

Scot McKnight, *The King Jesus Gospel: The Original Good News Revisited* (Zondervan, 2016).

N. T. Wright, *Simply Good News: Why the Gospel Is News and What Makes It Good* (HarperOne, 2017).

Christopher West, *Fill These Hearts: God, Sex, and the Universal Longing* (Image, 2013).

Ruth Chou and Troy Simons, *Foundations: 12 Biblical Truths to Shape a Family* (Harvest House, 2020).

For Families

Sally Lloyd Jones, *Thoughts to Make Your Heart Sing* (Zonderkidz, 2012), and *The Jesus Storybook Bible: Every Story Whispers His Name* (Zonderkidz, 2007).

Mariko Clark and Rachel Eleanor, *The Book of Belonging: Bible Stories for Kind and Contemplative Kids* (Convergent, 2024).

Our Daily Bread Ministries, *A Bible Memory Book* series (Our Daily Bread Publishing, 2019).

Louie Giglio, *The Wonder of Creation: 100 More Devotions About God and Science* (Tommy Nelson, 2021).

Shirley Raye Redmond, *Brave Heroes and Bold Defenders: 50 True Stories of Daring Men of God* (Harvest House, 2020) and *Courageous World*

Changers: 50 True Stories of Daring Women of God (Harvest House, 2020).

Songs

Shai Linne, "Only Jesus," track 5 on *Jesus Kids*, Shai Linne Music, 2018.

Bizzle, "The Gospel," track 16 on *Light Work 3*, God Over Money Records, 2023.

Brother Isaiah, "Love Song for the Bride," track 9 on *Poco a Poco*, Franciscan Friars of the Renewal, 2018.

Marriage and Singleness

For Parents

Laurie and Matt Krieg, *An Impossible Marriage: What Our Mixed-Orientation Marriage Has Taught Us About Love and the Gospel* (InterVarsity Press, 2020).

Preston Sprinkle, *Does the Bible Affirm Same-Sex Marriage? 21 Conversations from a Historically Christian View* (David C Cook, 2023).

Dani Treweek, *The Meaning of Singleness: Retrieving an Eschatological Vision for the Contemporary Church* (InterVarsity Press, 2023).

Timothy and Kathy Keller, *The Meaning of Marriage: Facing the Complexities of Commitment with the Wisdom of God* (Dutton, 2011).

Jackie Hill Perry, *Gay Girl, Good God: The Story of Who I Was, and Who God Has Always Been* (B&H, 2018).

Greg Coles, *Single Gay Christian: A Personal Journey of Faith and Sexual Identity* (InterVarsity Press, 2017).

Rachel Gilson, *Parenting Without Panic in an LGBT-Affirming World: Discipling Our Kids with Jesus' Truth and Love* (Good Book Company, 2024).

For Families

Sam Allberry, *God's Signpost: How Marriage Points Us to God's Love* (B&H Kids, 2023) and *God's Go-Togethers* (B&H Kids, 2024).

Gender

For Parents

Preston Sprinkle, *Embodied: Transgender Identities, the Church, and What the Bible Has to Say* (David C Cook, 2021).

Mark Yarhouse, *Talking to Kids About Gender Identity: A Roadmap for Christian Compassion, Civility, and Conviction* (Bethany House, 2023).

Abigail Favale, *The Genesis of Gender: A Christian Theory* (Ignatius, 2022).

Branson Parler, *Every Body's Story: 6 Myths About Sex and the Gospel Truth About Marriage and Singleness* (Zondervan, 2022).

Kelly M. Kapic, *Embodied Hope: A Theological Meditation on Pain and Suffering* (InterVarsity Press, 2017).

For Families

Marty Machowski, *God Made Boys and Girls: Helping Children Understand the Gift of Gender* (New Growth, 2019).

Processing Stories

For Parents

Alison Cook, *The Best of You: Break Free from Painful Patterns, Mend Your Past, and Discover Your True Self in God* (Thomas Nelson, 2022).

Aundi Kolber, *Try Softer: A Fresh Approach to Move Us out of Anxiety, Stress, and Survival Mode—and into a Life of Connection and Joy* (Tyndale Refresh, 2020) and *Strong Like Water: Finding the Freedom, Safety, and Compassion to Move through Hard Things—and Experience True Flourishing* (Tyndale Refresh, 2020).

Lysa Terkheurst, *I Want to Trust You, but I Don't: Moving Forward When You're Skeptical of Others, Afraid of What God Will Allow, and Doubtful of Your Own Discernment* (Nelson, 2024).

Michael Card, *A Sacred Sorrow: Reaching Out to God in the Lost Language of Lament* (NavPress, 2014).

Mark Vroegop, *Dark Clouds, Deep Mercy: Discovering the Grace of Lament* (Crossway, 2019).

The Allender Center, https://theallendercenter.org

Diane Langberg, *Redeeming Power: Understanding Authority and Abuse in the Church* (Brazos, 2020).

Laurie and Matt Krieg, *Hole in My Heart Podcast*, https://lauriekrieg.com/podcast.

Alison Cook, *The Best of You Podcast*, www.dralisoncook.com/podcast.

Curt Thompson, *Being Known Podcast*, www.beingknownpodcast.com.

For Families

Aubrey Sampson, *Big Feeling Days: A Book about Hard Things, Heavy Emotions, and Jesus' Love* (NavPress, 2023).

Discussing Sex and Reproduction

For Parents

Sam Jolman, *The Sex Talk You Never Got* (www.samjolman.com/the-sex-talk-you-never-got-book).

Julia Sadusky, *Start Talking to Your Kids About Sex: A Practical Guide for Catholics* (Ave Maria Press, 2023).

Birds & Bees, https://birds-bees.com.

Sex Ed Reclaimed, www.sexedreclaimed.com.

For Families

Luke Gilkerson, *The Talk: 7 Lessons to Introduce Your Child to Biblical Sexuality* (CreateSpace Independent Publishing, 2014).

Justin and Lindsey Holcomb, *God Made Babies: Helping Parents Answer the Baby Question* (New Growth, 2022).

Stan and Brenna Jones, *God's Design for Sex Series*, rev. ed. (NavPress, 2019).

Educate and Empower Kids, *30 Days of Sex Talks: Ages 3-7* (Rising Parent Media, 2015).

Body Safety and Screen Safety

For Parents

Jonathan Haidt, *The Anxious Generation: How the Great Rewiring of Childhood Is Causing an Epidemic of Mental Illness* (Penguin, 2024).

Protect Young Eyes, www.protectyoungeyes.com.

Common Sense Media, www.commonsensemedia.org.

Plugged In by Focus on the Family, www.pluggedin.com.

For Families

John Ortberg, *Your Magnificent Chooser: Teaching Kids to Make Godly Choices* (Tyndale House, 2017).

Justin and Lindsey Holcomb, *God Made All of Me: A Book to Help Children Protect Their Bodies* (New Growth, 2015).

Krystaelynne Sanders Diggs, *Where Hands Go* series (Diggs, 2021–2023).

Elizabeth Cole, *Body Boundaries Make Me Stronger* (Go2Publish, 2022).

Rachael DenHollender, *How Much Is a Little Girl Worth?* (Tyndale Kids, 2019) and *How Much Is a Little Boy Worth?* (Tyndale Kids, 2022).

APPENDIX A

How to Talk with Kids Between Ages Seven and Ten About Sex

ALTHOUGH PARENTS SHOULD BE SHARING about God's design for sex in little ways throughout their kids' lives, there is a moment when they should sit their children down and share specifics around age seven to ten. This is biologically around the time a child's body is preparing for puberty, and they need to learn why their body is changing and how to prepare for it. A parent might not choose to have this entire conversation in one sitting but instead split it up over a series of weeks. Because kids can get overwhelmed or have questions pop up later, and because we want parents to continue to be the anchoring source about God's design for sexuality, parents should follow up many times after this conversation.

When you are having this conversation, maintain this pattern: gospel big picture, specific biology of sex, check in with the child. Then repeat. Theology, biology, check in, repeat.

Specifically, we recommend the conversation (or series of conversations) go like this, but as always, feel free to adapt this to your preferences:

- Remind them of God's design for marriage.
- Ask what they know about babies and sex.
- Give specifics about sex.
- Talk about how God's design for the procreation of children is within the safety of a promise of a one-man and one-woman marriage.
- Tell them they don't have to worry about it now—this is just to help them understand why their body is changing.

- Remind them of family rules about private parts.
- Talk about girl- and boy-specific puberty things (for girls: periods, hair, bigger breasts, body odor; for boys: voices, wet dreams, erections, hair, body odor).
- Talk about what those puberty things are for (getting you ready to have a baby if God calls you to it).
- Talk about God's procreative heart for everyone. (He wants all believers to make disciples.)
- Remind them you will be with them every step of the way.
- Ask if they have questions throughout and at the end.

The Script

"Hey, I am going to share something with you about how your body is going to change in the next couple of years."

Wait and listen to see if they need or want to say anything.

"Do you know how boys and girls are created differently? How are they created differently?"

Wait, listen, and correct gently if they say something that isn't quite right.

"Have you heard about how babies are created?"

Wait and listen to what they have to say. Agree with anything they say that's right. No need to get nitpicky if they are slightly off. This is a tender topic, and you are about to teach what is true.

"God created moms and dads so cool and so different. You know that mamas are the ones to have the baby, but do you know how the baby gets in there?"

Listen.

"Well, God created mom's and dad's private parts to fit together."

Let them react. Don't correct their emotion but empathize while still leading.

"After moms and dads get married, they 'have sex.'"

Pause; listen; ask if they have heard that word.

"The mom and dad bring their private parts together. The dad puts his penis inside the mom's vagina, and sperm comes out of him. The sperm then goes into the mom's uterus, which is inside her tummy."

Ask, "How do you feel about what I just said?" Then listen. Respond empathetically. Answer questions.

Next, add something about the timing of sex: "You do not have to worry about it or think about it now. If God calls you to marriage, he will put a desire for closeness with your spouse inside your heart, but you don't have to want to do that now. I just want you to know about this, because it's part of how God made the world, and because your body is already preparing to turn into an adult body that could one day make a baby—if God calls you to it."

This is where a parent could end the conversation and come back to it another day if the child is overwhelmed. If not, the parent could show a children's puberty book with pictures that are not graphic but are clear about what happens inside the mom's body.

"Sperm look like little tadpoles, and they swim and find an egg that's in the mom, and together one sperm and one egg form a baby. What do you think about that?"

Listen. Respond. Then, depending on how they seem to be feeling, save this or gently address that people can choose to have sex outside of marriage.

"This is only something for you to do if God has called you to marriage. God wants people to do this in the safety of a promise. (Moms and dads vow or make a promise at the wedding.) God doesn't want adults to have sex if they are not married, but some people choose to disobey God and do that." Say this with grief and tenderness.

Listen. Respond. Explain more if needed. Then, go back to the gospel.

"Remember that marriage is something Jesus calls some of us to—and if he calls you to get married, he'll help you understand this part of marriage when it's time. If he calls you to stay single, that will be good too! Either way, we can trust Jesus with this part of how our bodies work."

Before talking about puberty, address body safety and family rules.

"You remember our family rules that we don't touch, see, or show private parts to anyone? Private parts are special for marriage, and for now we are to keep them clean and safe."

Listen, answer questions, empathize.

For Girls

"When you turn ten, eleven, or twelve your brain says, 'Oh! It's time to grow up! I want to prepare to possibly have a baby someday, if God calls me to it.' At this time, your body starts to turn from a little girl into a young woman. That time is called 'puberty.' Have you ever heard that word?"

Listen.

"Because you're not old enough to get married and have a baby yet, your body flushes out the lining of the uterus—the cozy little room inside your lower belly where the baby would grow—and gets it ready for the next month. When it cleans it out, you have what's called a period."

Moms, share your own age when you had your first period. Dads or male caregivers, mention a female friend and their age when they started puberty. "Women usually have periods every month until you are married and ready to have a baby. Yeah. Blood will come out of the middle hole in your private area—your vagina. But you are not dying. You are not sick. It's just cleaning out your insides. And don't worry at all; they make special pads to put in your underwear to keep you clean."

Listen. Respond. Show them a nongraphic kids' book that can help illustrate these words if it would help.

"I know. It's pretty intense, isn't it? What are you thinking?"

Listen. Empathize. If they have questions you don't know the answer to, tell her it's a great question, do some research, and circle back. Then go back to the gospel.

"Do you remember the purpose of marriage?"

Listen for something like, "The purpose of marriage is to show the world a picture of how much God loves me."

"Yup! And your body is getting ready to be married if that's what God calls you to. Every time you have a period, you can remember, 'This is my body getting ready to potentially make babies someday. Maybe I'll get married and have babies with my husband, or maybe I'll adopt kids, or maybe God will call me to be single and God will want me to focus on making disciples.[1] No matter what, I get to be part of what God does in creating new life, wherever I am.' What do you think?"

Listen, then go back to biology specifics.

"As you get older, you are also going to get taller. Your breasts will grow bigger, your body will grow hair under your armpits and on your legs . . . and even around your private area. You're also going to start needing deodorant. Let's get some together! And we can put pads in your backpack just in case. I'll show you how to use them."

Listen. Respond.

"I know this is a lot. But remember that I am going to be with you through this. I am going to be here for you. What are you thinking? What questions do you have?"

Listen. Respond. End when they are ready to end.

For Boys

"Have you heard that when boys get older, their voices get lower?"

Listen.

Dads, share your own age when your voice changed. Moms or female caregivers, mention a male friend and their age when they started puberty. Then say, "Well, when you turn ten, eleven, or fourteen, your brain says, 'Oh! It's time to grow up!' Your body starts to turn from a little boy into a young man. That time is called 'puberty.' Have you ever heard that word?"

Listen. Respond.

"Part of that process of turning from a young boy into an adult man is your voice deepening."

Ask if they have heard about that, listen, and respond.

"But God is also getting you ready to help make a baby someday—if he calls you to it when you are an adult man. Because you're not old enough to get married yet and can't help make a baby, your body practices while you sleep. You might wake up some morning and feel like your sheets are wet and it's not from pee. That's not your fault. It's called a 'wet dream.' You're not doing something wrong; you can just put your things in the laundry basket, change, no problem. No big deal."

Wait. Listen. Ask if he has questions and answer them. If you don't know the answer, tell him it's a great question, do some research, and circle back.

Consider mentioning erections next. Erections should be discussed starting around age three or four, as they can happen even in babies—without ejaculation. But it might also be helpful to talk about them here.

"Sometimes, when you're sleeping or even sitting down, your penis might get hard and stick up. Have you ever had that happen? It's normal, too. You didn't do anything wrong. It's blood rushing to the tip of your penis that makes it do that. That's part of growing up and of being a man. Just wait or walk around, and eventually it will relax again and you can go on with your day."

Listen. Empathize. Then go back to the gospel.

"Do you remember the purpose of marriage?"

Listen for something like, "The purpose of marriage is to show the world a picture of how much God loves me."

"Yup! And your body is getting ready to be married if that's what God calls you to do. Every time you wake up with a wet dream, you can remember, 'This is my body getting ready to potentially make babies someday. Maybe I'll get married and have babies with my wife, or maybe I'll adopt kids, or maybe God will call me to be single and God will want me to focus on making disciples. No matter what, I get to be part of what God does in creating new life, wherever I am.' What do you think?"

Listen. Then, go back to biology specifics.

"During puberty, you are going to get bigger! You will grow taller, and your penis will get bigger. You're going to get hairy like me [or name a male mentor if you are a female caregiver]! And stinky like me!"

Listen. Answer questions.

"Hey, this is a lot. But I want you to know that I am going to be with you through this. I am going to be here for you. What are you thinking? What questions do you have?"

Listen. Respond. End when they are ready to end.

APPENDIX B

What If We Suspect Something Sexually Abusive Has Happened to Our Kids?

If anyone causes one of these little ones . . . to stumble, it would be better for them to have a large millstone hung around their neck and to be drowned in the depths of the sea.
JESUS, MATTHEW 18:6 NIV

WHAT DO IF WE SUSPECT SOMETHING has happened to our kids that is beyond normal childhood curiosity and play? Here is what would spark my wondering: If I heard my child allude to something that "might have happened," or their once bubbly personality changed quickly to sullen, their usually picky eating turned to fasting, or they had persistent stomachaches or night terrors. I would ask open-ended, curious questions to hear if what happened was in the category of "normal" play or something else, and I would reach out to a trusted trauma therapist for children to help me officially discern.[1] It is always wise to have a professional opinion (or two) clarify "normal" and "abnormal" behavior, as most of us parents were not trained to know the difference.

Then what? No matter what our child says, we need to believe them. The research shows that children almost never make up stories about being sexually abused.[2] They may not reveal it right away for various reasons, but rarely (less than 5 percent of the time) do they lie.[3]

Next, we need to put our own triggers and suffering aside and attune to our kids. We can receive care later. They need care now.

Research shows that kids long for comfort after something as blatant as a sexual violation (of course they do), and if the parent is overly distressed, it can exacerbate the child's ability to process. This can lead to heightened levels of emotional and behavioral problems, including PTSD and depression.[4] Furthermore, if our lack of calmness escalates to leaning on our kids to comfort us in this time, our kids can experience long-term suffering.[5]

Let's focus a bit more on how we can begin to discern the severity of what happened as we are scheduling with a professional trauma therapist. First, ask open-ended questions, such as, "What happened?" or "What exactly did they do?" If I'm sensing that they are withholding something, I'll ask something like, "Did they do anything to make you feel uncomfortable?" If a child were to mention touching, I wouldn't ask directly about private parts but ask, "Where did they touch you? Circle with one finger everywhere on your body they touched you." And, "Did they ask you to touch them? Can you circle on me where you did that?"

After that, if their response was unclear, I would ask about body parts in a series: "Did they touch your shoulder? Your butt? Your knee? Your private parts?" No matter their response, if there was an uncomfortable boundary crossing of any kind, I would say, "I am so sorry that happened to you. That is not right." Even "normal" play is not necessarily healthy. If my kid was the one who initiated the play, I would tenderly review our family rules about not touching, looking at, laughing at, or asking to see another's private parts.[6]

If my questioning revealed not an innocent situation but a suspicion that my child had been subjected to more concerning behavior—perhaps by someone at school, the gym, or church—my follow-up would escalate. For example, let's say that after school one of my girls said, "A boy touched my private parts when we were playing a game. I think it was an accident. But then he laughed at me when I said not to do that."

I would show her I was taking the situation seriously. I would call or email the person in charge to share what my child told me, ask for clarity, and inquire about the plan for follow-up. If it seemed worthy, I would call administrators, medical providers, and even the police. When it comes to protecting and caring for our kids, over-responding is better than under-responding. No matter what, I would contact a mental health provider to help me discern wise next steps.

Another situation parents may encounter is a son saying something like, "This girl likes me, and she keeps hugging me."

I would first ask how he feels. Likely, he's confused ("Am I supposed to like that?"). I'd say calmly but strongly, "Honey, that is not okay. No one should hug you when you don't want to be hugged. They should ask first. She crossed your boundaries. I am so sorry. How do you feel?"

After listening, attuning, and sympathizing, I would tell him what happens next. I want him to know I will defend him. I will stand up for his body. I will believe him.

"I am going to talk with your teacher about that, because it is not okay."

Then I'd email or call the teacher, saying something to the effect of: "This happened. I am not okay if my child's boundaries are crossed even if someone likes him. We practice asking for hugs before touching. I trust you will take care of this. Please let me know the follow-up."

If they were to sweep it under the rug or say, "She probably has a crush on him!" that is not walking in the way of Jesus, who defends the helpless and stands up for the oppressed. So they would lose trust with me. If they were flippant about the situation, or if the hugging kept happening even after several conversations, I would reach out to administrators, and if they responded similarly, I might pull my kid from the class or institution.[7]

What if my child is exhibiting signs of extreme distress or reporting that someone is engaging in the "very abnormal" behaviors we discussed in chapter ten? My immediate response would initially sound the same as in the other situations: I would listen to my child tenderly, offer compassion and care, tell my child I was going to follow up, and ask a therapist for help discerning. However, I would not follow up with the offender or even the institution directly. I would immediately go to something like a child advocacy center, the police, and/or a medical professional.[8]

Let me say that more clearly: If our children are showing major symptoms of distress and disclose a situation of abuse, we need to believe them and go to the authorities. Even if the offense happened in a church, abuse is abuse. Even if another adult is saying, "Nothing happened!" bring in another party for help. Adults often lie. Kids don't.[9] In believing them and getting them help, we are shaping our child's future story about what happened. Instead of a narrative of neglect, they can say, "My mom and dad did everything they could to get me healed and for justice to be served. I hate what happened, but the aftercare was what I needed."

If any of the above happened to one of my kids, outside of their therapy sessions I would invite them to journal their feelings by coloring dark colors with me, saying, "This stinks so much! I am so mad!" We could also punch a pillow together to "get our mad out." Or, if they are old enough, write to Jesus telling him how they feel about what happened. I would be very gentle and not push this process and be sure to surround it with lots of play and normal family fun. But if our kids are angry and hurting, inviting them to get it out with you by their side and Jesus before them can be very healing.

Finally, forgiveness is an important part in this process, but it must not be rushed or pressured. Our kids may need to wait until adulthood to truly process it all. When they are young, however, I would say things like, "When they did that, they shot an arrow in you. What does that arrow say to you? 'You are worthless?' 'You don't matter?'" (Help them name the language of the lie.) "Let's take that arrow-lie out of you and give it to Jesus. He died for that lie. You are valuable. You matter so much." And then we would physically act out pulling the "arrow" from our bodies and say, "We give this lie to Jesus! We believe what is true!" And then we would speak the truth together. I have found this practice to be very healing for my kids no matter how they have experienced someone sinning against them.

Okay, guys, that's it. This is heavy, but I'm happy to be a fellow mom in the trenches trying to discern how to love and protect these kids like Jesus loves and protects us.

APPENDIX C

Where Should I Send My Kids to School?

THIS FEELS LIKE A TRICK QUESTION.
Laurie: *Tries to answer it with a definitive answer.*
Laurie: *Dies.*
Y'all, I am brave but not stupid. So I am not going to try to answer this definitively, but rather my aim is to offer a framework for thinking about school systems for our kids.

The Research

The research around school choices does not show much of a longitudinal difference between public and private/religious school kids. An examination of the social, physical, and mental health trends of twelve thousand children through adulthood found that those who went to private school were only marginally more likely to register to vote, less likely to be obese, and more likely to have fewer sexual partners by the time they became young adults.[1] On the other hand, they were slightly more likely to engage in excessive drinking, and another study found that teens are 21 percent more likely to see pornography in a private school than they are in public school.[2]

The benefits of homeschooling do shine through the studies. (I hear you homeschooling parents saying, "I told you!") Homeschoolers were 51 percent more likely to attend religious services frequently, and they were also more likely to volunteer, forgive others, and possess a sense of mission and purpose; they had notably fewer lifetime sexual partners. They were also 23 percent less likely to attend college. As much as it may seem like home-schooling is the clear winner from this study, a study cannot measure a heart. God knows the best place that will help our kids love Jesus and love their neighbor from the heart.

Our Kids Need Good Wind and Good Soil

When I think about choosing a school for our kids, I think about trees. As we discussed in the introduction, social psychologist Jonathan Haidt reports that kids are similar to trees—they can have the perfect amount of sunlight, nutrients, and water in their soil, but without wind, many will fall over and die from their own weight.[3] Researcher Nassim Taleb coined the term *antifragile* to describe things that need to bump up against other things to get stronger.[4] Wine glasses and windows break when they bump up against things, but trees, our immune systems, our muscles, and kids are antifragile. They need challenge in order to grow strong.

"Children are intrinsically antifragile, which is why overprotected children are more likely to become adolescents who are stuck in defend mode," Haidt says. "In defend mode, they're likely to learn less, have fewer close friends, be more anxious, and experience more pain from ordinary conversations and conflicts."[5] Kids need good soil and the right amount of wind in order to thrive as adults.

A biblical way we could look at this is they need a balance of "love God" and "love your neighbor." Or a balance of "being with God" and "being on mission with God." When our kids are infants, their entire life is "be." There is very little wind other than learning to sleep and eat. (For some of us parents, this still feels like too much—for them and us!) As infants grow, they start to experience more of the missional life as they spend time with a babysitter. As they enter school years, they start to meet kids who aren't Christians and go to activities with people who don't know Jesus. The wind picks up, but hopefully they have enough muscles to withstand it. By the time they are ready for college or career, they have hopefully found a beautiful balance of experiencing wind versus receiving good nutrients (but truly, that is a lifelong battle).

As we consider schools for our kids, the soil-wind equation is a helpful lens with which to view the options. How "on mission" do they need to be right now, and how much "receiving love, truth, and nutrients" do they need right now?

Public school parents, if we have our kids in a public school all day, are we ensuring they are getting enough of the filling/receiving/love-fueling side of life to balance out a life on mission? Are we intentionally helping our kids process what they see and hear there? Are we volunteering and caring for the staff and administration so we can, one, be like Jesus, and two, earn relational equity with the administration in case there are serious conversations that need to be had in the future? If the wind is becoming a hurricane, can we pivot classrooms? Switch to another school in the district? Is there a charter school option to consider?

Homeschool parents, are we ensuring our kids are getting enough of the missional/giving/doing side of participating in the kingdom of God? Are we intentionally looking for opportunities for our kids to experience the world's missional wind? If not, in what creative ways can we help our kids grow to become the strong men and women of God we pray they will be?

Christian school parents, where are our kids in the equation? Is their school truly growing them? Are we intentionally pouring nutrients into their soil at home, or are we depending too much on the school to do the job for us? Are they experiencing enough wind to grow their roots and become the missional people of God he wants them to be?

How We Can Think Through School Choices

With that, here is a more specific list of questions we can ask ourselves about where to educate our kids:

- How is God asking us to steward our finances? (If we can't afford Christian school, that is likely not an option for us. And if God is calling us to homeschool, someone will likely not be able to work. Can we afford that?)
- How is God asking us to steward our time? (Is he asking one of us to stay home with the kids and homeschool? Is he asking both of us to work outside the home, so that we need to look at options other than homeschool?)
- What are the school systems like in our area? How godly or ungodly are they?
- Who can we ask to understand more about the schooling options in our area? (Are there co-ops for homeschooling? Are there friends I know in the Christian schools who could help me decide? Are there Christians who have their kids in public school I could talk to?)
- What is the "If this happens, we will make a different schooling decision" line for us?
- What are the social, academic, and extracurricular activities available at the school system we're considering? How much do we prioritize each area? (If our child really wants to play soccer or orchestra for their school, but that is not an option, how important is that to our decision-making? If our child needs specific help with their neurological or emotional needs, do they offer that?)
- If we are married, what does our spouse say? What do our friends recommend? What about our mentors, spiritual advisers, and pastors?
- What is God prompting us to do this year?
- That final question is the one that relieves stress for me. It lets me say, "I can change my mind at any time." We currently have two of our kids in public school and one in Christian school, and we hold it all with open hands. We are

listening for sounds of good wind, as well as wind that has become a hurricane. Our kids are God's, and we want to be prayerful and intentional about where they can be best formed into the image of Christ and as they get equipped for the mission God has prepared for them long ago (Eph 2:10).

NOTES

Introduction

[1] *A Political and Cultural Glimpse into America's Future: Generation Z's Views on Generational Change and the Challenges and Opportunities Ahead,* Public Religion Research Institute, January 2024, www.prri.org/wp-content /uploads/2024/01/PRRI-Jan-2024-Gen-Z-Draft.pdf.

[2] "Religious Dating Sites: More than Half of Users Surveyed Are OK with Premarital Sex," *Relevant,* January 27, 2014, http://relevantmagazine.com/slices /religious-dating-sites-more-half-users-surveyed-are-ok-premarital-sex.

[3] Maria Baer, "More Christians Are Watching Porn, but Fewer Think It's a Problem," *Christianity Today,* www.christianitytoday.com/2024/09/pornography -use-christians-study-barna-research-pure-desire-ministries.

[4] Lorena Taboas, "New Report Reveals Truths About How Teens Engage with Pornography," Common Sense Media, January 10, 2023, www.common sensemedia.org/press-releases/new-report-reveals-truths-about-how-teens-engage -with-pornography.

[5] As quoted by Abigail Favale in *The Genesis of Gender: A Christian Theory* (Ignatius, 2022), 167. See also "Regional Model for Gender Care Announced for Children and Young People," The Tavistock and Portman NHS Foundation Trust, NHS, July 28, 2022, http://tavistockandportman.nhs.uk/news/regional -model-for-gender-care-announced-for-children-and-young-people.

[6] *The National Intimate Partner and Sexual Violence Survey,* National Center for Injury Prevention and Control, Centers for Disease Control and Prevention, 2016 2017, www.cdc.gov/nisvs/documentation/nisvsReportonSexualViolence .pdf.

[7] Laurie Krieg and Matt Krieg, *An Impossible Marriage: What Our Mixed-Orientation Marriage Has Taught Us About Love and the Gospel* (InterVarsity Press, 2020).

[8] Dan Pilat and Sekoul Krastev, "Why Do We Compare Everything to the First Piece of Information We Received?" The Decision Lab, copyright 2025, http:// thedecisionlab.com/biases/anchoring-bias.

[9] Jonathan Haidt, *The Anxious Generation* (Penguin, 2024), 70-72.

[10] Haidt, *Anxious Generation,* 72.

[11] Haidt, *Anxious Generation,* 75.

[12] Taboas, "New Report Reveals."

[13] "How Porn Can Normalize Sexual Objectification," Fight the New Drug, copyright 2025, https://fightthenewdrug.org/how-porn-can-normalize-sexual -objectification.

[14] Taboas, "New Report Reveals."

1. The Gospel: Lay the Foundation

[1] Vivek H. Murthy, "Parents Under Pressure: The U.S. Surgeon General's Advisory on the Mental Health and Well-Being of Parents," Office of the Surgeon General,

U.S. Department of Health and Human Services, 2024, www.hhs.gov/surgeon general/reports-and-publications/parents/index.html.

2 Murthy, "Parents Under Pressure."

3 Murthy, "Parents Under Pressure."

4 Daniel J. Ebert IV, "The Wisdom of God," The Gospel Coalition, copyright 2025, www.thegospelcoalition.org/essay/the-wisdom-of-god.

5 Douglas J. Moo, *The Letters to the Colossians and to Philemon*, Pillar New Testament Commentary (Eerdmans, 2008), 170.

6 Tim Keller, "The Freedom of True Love," Gospel in Life, September 21, 2003, https://gospelinlife.com/downloads/the-freedom-of-true-love-5327.

7 Christopher West with Laurie Krieg, "Episode 80: Fill These Hearts," *Hole in My Heart Podcast*, June 29, 2019, https://lauriekrieg.com/podcast/fill-these-hearts.

8 Cornelius Plantinga, *Not the Way It's Supposed to Be: A Breviary of Sin* (Eerdmans, 1995), 10.

9 Scot McKnight, *The King Jesus Gospel* (Zondervan, 2016), 138.

10 McKnight, *King Jesus Gospel*, 138.

2. The Gospel: Walk the Foundation

1 Callie L. Brown et al., "Eating Family Meals Together at Home," JAMA Pediatrics Patient Page, March 25, 2024, https://jamanetwork.com/journals/jama pediatrics/fullarticle/2816155.

2 Ying Chen et al., "Religious-Service Attendance and Subsequent Health and Wellbeing Throughout Adulthood: Evidence from Three Prospective Cohorts," *International Journal of Epidemiology* 49, no. 6 (December 2020): 2030-40, https://academic.oup.com/ije/article/49/6/2030/5892419#.

3 N. T. Wright, *Simply Good News: Why the Gospel Is News and What Makes It Good* (HarperOne, 2017), 99.

3. Marriage and Singleness: Lay the Foundation

1 Tim Keller, "The Freedom of True Love," Gospel in Life, September 21, 2003, https://gospelinlife.com/downloads/the-freedom-of-true-love-5327.

2 See Laurie Krieg and Matt Krieg, *An Impossible Marriage: What Our Mixed-Orientation Marriage Has Taught Us About Love and the Gospel* (InterVarsity Press, 2020), 14-15. The entire book is a story-driven argument for God's design for marriage and sex in marriage.

3 See Courtenay E. Cavanaugh et al., "Experiences of Mothers Who Are Child Sexual Abuse Survivors: A Qualitative Exploration," *Journal of Child Sexual Abuse* 24, no. 5 (2015): 506-25, www.ncbi.nlm.nih.gov/pmc/articles /PMC5933442 and Patricia Grisafi, "Mothers Who've Suffered Abuse and Trauma Can Be Triggered by Their Toddlers. What to Do," Think, NBC News, August 21, 2021, www.nbcnews.com/think/opinion/mothers-who-ve-suffered -abuse-trauma-can-be-triggered-their-ncna1277326.

4 Christopher West, *Fill These Hearts: God, Sex, and the Universal Longing* (Image, 2013), 92.

5 N. T. Wright (@ntwrightonline), "From @premierradio's 'Ask NT Wright Anything' podcast with @justin.brierley," Instagram Reel, August 22, 2022, www .instagram.com/reel/ChkJb5igNUj.

6 Dani Treweek with Laurie Krieg, "Episode 213: The Value of Singleness," *Hole in My Heart Podcast*, January 12, 2024, https://lauriekrieg.com/podcast/episode-213-the-value-of-singleness-with-dani-treweek.

7 Stanley Hauerwas, *A Community of Character: Toward a Constructive Christian Social Ethic* (University of Notre Dame Press, 1981), 174, 190.

8 "A Survey of LGBT Americans: Chapter 3: The Coming Out Experience," Pew Research Center, June 13, 2013, www.pewresearch.org/social-trends/2013/06/13/chapter-3-the-coming-out-experience.

9 Jay Stringer and Heather Stringer, "Body Talks" seminar, The Journey Course, June 1, 2024, www.thejourneycourse.com/courses/bodytalks.

10 "These Neurons Are the Reason You Yawn when You See Others Do It, and They Could Help Us Teach Children More Creatively Too," NeuroscienceNews.com, April 2, 2023, https://neurosciencenews.com/mirror-neurons-empathy-creativity-22921.

11 Sarah Epstein, "The Long-Term Harm of Emotional Parentification," Between the Generations (blog), *Psychology Today*, May 23, 2023, www.psychologytoday.com/us/blog/between-the-generations/202305/were-you-your-parents-therapist.

12 See, for example, Leon F. Seltzer, "What Your Anger May Be Hiding," Evolution of the Self (blog), *Psychology Today*, July 11, 2008, www.psychologytoday.com/us/blog/evolution-of-the-self/200807/what-your-anger-may-be-hiding.

4. Marriage and Singleness: Walk the Foundation

1 "Sticky Faith Parents: Building Lifelong Faith," Fuller Youth Institute, copyright 2025, https://fulleryouthinstitute.org/stickyfaith/parents.

2 Kara Powell et al., "The Church Sticking Together," *Lifelong Faith*, Spring 2012, www.intergenerationalfaith.com/uploads/5/1/6/4/5164069/the_church_sticking_together.pdf.

3 "Sticky Faith Parents."

4 Powell et al., "The Church Sticking Together." See also Erika C. Knuth, "Intergenerational Connections and Faith Development in Late Adolescence" (unpublished doctoral diss., Fuller Theological Seminary, 2010).

5 "Marriages and Divorces," Our World in Data, revised February 2025, https://ourworldindata.org/marriages-and-divorces.

6 Anna Harris, "Global Marriage Statistics: Trends, Patterns, and Insights," Online MFT Programs, March 19, 2025, https://onlinemftprograms.com/worldwide-marriage-statistics.

7 The fact that spiritual children are valuable does not negate the earlier argument about God's desire for physical children to be born and created into this world.

8 This question can get blurry when we are talking about sex with our older kids (ages eight to ten). Isn't every description of sex explicit or graphic? We can talk about sex with our kids without talking sexually. More on this in later chapters.

9 Miran Lavrič and Andrej Naterer, "The Power of Authoritative Parenting: A Cross-National Study of Effects of Exposure to Different Parenting Styles on Life Satisfaction," *Children and Youth Services Review* 116 (September 2020): 105274, www.sciencedirect.com/science/article/abs/pii/S0190740920 30918X.

10 See appendix C for more thoughts on how we can choose schools.

[11] We have other boundaries on shows and books such as swearing (we have a three-strikes and we won't watch it rule), rudeness, disrespect of parents or others (without resolving it), racism, celebration of greed, or generally consuming things that are antibiblical, we will turn it off too. I am simply highlighting how we engage sexual sin.

[12] Emily Falk, "Why Storytelling Is an Important Tool for Social Change," *Los Angeles Times,* June 27, 2021, www.latimes.com/opinion/story/2021-06-27/stories -brain-science-memory-social-change.

5. Gender: Lay the Foundation

[1] Becky Kennedy, *Good Inside: A Guide to Becoming the Parent You Want to Be* (Harper Wave 2022), 97.

[2] Dan Siegel and Tina Payne Bryson, *The Whole Brain Child: 12 Revolutionary Strategies to Nurture Your Child's Developing Mind* (Bantam, 2012), 29.

[3] Kennedy, *Good Inside,* 97.

[4] Matthew Mason, "A Theological and Pastoral Response to Gender Dysphoria," in *Cultural Engagement: A Crash Course in Contemporary Issues,* ed. Joshua D. Chatraw and Karen Swallow Prior (Zondervan, 2019), 90-92.

[5] Mark A. Yarhouse and Julia Sadusky, "A Christian Psychological Assessment of Gender Dysphoria," in *Cultural Engagement,* ed. Joshua D. Chatraw and Karen Swallow Prior (Zondervan, 2019), 93-99.

[6] Mark Yarhouse, *Talking to Kids About Gender Identity* (Bethany House, 2023), 19.

[7] Jeffrey M. Jones, "LGBTQ+ Identification in U.S. Now at 7.6 percent," Gallup, March 13, 2024, https://news.gallup.com/poll/611864/lgbtq-identification.aspx.

[8] As quoted by Abigail Favale in *The Genesis of Gender: A Christian Theory* (Ignatius, 2022), 167. See also "Regional Model for Gender Care Announced for Children and Young People," The Tavistock and Portman NHS Foundation Trust, NHS, July 28, 2022, http://tavistockandportman.nhs.uk/news /regional-model-for-gender-care-announced-for-children-and-young-people.

[9] Robin Respaut and Chad Terhune, "Putting Numbers on the Rise in Children Seeking Gender Care," Youth in Transition, Reuters, October 6, 2022, www .reuters.com/investigates/special-report/usa-transyouth-data.

[10] Lisa Littman, "Parent Reports of Adolescents and Young Adults Perceived to Show Signs of a Rapid Onset of Gender Dysphoria," PLOS One, August 16, 2018, https:// journals.plos.org/plosone/article?id=10.1371/journal.pone.0202330.

[11] *A Political and Cultural Glimpse into America's Future: Generation Z's Views on Generational Change and the Challenges and Opportunities Ahead,* Public Religion Research Institute, January 2024, www.prri.org/wp-content/uploads /2024/01/PRRI-Jan-2024-Gen-Z-Draft.pdf.

[12] "Gender Identities Explained: Everything You Need To Know," Rainbow & Co., June 9, 2021, https://rainbowandco.uk/blogs/what-were-saying /gender-identities-what-you-need-to-know.

[13] For more, read Yarhouse, *Talking to Kids,* 21-24.

[14] In 2011, 77 percent of American teens had a phone but just 23 percent had a smartphone. By 2016, 79 percent of teens had a smartphone, as well as 28 percent of kids ages eight to twelve. Jonathan Haidt, *The Anxious Generation* (Penguin, 2024), 32-34.

[15] Haidt, *Anxious Generation,* 119. Haidt also notes that LGBTQ youth spend an extra three hours per day on their phones compared with their cisgender, heterosexual counterparts (315).

[16] Haidt, *Anxious Generation,* 175.

[17] Haidt, *Anxious Generation,* 155.

[18] Haidt, *Anxious Generation,* 43.

[19] "Like people with heroin and cocaine addictions, those addicted to digital activities found that 'nothing feels good anymore' when they were not doing their preferred activity. The reason is that the brain adapts to long periods of elevated dopamine by changing itself in a variety of ways to maintain homeostasis." Haidt, *Anxious Generation,* 58.

[20] See KK Pitchers et al., "DeltaFosB in the Nucleus Accumbens Is Critical for Reinforcing Effects of Sexual Reward," *Genes, Brain, and Behavior* 9 (2010): 831-40; Aline Wéry and J. Billieux, "Online Sexual Activities: An Exploratory Study of Problematic and Non-problematic Usage Patterns in a Sample of Men," *Computers in Human Behavior* 56 (March 2016): 257-66; and Simone Kühn and Jürgen Gallinat, "Brain Structure and Functional Connectivity Associated with Pornography Consumption: The Brain on Porn," *JAMA Psychiatry* 71, no. 7 (2014): 827-34.

[21] Ingrid Solano et al., "Pornography Consumption, Modality and Function in a Large Internet Sample," *Journal of Sex Research* 57, no. 1 (2020): 92-103.

[22] Daniel A. Cox et al., "Politics, Sex, and Sexuality: The Growing Gender Divide in American Life," Survey Center on American Life, April 27, 2022, www.americansurveycenter.org/research/march-2022-aps.

[23] "National Survey Reveals 73 percent of Teens Have Seen Porn—Many Watching It at School," Fight the New Drug, copyright 2025, https://fightthenewdrug.org/national-survey-reveals-73-of-teens-have-seen-porn-many-watching-it-at-school.

[24] "2023 State of Deepfakes," Security Hero, August 29, 2023, www.securityhero.io/state-of-deepfakes.

[25] *How AI Is Being Abused to Create Child Sexual Abuse Imagery,* Internet Watch Foundation, October 2023, www.iwf.org.uk/media/q4zll2ya/iwf-ai-csam-report_public-oct23v1.pdf; "State of Deepfakes," Security Hero.

[26] Maria Baer, "More Christians Are Watching Porn, but Fewer Think It's a Problem," *Christianity Today,* September 26, 2024, www.christianitytoday.com/2024/09/pornography-use-christians-study-barna-research-pure-desire-ministries; Michal Privara and Petr Bob, "Pornography Consumption and Cognitive-Affective Distress," *The Journal of Nervous and Mental Disease* 211, no. 8 (August 2023): https://journals.lww.com/jonmd/fulltext/2023/08000/Pornography_Consumption_and_Cognitive_Affective.14.aspx.

[27] "How Porn Can Normalize Sexual Objectification," Fight the New Drug, copyright 2025, https://fightthenewdrug.org/how-porn-can-normalize-sexual-objectification.

[28] Matt Brzycki, "Gender Differences in Strength: A Comparison of Male and Female World-Record Performances In Powerlifting," Princeton University, 2004, https://brzycki.scholar.princeton.edu/sites/g/files/toruqf4561/files/brzycki/files/mb-2002-01.pdf.

[29] Favale, *Genesis of Gender,* 199.

[30] Favale, *Genesis of Gender*, 199.

[31] Dietrich Bonhoeffer, *Creation and Fall* (Fortress, 1997), 77.

[32] Kelly M. Kapic, *Embodied Hope* (InterVarsity Press, 2017), 50.

[33] Favale, *Genesis of Gender*, 36

[34] Favale, *Genesis of Gender*, 40.

[35] "Intersex Variation," HealthDirect, May 2024, www.healthdirect.gov.au /intersex-variation.

[36] Favale, *Gensis of Gender*, 126-27.

6. Gender: Walk the Foundation

[1] Abigail Favale, *The Genesis of Gender: A Christian Theory* (Ignatius, 2022), 121.

[2] Mark Yarhouse, *Talking to Kids About Gender Identity* (Bethany House, 2023), 68.

[3] Someone can get testosterone at Planned Parenthood now without much vetting.

[4] "A Survey of LGBT Americans: Chapter 3: The Coming Out Experience," Pew Research Center, June 13, 2013, www.pewresearch.org/social-trends/2013/06/13 /chapter-3-the-coming-out-experience.

[5] Andy Crouch, *Culture Making: Recovering Our Creative Calling* (InterVarsity Press, 2013), 23.

[6] Duane Elmer, *Cross-Cultural Servanthood: Serving the World in Christlike Humility* (InterVarsity Press, 2006), 131.

[7] John Lightfoot, *The Whole Works of the Rev. John Lightfoot*, ed. John Rogers Pitman, vol. 12 (J. F. Dove, 1822), 265, www.google.com/books/edition/The _Whole_Works_of_the_Rev_John_Lightfoo/taArStIFd1MC?hl=en&gbpv=1& pg=PA265.

[8] Yarhouse, *Talking to Kids*, 108-9.

7. God's Design for Sex: Lay the Foundation

[1] T. D. Afifi et al., "Why Can't We Just Talk About It? An Observational Study of Parents' and Adolescents' Conversations About Sex," *Journal of Adolescent Research* 23, no. 6 (2008): 689-721. https://doi.org/10.1177/0743558408323841.

[2] Doreen A. Rosenthal and S. Shirley Feldman, "The Importance of Importance: Adolescents' Perceptions of Parental Communication About Sexuality," *Journal of Adolescence* 22, no. 6 (December 1999): 835-51. https://doi.org/10.1006 /jado.1999.0279.

[3] Afifi et al., "Why Can't We?" 690.

[4] Kathleen C. Basile et al., *The National Intimate Partner and Sexual Violence Survey: 2016/2017 Report on Sexual Violence*, National Center for Injury Prevention and Control, Centers for Disease Control and Prevention, June 2022, www.cdc.gov/nisvs/documentation/nisvsReportonSexualViolence.pdf.

[5] Julia Sadusky, *Start Talking to Your Kids About Sex* (Ave Maria Press, 2023), 9.

[6] Linda Padou Burkett, "Parenting Behaviors of Women Who Were Sexually Abused as Children in Their Families of Origin," *Family Process* 30, no. 4 (December 1991): 421-34, https://onlinelibrary.wiley.com/doi/abs/10.1111/j.1545 -5300.1991.00421.x.

[7] Sadusky, *Start Talking*, 139

[8] Jay Stringer, *Unwanted: How Sexual Brokenness Reveals Our Way to Healing* (NavPress, 2018), 39.

9 K.L. Pariera and E. Brody, "'Talk More About It': Emerging Adults' Attitudes About How and When Parents Should Talk About Sex," *Sexuality Research and Social Policy* 15 (2018): 219-29. https://doi.org/10.1007/s13178-017-0314-9.

10 Sheila Wray Gregoire, *She Deserves Better: Raising Girls to Resist Toxic Teachings on Sex, Self, and Speaking Up* (Baker, 2023), 14.

11 Lisa Wade, *American Hookup: The New Culture of Sex on Campus* (W. W. Norton, 2017), 48.

12 Wade, *American Hookup*, 15.

13 Kevin Leman and Kathy Flores Bell, *A Chicken's Guide to Talking Turkey with Your Kids About Sex* (Zondervan, 2009), 18.

14 The lament process has been important for both Matt and me as we teach our kids about sex and sexuality while each carrying our own stories of broken sexuality. As you process your own story, I recommend listening to our *Hole in My Heart Podcast* (https://lauriekrieg.com/podcast); you could start with episode 192. Also helpful are *The Best of You Podcast* with Dr. Alison Cook (www.dralisoncook.com/podcast) and Curt Thompson's *Being Known Podcast* (www.beingknownpodcast.com).

15 Afifi et al., "Why Can't We?" 714.

16 Afifi et al., "Why Can't We?" 704.

17 Afifi et al., "Why Can't We?" 715.

18 Afifi et al., "Why Can't We?" 692.

19 Afifi et al., "Why Can't We?" 692.

20 Vincent Guilamo-Ramos et al., "Parental expertise, trustworthiness, and accessibility: Parent-adolescent communication and adolescent risk behavior," *Journal of Marriage and Family* 68, no. 5 (2006): 1229-46.

21 Jack Stoltzfus, "Am I a 'Good Enough' Parent?" Parents Letting Go, September 5, 2023, https://parentslettinggo.com/am-i-a-good-enough-parent.

22 L. Alan Sroufe, "Then and Now: The Legacy and Future of Attachment Research," *Attachment and Human Development* 23, no. 4 (2021): 396-403. doi: 10.1080/14616734.2021.1918450.

23 Adapted from "The 4 Attachment Styles and How They Impact You," Health Essentials, Cleveland Clinic, September 23, 2022, https://health.clevelandclinic.org/attachment-theory-and-attachment-styles.

24 Anna Zdolska-Wawrzkiewicz et al., "Attachment Styles, Various Maternal Representations and a Bond to a Baby," *International Journal of Environmental Research and Public Health* 17, no. 10 (2020): 3,363. https://doi.org/10.3390/ijerph17103363.

25 See "4 Attachment Styles," Cleveland Clinic, as well as works by Alison Cook and Aundi Kolber.

26 E. Z. Tronick and A. Gianino, "Interactive Mismatch and Repair: Challenges to the Coping Infant," *Zero to Three* 6, no. 3 (1986): 1-6.

27 Diana Divecha, "Family Conflict Is Normal; It's the Repair That Matters," *Greater Good Magazine*, October 27, 2020, https://greatergood.berkeley.edu/article/item/family_conflict_is_normal_its_the_repair_that_matters.

28 Becky Kennedy, *Good Inside: A Guide to Becoming the Parent You Want to Be* (Harper Wave 2022), 53.

29 These are all adapted from Miran Lavrič and Andrej Naterer, "The Power of Authoritative Parenting: A Cross-National Study of Effects of Exposure to

Different Parenting Styles on Life Satisfaction," *Children and Youth Services Review* 116 (September 2020): 105274, https://doi.org/10.1016/j.childyouth.2020.105274.

[30] I realize there are circumstances where such a consummation is not possible due to disability or other reasons. God is sovereign over all.

[31] Tim Keller, "The Gospel and Sex," Gospel in Life, April 27, 2010, https://gospelinlife.com/manual-paper/the-gospel-and-sex.

[32] Branson Parler, *Every Body's Story: 6 Myths About Sex and the Gospel Truth About Marriage and Singleness* (Zondervan, 2022), 171

8. God's Design for Sex: Walk the Foundation

[1] "Begins to Show the Emotion of Embarrassment (19-25 Months)," Parenting Counts, copyright 2025, www.parentingcounts.org/begins-to-show-the-emotion-of-embarrassment-19-25-months.

[2] Did you know that after Acts 21:4, the word *disciple* is not used anywhere in the Bible? Instead, the writers of the Epistles use the language of parenting to help Gentile believers understand what it means to conform to the image of Christ. See 1 Corinthians 4:14-17 as a prime example.

[3] I have single friends who have fostered and adopted kids. This is a beautiful vision of God's adopting us into his family. But I find it unrealistic to explain every single way people can "have kids" to my children every time the subject comes up. Talking about adoption would be a gorgeous way to teach the metaphor of adoption in the Bible, but this was not that conversation. As always, feel free to adopt, adjust, or completely alter my suggestions.

[4] Matthew Halverson, "Puberty Lady Julie Metzger Talks About Sex," *Seattle Met*, March 23, 2012, www.seattlemet.com/news-and-city-life/2012/03/puberty-lady-julie-metzger-talks-about-sex-april-2012.

[5] I first heard this advice from ministry leaders, researchers, and authors Josh Glaser and Daniel Weiss, who wrote *Treading Boldly Through a Pornographic World* (Salem, 2021). You might hear me do a near spit-take when they suggest it in "Episode 180: Helping Kids Navigate a P*rn-Saturated World," *Hole in My Heart Podcast*, September 17, 2021, https://lauriekrieg.com/podcast/helping-kids-navigate-a-porn-saturated-world-with-josh-glaser-daniel-weiss.

[6] Two of the experts who influence my advice in this chapter include Covenant Eyes' Luke Gilkerson, who wrote *The Talk: 7 Lessons to Introduce Your Child to Biblical Sexuality* (CreateSpace Independent Publishing, 2014), and Julia Sadusky, author of *Start Talking to Your Kids about Sex* (Ave Maria Press, 2023). Although the American Academy of Pediatrics does not say it explicitly, experts do talk about puberty beginning at age eight for girls and needing to "start these conversations early." See Brittany Allen and Katy Miller, "Physical Development in Girls: What to Expect During Puberty," HealthyChildren.org, American Academy of Pediatrics, June 4, 2019, www.healthychildren.org/English/ages-stages/gradeschool/puberty/Pages/Physical-Development-Girls-What-to-Expect.aspx.

[7] There has been an increasing phenomenon of early puberty in girls since 2020. Some don't just form breast buds at eight; they get their periods then. See Jessica Winter, "Why More and More Girls Are Hitting Puberty Early," *The New*

Yorker, October 27, 2022, www.newyorker.com/science/annals-of-medicine/why-more-and-more-girls-are-hitting-puberty-early.

8 Jasmine Reese, "The Stages of Puberty for Girls," Johns Hopkins Medicine, copyright 2025, www.hopkinsmedicine.org/health/wellness-and-prevention/the-stages-of-puberty-for-girls; Allen and Miller, "Physical Development in Girls."

9 "Puberty," Cleveland Clinic, August 26, 2024, https://my.clevelandclinic.org/health/body/puberty.

10 Charles E. Schaefer and Theresa Foy DiGeronimo, *Ages and Stages: A Parent's Guide to Normal Childhood Development* (John Wiley & Sons, 2000), 195; Gilkerson also talks about this tendency in *The Talk,* 9-10.

11 Schaefer and DiGeronimo, *Ages and Stages,* 190.

12 Schaefer and DiGeronimo, *Ages and Stages,* 170, 200.

13 Emily Nagoski, *Come as You Are: The Bestselling Guide to the New Science that Will Transform Your Sex Life* (Simon & Schuster, 2015), 226, 237-8. Find more about Sam's ebook here: www.samjolman.com/the-sex-talk-you-never-got-book.

14 Sadusky is especially tender toward parents in *Start Talking*; see page 20, for example.

15 Maureen C. Kenny and Sandy K. Wurtele, "Toward Prevention of Childhood Sexual Abuse: Preschoolers' Knowledge of Genital Body Parts," in *Proceedings of the Seventh Annual College of Education Research Conference: Urban and International Education Section,* ed. M. S. Plakhotnik and S. M. Nielsen (Florida International University, 2008), 74-9. https://digitalcommons.fiu.edu/cgi/viewcontent.cgi?article=1121&context=sferc.

16 For example, see Robbie H. Harris's bestselling kids' book *It's Not the Stork* (Candlewick, 2008).

17 Strong's Lexicon, "2588. kardia," copyright 2021, https://biblehub.com/greek/2588.htm; A. Craig Troxel, "One of the Most Misused Words Today," Crossway, February 21, 2020, www.crossway.org/articles/one-of-the-most-misused-words-today.

18 I have already mentioned this, but it's worth repeating that sex is not only for creating babies. It is a covenant renewal ceremony that produces fruit—one of which (ideally) is children. Other fruits are intimacy, connectedness, etc.

19 From my friend and adoptive dad Andrew Klum, email exchange, October 12, 2024. Shared with permission.

20 Dan Siegel and Tina Payne Bryson, *The Whole Brain Child: 12 Revolutionary Strategies to Nurture Your Child's Developing Mind* (Bantam, 2012), 24.

21 Becky Kennedy, *Good Inside: A Guide to Becoming the Parent You Want to Be* (Harper Wave 2022), 33.

22 Some people recommend having these talks in the car or during a walk. For boys especially, having an eye-to-eye conversation can feel threatening. Being side by side can be more comfortable.

23 Louann Brizendine, "Love, Sex and the Male Brain," Opinion, CNN, March 25, 2010, www.cnn.com/2010/OPINION/03/23/brizendine.male.brain.

24 A.-L. Goddings et al., "Puberty and Risky Decision-Making in Male Adolescents," *Developmental Cognitive Neuroscience* 60 (April 2023): 101230. https://doi.org/10.1016/j.dcn.2023.101230.

[25] "Girls and Puberty," FamilyDoctor.org, April 2025, https://familydoctor.org/girls-and-puberty.

[26] A. Angold et al., "Pubertal Changes in Hormone Levels and Depression in Girls," *Psychological Medicine* 29, no. 5 (1999): 1043-53. doi:10.1017/s0033291799008946.

9. Honor Our Bodies: Lay the Foundation

[1] David Finkelhor et al., "The Lifetime Prevalence of Child Sexual Abuse and Sexual Assault Assessed in Late Adolescence," *Journal of Adolescent Health* 55, no. 3 (September 2014): 329-33.

[2] Kathleen C. Basile et al., *The National Intimate Partner and Sexual Violence Survey: 2016/2017 Report on Sexual Violence*, National Center for Injury Prevention and Control, Centers for Disease Control and Prevention, June 2022, www.cdc.gov/nisvs/documentation/nisvsReportonSexualViolence.pdf.

[3] Basile et al., *National Intimate Partner.*

[4] D. B. Allender, *Healing the Wounded Heart: The Heartache of Sexual Abuse and the Hope of Transformation* (Baker, 2016), 36.

[5] Michael H. Keller, "On These Apps, the Dark Promise of Mothers Sexually Abusing Children," *New York Times*, December 8, 2024, www.nytimes.com/2024/12/07/us/child-abuse-apple-google-apps.html.

[6] Even if our kids are not yet a part of the body of Christ (they have not said "yes" to his invitation), the call of Jesus to "love our neighbor as you love yourself" applies to believers and nonbelievers alike (Mk 12:31).

[7] "Rom 12:9-13," in *Moody Bible Commentary* (Moody Publishers, 2014), 1766.

[8] Charlotte M. Handford et al., "The Influence of Maternal Modeling on Body Image Concerns and Eating Disturbances in Preadolescent Girls," *Behaviour Research and Therapy* 100 (2018): 17-23. https://doi.org/10.1016/j.brat.2017.11.001.

[9] Erica Cirino, "What Are the Benefits of Hugging?" Healthline, April 11, 2018, www.healthline.com/health/hugging-benefits.

[10] Julia Sadusky, *Start Talking to Your Kids about Sex* (Ave Maria Press, 2023), 28.

[11] Kevin Collier, "Here's Why You Shouldn't Publicly Post Photos of Your Kid Online," Cyber Dad (blog), June 16, 2024, https://cyberdad.info/p/heres-shouldnt-publicly-post-photos-kid-online.

[12] "2023 State of Deepfakes," Security Hero, August 29, 2023, www.securityhero.io/state-of-deepfakes.

[13] Nicholas Kristof, "The Online Degradation of Women and Girls That We Meet With a Shrug," Opinion, *The New York Times*, March 23, 2024, www.nytimes.com/2024/03/23/opinion/deepfake-sex-videos.html.

[14] Carolyn was trained in a lament and listening prayer process at Healing Care Ministries (see www.healingcare.org).

[15] Ann Voskamp, *The Broken Way: A Daring Path into the Abundant Life* (Zondervan, 2016), 237.

[16] "Fact: What Is a Psalm of Lament?" ESV, Crossway, copyright 2021-2025, www.esv.org/resources/esv-global-study-bible/facts-psalms-6.

[17] Timothy Keller, "Truth, Tears, Anger, and Grace," Timothy Keller Sermons Podcast, Gospel in Life, September 16, 2001, https://podcast.gospelinlife.com/e/truth-tears-anger-and-grace.

10. Honor Our Bodies: Walk the Foundation

1 Alexis Jay et al., "3.2 The Effects of Child Sexual Abuse," in *Interim Report of the Independent Inquiry into Child Sexual Abuse,* April 2018, www.iicsa.org .uk/reports-recommendations/publications/inquiry/interim/nature-effects-child -sexual-abuse/effects-child-sexual-abuse.html.

2 Laurie Krieg with Julia Sadusky, "Episode 223: Protecting Our Kids in This Wild World," *Hole in My Heart Podcast,* May 31, 2024, https://lauriekrieg.com/ podcast/episode-223-protecting-our-kids-in-this-wild-world-with-julia -sadusky.

3 Maureen C. Kenny and Sandy K. Wurtele, "Toward Prevention of Childhood Sexual Abuse: Preschoolers' Knowledge of Genital Body Parts," in *Proceedings of the Seventh Annual College of Education Research Conference: Urban and International Education Section,* ed. M. S. Plakhotnik and S. M. Nielsen (Florida International University, 2008), 74-9. https://digitalcommons.fiu.edu/cgi /viewcontent.cgi?article=1121&context=sferc.

4 Krieg with Sadusky, "Protecting Our Kids."

5 Kenny and Wurtele, "Toward Prevention."

6 Krieg with Sadusky, "Protecting Our Kids." See Michele Elliott et al., "Child Sexual Abuse Prevention: What Offenders Tell Us, *Child Abuse & Neglect* 19, no. 5 (1995): 579-94; and additional research here: www.coffeecountycac.org /tea.

7 Terry Gross with Robert Downen, "How the Southern Baptist Convention Covered Up Its Widespread Sexual Abuse Scandal," Fresh Air, NPR, June 2, 2022, www.npr.org/2022/06/02/1102621352/how-the-southern-baptist-con- vention-covered-up-its-widespread-sexual-abuse-scand; Ruth Graham, "What the Latest Investigations Into Catholic Church Sex Abuse Mean," *The New York Times,* June 2, 2023, www.nytimes.com/2023/06/02/us/catholic-church-sex -abuse-investigations.html.

8 *The National Intimate Partner and Sexual Violence Survey,* National Center for Injury Prevention and Control, Centers for Disease Control and Prevention, 2016-2017, www.cdc.gov/nisvs/documentation/nisvsReportonSexualViolence .pdf.

9 Andy Jones, "Sexcam Therapy," The Face, September 16, 2019, https://theface .com/life/sex-webcam-therapy-porn-addiction.

10 "Studies Show Pornography Changes the Brain," National Center on Sexual Exploitation, January 24, 2022, https://endsexualexploitation.org/articles /pornography-changes-the-brain.

11 V. Bouché, "Survivor Insights: The Role of Technology in Domestic Minor Sex Trafficking," Thorn, January 2018, www.thorn.org/wp-content /uploads/2019/12/Thorn_Survivor_Insights_090519.pdf.

12 M. L. Bourke and A.E. Hernandez, "The 'Butner Study' Redux: A Report of the Incidence of Hands-on Child Victimization by Child Pornography Of- fenders," *Journal of Family Violence* 24 (2009): 183-91. https://doi .org/10.1007/s10896-008-9219-y.

13 These guidelines are adapted from Darkness to Light, a nonprofit focused on child sexual abuse prevention. See "Tips for Selecting Youth-Serving Organiza- tions," Darkness to Light, 2024, www.d2l.org/wp-content/uploads/2024/11 /Selecting-YSOs.pdf.

[14] Justin and Lindsey Holcomb, *God Made All of Me* (New Growth, 2015).

[15] Virginia Duan, "I Won't Force My Kids to Hug Me or Anyone Else," *Parents*, November 21, 2022, www.parents.com/i-won-t-force-my-kids-to-hug-me-or-anyone-else-6830853.

[16] Beth Sissons, "What Is Parent Codependency?" Medical News Today, August 1, 2023, www.medicalnewstoday.com/articles/parent-codependency.

[17] Kate Motaung, "5 Codependency Symptoms of an Adult Child and Codependent Parent," Mill Creek Christian Counseling, April 29, 2021, https://millcreekchristiancounseling.com/5-codependency-symptoms-of-an-adult-child-and-codependent-parent.

[18] Educate and Empower Kids, *30 Days of Sex Talks* (Rising Parent Media, 2015), 21.

[19] Julia Sadusky, *Start Talking to Your Kids about Sex* (Ave Maria Press, 2023), 70-71.

[20] I. Meizner, "Sonographic Observation of In Utero Fetal 'Masturbation,'" *Journal of Ultrasound in Medicine* 6, no. 2 (February 1987): 111. https://doi.org/10.7863/jum.1987.6.2.111.

[21] C. Mallants and K. Casteels, "Practical Approach to Childhood Masturbation—A Review," *European Journal of Pediatrics* 167 (2008): 1111-7. https://doi.org/10.1007/s00431-008-0766-2.

[22] M. Izadi-Mazidi and F. Riahi, "Pathological Childhood Masturbation in Children Who Referred to a Child and Adolescent Psychiatric Clinic," *Journal of Comprehensive Pediatrics* 11, no. 3 (2020): e65121. https://doi.org/10.5812/compreped.65121.

[23] Joseph H. Beitchman et al., "A Review of the Long-Term Effects of Child Sexual Abuse," *Child Abuse & Neglect* 16, no. 1 (1992): 101-18. Other symptoms that appear in studies include anxiety, depression, withdrawn behavior, somatic complaints, aggression, and school problems. K. A. Kendall-Tackett et al., "Impact of Sexual Abuse on Children: A Review and Synthesis of Recent Empirical Studies," *Psychological Bulletin* 113, no. 1 (1993): 164-80. https://doi.org/10.1037/0033-2909.113.1.164.

[24] G. M. McCray, "Excessive Masturbation of Childhood: A Symptom of Tactile Deprivation?" *Pediatrics* 62, no. 3 (September 1978): 277-9.

[25] I recognize this could sound like marriage is a guarantee. It would be very complicated to explain to a small child about sexual stewardship for single people as it relates to masturbation in this moment. That's for another day.

[26] Nancy D. Kellogg and Committee on Child Abuse and Neglect, "Clinical Report—The Evaluation of Sexual Behaviors in Children," *Pediatrics* 124, no. 3 (September 2009; reaffirmed October 2018): 992-8. https://doi.org/10.1542/peds.2009-1692.

[27] "Sexual Behaviors in Young Children: What's Normal, What's Not?" HealthyChildren.org, American Academy of Pediatrics, April 17, 2023, www.healthychildren.org/English/ages-stages/preschool/Pages/Sexual-Behaviors-Young-Children.aspx.

[28] Kellogg and Committee on Child Abuse and Neglect, "Clinical Report."

[29] Kelly Newcom, "5 Crucial Answers You Need Before Sleepovers," Brave Parenting, https://braveparenting.net/5-crucial-answers-before-sleepovers, accessed May 1, 2025.

30 Brené Brown, "SuperSoul Sessions: The Anatomy of Trust," November 1, 2015, https://brenebrown.com/videos/anatomy-trust-video.

11. Honor God with Our Minds: Lay the Foundation

1 In 1 Corinthians 5:12-13, for example, Paul assumes church members are judging each other eye-to-eye as equals under God. We are not to judge hypocritically, nor are we to do so pridefully—which would be judgmentalism (see Mt 7:3-5).

2 Kevin B. Skinner, *Treating Pornography Addiction* (GrowthClimate, 2017), 41.

3 Fight the New Drug's beautiful documentary *Brain Heart World* does a great job at explaining this in a winsome way.

4 Jay Stringer, *Unwanted: How Sexual Brokenness Reveals Our Way to Healing* (NavPress, 2018), 98.

5 Saint Augustine, *The Confessions,* trans. Maria Boulding (New City Press, 1997), 35.

6 *Beyond the Porn Phenomenon,* Pure Desire Ministries and Barna Research Group, September 2024, https://puredesire.org/beyond-porn-phenomenon.

7 *Beyond the Porn Phenomenon,* Pure Desire and Barna.

8 Maria Baer, "More Christians Are Watching Porn, but Fewer Think It's a Problem," *Christianity Today,* www.christianitytoday.com/2024/09/pornography -use-christians-study-barna-research-pure-desire-ministries.

9 Baer, "More Christians."

10 Raymond M. Bergner and Ana J. Bridges, "The Significance of Heavy Pornography Involvement for Romantic Partners: Research and Clinical Implications," *Journal of Sex & Marital Therapy* 28, no. 3 (2002): 193-206. https://doi .org/10.1080/009262302760328235; C. Hesse and K. Floyd, "Affection Substitution: The Effect of Pornography Consumption on Close Relationships," *Journal of Social and Personal Relationships* 36, no. 11-12 (2019): 3887-907. https://doi.org/10.1177/0265407519841719.

11 "How Porn Can Distort Consumers' Understanding of Healthy Sex," Fight the New Drug, copyright 2025, https://fightthenewdrug.org/how-porn-can-distort -consumers-understanding-of-healthy-sex; "How Porn Can Harm Consumers' Sex Lives," Fight the New Drug, copyright 2025, https://fightthenewdrug.org /how-porn-can-harm-consumers-sex-lives.

12 Kyle K. Pitchers et al., "ΔFosB in the Nucleus Accumbens Is Critical for Reinforcing Effects of Sexual Reward," *Genes, Brain and Behavior* 9, no. 7 (2010): 831-40; "Watching Pornography Rewires the Brain to a More Juvenile State," NeuroscienceNews.com, December 29, 2019, https://neurosciencenews.com /neuroscience-pornography-brain-15354; "How Porn Can Become an Escalating Behavior," Fight the New Drug, copyright 2025, https://fightthenewdrug.org /how-porn-can-become-an-escalating-behavior.

13 A. Wéry and J. Billieux, "Online Sexual Activities: An Exploratory Study of Problematic and Non-problematic Usage Patterns in a Sample of Men," *Computers in Human Behavior* 56 (2016): 257-66. https://doi.org/10.1016/j .chb.2015.11.046; Anna Fleck, "Online Child Pornography Skyrockets," Statista, October 5, 2023, www.statista.com/chart/30964/total-number-of-urls -confirmed-as-containing-child-sexual-abuse-imagery.

14 P. Banca et al., "Novelty, Conditioning and Attentional Bias to Sexual Rewards," *Journal of Psychiatric Research* 72 (2016): 91-101. https://doi

.org/10.1016/j.jpsychires.2015.10.017; V. Bouché, "Survivor Insights: The Role of Technology in Domestic Minor Sex Trafficking," Thorn, January 2018, www.thorn.org/wp-content/uploads/2019/12/Thorn_Survivor_Insights_090519.pdf.

[15] M. L. Bourke and A.E. Hernandez, "The 'Butner Study' Redux: A Report of the Incidence of Hands-on Child Victimization by Child Pornography Offenders," *Journal of Family Violence* 24 (2009): 183-91. https://doi.org/10.1007/s10896-008-9219-y.

[16] Ana J Bridges, Robert Wosnitzer, Erica Scharrer, Chyng Sun, and Rachael Liberman, "Aggression and Sexual Behavior in Best-Selling Pornography Videos," PubMed, 2010, https://pubmed.ncbi.nlm.nih.gov/20980228/#:~:text=The%20study's%20findings%20include:%20*%20High%20levels,the%20University%20of%20Arkansas%2C%20Fayetteville%2C%20AR%2072701.

[17] Nicholas Kristof, "The Children of Pornhub," Opinion, *The New York Times*, December 4, 2020, www.nytimes.com/2020/12/04/opinion/sunday/pornhub-rape-trafficking.html.

[18] V. Bouché, "Survivor Insights."

[19] Baer, "More Christians."

[20] Michael B. Robb and Supreet Mann, *Teens and Pornography*, Common Sense Media, 2023, www.commonsensemedia.org/sites/default/files/research/report/2022-teens-and-pornography-final-web.pdf.

[21] Lorena Taboas, "New Report Reveals Truths About How Teens Engage with Pornography," Common Sense Media, January 10, 2023, www.commonsensemedia.org/press-releases/new-report-reveals-truths-about-how-teens-engage-with-pornography.

[22] Robb and Mann, *Teens and Pornography*, 15.

[23] Robb and Mann, *Teens and Pornography*, 6, 11.

[24] Robb and Mann, *Teens and Pornography*, 6. See also K. Kubicek et al., "In the Dark: Young Men's Stories of Sexual Initiation in the Absence of Relevant Sexual Health Information," *Health Education & Behavior* 37, no. 2 (2009): 243-63. https://doi.org/10.1177/1090198109339.

[25] Julia Sadusky, *Start Talking to Your Kids About Sex* (Ave Maria Press, 2023), 115.

[26] Taboas, "New Report Reveals."

[27] Robb and Mann, *Teens and Pornography*, 25.

[28] Robb and Mann, *Teens and Pornography*, 24.

[29] Robb and Mann, *Teens and Pornography*, 24.

[30] Robb and Mann, *Teens and Pornography*, 24.

[31] Matt often uses this framework to talk about social media consumption as well.

12. Honor God with Our Minds: Walk the Foundation

[1] I often use Common Sense Media (www.commonsensemedia.org). It's a secular site, but it has been helpful for me to get at least a cursory look at reviews and see if there is generally any content that could unwise for my kids to see. I also appreciate PluggedIn.com.

[2] The book was a secular cartoon book designed to help kids keep their bodies safe and prepare for puberty, but it was too graphic for Juliette. There was a sweet childhood storyline, but then suddenly there were graphic images of the little

girl's sexual parts on display. Kids should not get used to graphic images of sexual body parts showing up in the midst of a story. That's what porn does.

3 Julia Sadusky, *Start Talking to Your Kids about Sex* (Ave Maria Press, 2023), 139.

4 Lorena Taboas, "New Report Reveals Truths About How Teens Engage with Pornography," Common Sense Media, January 10, 2023, www.commonsensemedia.org/press-releases/new-report-reveals-truths-about-how-teens-engage-with-pornography.

5 For specific screen time recommendations by age, see "Screen Time and Children," American Academy of Child and Adolescent Psychiatry, May 2024, www.aacap.org/AACAP/Families_and_Youth/Facts_for_Families/FFF-Guide/Children-And-Watching-TV-054.aspx.

6 J. M. Nagata et al., "Associations Between Media Parenting Practices and Early Adolescent Screen Use," *Pediatric Research* 97 (2025): 403-10. https://doi.org/10.1038/s41390-024-03243-y.

7 For a helpful guide to YouTube, see "The Ultimate Guide to YouTube for Caregivers," Protect Young Eyes, May 1, 2024, https://protectyoungeyes.com/the-ultimate-guide-to-youtube-for-caregivers.

8 We got a Gabb watch (see https://gabb.com), but there are others on the market similar to this.

9 Our kids like to watch Art for Kids Hub, for example, on Youtube (www.youtube.com/user/ArtforKidsHub). But while they are watching it, it is out in the open, I am listening in, I am able to step in if some random inappropriate commercial pops up.

10 Jonathan Haidt, *The Anxious Generation* (Penguin, 2024), 119, 63.

11 Haidt, *Anxious Generation*, 175.

12 Elizabeth M. White et al., "Associations Between Household Chores and Childhood Self-Competency," *Journal of Developmental & Behavioral Pediatrics* 40, no. 3 (April 2019): 176-82; Joan E. Grusec et al., "Household Work and the Development of Concern for Others," *Developmental Psychology* 32, no. 6 (November 1996): 999-1007.

13 M. Privara and P. Bob, "Pornography Consumption and Cognitive-Affective Distress," *Journal of Nervous and Mental Disease* 211, no. 8 (August 1, 2023): 641-6.

14 Maria Baer, "More Christians Are Watching Porn, but Fewer Think It's a Problem," *Christianity Today*, www.christianitytoday.com/2024/09/pornography-use-christians-study-barna-research-pure-desire-ministries.

15 Sherry Turkle, as quoted in Kelsi Klembara, "Forever Elsewhere," 1517, May 8, 2024, www.1517.org/articles/forever-elsewhere.

16 See L. Veldhuis et al., "Parenting Style, the Home Environment, and Screen Time of 5-Year-Old Children; The 'Be Active, Eat Right' Study," PLoS One 9 (2014): e88486; S. Geurts et al., "Rules, Role Models or Overall Climate at Home? Relative Associations of Different Family Aspects with Adolescents' Problematic Social Media Use," *Comprehensive Psychiatry* 116 (2022): 152318.

17 Nagata et al., "Associations Between Media."

18 Beata Mostafavi, "Frequently Using Digital Devices to Soothe Young Children May Backfire," Michigan Medicine, University of Michigan, December 12, 2022, www.michiganmedicine.org/health-lab/frequently-using-digital-devices-soothe-young-children-may-backfire.

[19] Hanna Rosin, "The Touch-Screen Generation," *The Atlantic*, April 2013, www.theatlantic.com/magazine/archive/2013/04/the-touch-screen-generation/309250.

[20] Liraz Margalit, "What Screen Time Can Really Do to Kids' Brains," *Psychológia šťastia*, April 17, 2016, https://psychologiastastia.sk/wp-content/uploads/2017/12/what-screen-time-can-really-do-kids-brains.

[21] David Brooks, "How Evil Is Tech?" Opinion, *The New York Times*, November 20, 2017, www.nytimes.com/2017/11/20/opinion/how-evil-is-tech.html.

Appendix A: How to Talk with Kids Between Ages Seven and Ten About Sex

[1] I recognize that married and single people with children are also called to make disciples outside of their own children. However, explaining that theological reality in this moment is probably a bit much.

Appendix B: What If We Suspect Something Sexually Abusive Has Happened to Our Kids?

[1] For a full, helpful list of signs and symptoms, see "The Issue of Child Sexual Abuse," Darkness to Light, www.d2l.org/wp-content/uploads/2025/02/Child-Sexual-Abuse-All-Statistics.pdf, accessed June 7, 2025.

[2] Kathleen Coulborn Faller, "Is the Child Victim of Sexual Abuse Telling the Truth?" *Child Abuse & Neglect* 8, no. 4 (1984): 473-81. https://doi.org/10.1016/0145-2134(84)90029-2.

[3] Paula Schaeffer et al., "Children's Disclosures of Sexual Abuse: Learning from Direct Inquiry," *Child Abuse & Neglect* 35, no. 5 (2011): 343-52, https://doi.org/10.1016/j.chiabu.2011.01.014; N. Trocmé and N. Bala, "False Allegations of Abuse and Neglect when Parents Separate," *Child Abuse & Neglect* 29, no. 12 (2005): 1333-45, https://doi.org/10.1016/j.chiabu.2004.06.016.

[4] A. Talmon et al., "Maltreatment in Daycare Settings: A Review of Empirical Studies in the Field," *Trauma, Violence & Abuse* 25, no. 1 (January 2024): 512-25.

[5] James L. Sack, "The Impact of Codependency on Relationships," https://core.ac.uk/download/pdf/228945511.pdf, accessed May 4, 2025.

[6] When I say "laughing at," I mean in a shame-provoking way. If we are all laughing at someone passing gas (including the one who did it), that's different from staring at someone's private part, pointing, and laughing at how goofy it is. The former is a together joke; the latter induces shame.

[7] Please note that I don't pull our kids away from every issue they bump up against. I want them to develop resilience in tough situations like relational or intellectual struggles. But sexual boundary crossing is a no-fly zone for me. It requires special honor and follow-up, and if institutions do not see that as important, I can't trust them.

[8] Visit the National Children's Alliance Coverage Maps page (www.nationalchildrensalliance.org/cac-coverage-maps) to find one in the United States. Usually these resources are free.

[9] Faller, "Is the Child Victim?"; see also "For Our Daughters Official Film," posted by Kristin Kobes Du Mez, YouTube, September 26, 2024, www.youtube.com/watch?v=IkES4X_qb6c for powerful stories of bravery in the face of church abuse.

Appendix C: Where Should I Send My Kids to School?

1 Stefani McDade, "Taking Kids to Church Matters More Than the 'Right' School, Study Suggests," *Christianity Today*, January 25, 2022, www.christianitytoday.com/2022/01/education-schooling-private-public-church-attendance-study.

2 Lorena Taboas, "New Report Reveals Truths About How Teens Engage with Pornography," Common Sense Media, January 10, 2023, www.commonsensemedia.org/press-releases/new-report-reveals-truths-about-how-teens-engage-with-pornography.

3 Jonathan Haidt, *The Anxious Generation* (Penguin, 2024), 75.

4 Nassim Nicholas Taleb, *Antifragile: Things That Gain from Disorder* (Random House, 2014).

5 Haidt, *Anxious Generation*, 75.

Like this book?

Scan the code to discover more content like this!

Get on IVP's email list to receive special offers, exclusive book news, and thoughtful content from your favorite authors on topics you care about.

ivp | InterVarsity Press